HITLER'S WAR

World War II as portrayed by

the International Nazi Propaganda Magazine

JEREMY HARWOOD

ZENITH PRESS

ZENITH PRESS

First published in the United States in 2014 by Zenith Press, a member of Quayside Publishing Group, 400 First Avenue North, Suite 400, Minneapolis, MN 55401 USA

© 2014 Quantum Books

This book is produced by
Quantum Publishing
6 Blundell Street
London
N7 9BH

All photographs are from the author's collection unless noted otherwise.

The information in this book is true and complete to the best of our knowledge. All recommendations are made without any guarantee on the part of the author or Publisher, who also disclaims any liability incurred in connection with the use of this data or specific details.

We recognize, further, that some words, model names, and designations mentioned herein are the property of the trademark holder. We use them for identification purposes only. This is not an official publication.

Zenith Press titles are also available at discounts in bulk quantity for industrial or sales-promotional use. For details write to Special Sales Manager at Quayside Publishing Group, 400 First Avenue North, Suite 400, Minneapolis, MN 55401 USA.

To find out more about our books, visit us online at www.zenithpress.com.

ISBN: 978-0-7603-4621-1

Editor: Sam Kennedy
Cover Designer: Amazing 15
Layout Designer: Andrew Easton

Printed in China

10 9 8 7 6 5 4 3 2 1

Contents

Genesis

Signal, Nazi Germany's most successful wartime propaganda magazine, published its first issue in April 1940 and its last in March, 1945—just weeks before VE Day and the end of the war in Europe. Its success was such that, at its peak, it sold around two and a half million copies per issue in twenty languages ranging from French, Italian, and Slovakian to Arabic, Finnish, and Dutch.

Modeled on other well-known magazines of the time—notably Britain's *Picture Post* and *Life,* and *National Geographic* in the United States—*Signal's* genesis in early 1940 stemmed from Nazi determination to produce a mass-circulation magazine that would promote Germany's claim to be the indisputable guardian of European civilization, and proclaim the virtues of National Socialism to the world beyond the immediate confines of the Third Reich. It would gain, it was hoped, "the trust of the population in the occupied territories." Particularly in South America, it would also influence neutral states to adopt a pro-German stance.

With its catchy layout and lavish use of color and black-and-white photographs, cutting cartoons, explicative graphics, and highly visual maps, *Signal* was an immediate success practically everywhere it appeared. Such was German confidence that it would be a hit that, even before the Reich struck in the West, they were already preparing to launch a French-language edition, though, in the event, an Italian one was the first to appear. Others followed. Soon, *Signal* was on sale in Belgium, Bohemia and Moravia, Bulgaria, Croatia, Denmark, Estonia, Finland, France, Greece, Hungary, Iran, Italy, Luxembourg, the Netherlands, Norway, Portugal, Romania, Sweden, Switzerland, Serbia, Slovakia, Spain, and Turkey. Even an English-language version was produced for sale in the occupied Channel Islands, neutral Ireland and, until the Americans entered the war, the United States. There, *Signal* could be purchased for just ten cents.

By 1943, when its circulation peaked at an amazing two and a half million copies, *Signal* had clearly established itself as wartime Europe's number one propaganda publication. The Finnish periodical *Kustaa Vaasa* described it as "the most remarkable and stunning magazine." The same year, across the Atlantic, *Life* itself paid reluctant tribute to its success. "The chief US foreign propaganda magazine *Victory*," it stated baldly, "is but a pallid imitation of the German *Signal*. It has less than half the circulation and contains no terrific propaganda shock like its Nazi counterpart." *Signal* was, *Life* concluded, "the great arsenal of Axis propaganda." As a consequence, the United States was in imminent danger of losing "the war of words."

Rise and fall

The lightning attack on the Poles that began the Second World War had no *Signal* to publicize it. The first issue of the fledgling magazine was not published until April 1940, when, after months of what many Germans dubbed the Sitzkrieg and the Allies the "Phoney War," Hitler's armies invaded Denmark and Norway. The following month, they struck at Holland, Belgium, and France. From their offices in the Deutscher Verlag building, the magazine's editorial staff—there were ten to fifteen of them—put each issue together. They were supported by some 120 translators, all of whom were foreign volunteers, plus a corps of freelance journalists, reporters, economists, and historians. For its striking war photographs, *Signal* could count on the thousand or so Propaganda Company cameramen who accompanied the Wehrmacht into action on all the major battlefronts. They were lavishly supplied with the best and most modern photographic equipment available—notably Agfa-Gevaert color cameras, which shot the photographs for which the magazine became particularly renowned.

Until September 1941, Harald Lechenberg was the magazine's editor-in-chief. Heinz von Medenfind took his place until spring 1942, when he was succeeded by Wilhelm Reetz, who held the position until February 1945. Giselher Wirsing, who had been de facto editor-in-chief since May 1943, then formally succeeded him. A dedicated Nazi, who had joined the SS in 1933 and who had worked off and on in the Institute for Research on the Jewish Question, Wirsing organized the evacuation of the magazine's staff

from Berlin—first to a village some 43 miles (70km) outside the capital to dodge the incessant Allied air raids, and then to Wattendorf, near Bamberg. It was there that the last issue of *Signal* was compiled in March 1945; the following month, Wirsing and his staff were captured by the advancing Americans.

Even toward the end of the war, *Signal* managed to hang on to many of its readers, though its circulation was steadily dwindling. Some editions—notably the French and eastern European ones—ceased publication as the territories where they circulated were liberated by the Allies. The content of the magazine, too, was now somewhat different. Though *Signal* was never intended to be just a news magazine, the majority of its pages during the early years of the war had been devoted to celebrating the

Reich's string of stunning military triumphs. Now, the emphasis changed. As the victories ground to a halt, and the Reich started to suffer major military reverses, *Signal* devoted more and more of its space to gossip about movie stars, sports events, concerts, theater, and fashion. Defeats like El Alamein, which proved to be the turning point in the North African desert war, were never mentioned at all. Nor was the Axis capitulation in Tunisia, or the loss of the Battle of the Atlantic. The surrender of the Sixth Army at Stalingrad was admitted only months after the event and, even then, the magazine assured its readers that it was only a temporary setback on the inevitable road to victory. The Axis evacuation of Sicily was described as a straightforward tactical withdrawal.

By 1944, pictures taken in 1941

and even earlier were being used to illustrate accounts of supposed German counter-offensives that in reality were totally illusionary. Even the carpet bombing that was steadily reducing the great industrial cities of the Reich to rubble received little coverage. On the rare occasions it was mentioned, the articles stressed its wantonness, brutality, and inhumanity. The attacks were "terror raids," and the RAF and USAAF aircrew who carried them out nothing more than "terror flyers." As the inevitable end approached, the tone became ever more strident. Europe, said *Signal*, was threatened by two barbarisms—Russian Bolshevism and American capitalism. It naturally failed to recognize that the greatest threat to European civilization undoubtedly came from the Third Reich itself.

BLITZKRIEG

It was a new type of war—a "lightning war" of rapid movement, led by tanks and other motorized formations, and closely supported by dive bombers to terrorize any opposition into submission. From the outbreak of war in 1939, until the Wehrmacht finally ground to a halt in the snows of the Russian winter, the ferocious knockout punches landed by Hitler's armies totally demoralized all their defeated foes.

From Poland to Norway

Just six weeks after the Nazis stormed into Poland on September 1, 1939, the Poles capitulated. Months of so-called "phoney war" followed. Hitler was not ready to strike in the West, where the French and British stood waiting for an attack that never came. It was not until April 1940—the month that *Signal* made its first appearance—that the Wehrmacht went on the offensive again. Hitler deemed it necessary to attack neutral Denmark and Norway to secure Nazi control of the iron ore route from Sweden to the Reich. The swift campaign that followed ended in a military debacle that brought about the fall of the British government.

No one was more disconcerted than Hitler when, following his invasion of Poland, the "little worms" he had humiliated at Munich declared war on the Third Reich on September 3, 1939. So, too, were millions of Germans. Memories of the 1918 capitulation were still fresh enough to lower civilian morale. Bloodless triumphs were one thing; war with Britain and France again was quite another. Even the successful Blitzkrieg against the Poles—the war in Poland was over in six weeks—did not raise morale on the home front. Nor did the imposition of food rationing, the tightening of other strict controls, and the onset of the harshest winter for many years do anything to lift German spirits.

The Polish Blitzkrieg

The actual campaign went according to plan. On September 1, the first of a grand total of sixty Divisions, numbering nearly one-and-a-half million men, crossed the Polish border. The advance was spearheaded by the army's five panzer divisions, together with four fully motorized divisions of infantry. The other troops relied in the main on horse-drawn transport and their feet. The Luftwaffe supported this imposing force with 897 bombers, 426 fighters and various transport and reconnaissance airplanes.

German military supremacy was overwhelming. Hoping against hope that the threat of Anglo-French intervention would force Hitler to cancel—or, at the worst, postpone—the invasion, the Poles had delayed mobilizing their armed forces until the last moment, and were poorly placed to resist the Wehrmacht's onslaught as a result. Though they notionally could put more than a million men into the field, much of their equipment was obsolete. They possessed far fewer tanks than their opponents, while their air force, with its 154 bombers and 159 fighters, was pitifully unready to take on the massed might of the Luftwaffe. In any event, much of it was destroyed on the ground. Its remnants were driven from the skies in a matter of days.

Taking the offensive

The main German thrust came from Slovakia in the south. Other German divisions attacked from East Prussia, while still more advanced from the west, slicing through the Polish Corridor, created by the Allies in the 1919 peace settlement at Versailles to give newly-independent Poland access to the Baltic Sea. Hitler's forces were divided into two Army Groups—Army Group North, commanded by General Fedor von Bock and consisting of the 3rd and 4th Armies, and Army Group South, under General Gerd von Rundstedt (8th, 10th and 14th Armies). The Poles resisted as best they could, but soon were in full retreat. Within a week, they were in total disarray with their command structure completely shattered.

Worse was to come. On September 17—the day the Polish government fled to Romania, where its members were promptly interned—the Red Army crossed Poland's eastern border, moving swiftly forward toward the demarcation line stipulated in the secret clauses of the Nazi-Soviet Non-Aggression Pact. The hapless Poles were now being forced to fight on two fronts.

Meanwhile, the Germans were encircling Warsaw. A desperate Polish counter-attack at Kutno on September 9 only delayed the inevitable. The city's 120,000-strong garrison capitulated on September 27 after a bitter siege, with the Luftwaffe dropping ton after ton of incendiary and high-explosive

bombs on the beleaguered capital. Before the encirclement was completed, many fled the city, joining the thousands of refugees already clogging the roads. Zygmunt Klukowski, a Polish hospital superintendent, noted in his diary: "The entire highway was crowded with military convoys, all types of motorized vehicles, horse-drawn wagons, and thousands of people on foot. Everyone was moving in one direction only—east. When daylight came, a mass of people on foot and on bicycles added to the confusion. It was completely weird. This whole mass of people, seized with panic, was going ahead, without knowing where or why, and without any knowledge of where the exodus would end."

From Blitzkrieg to Sitzkrieg

All fighting finally ceased on October 6. Altogether, the Poles lost an estimated 70,000 troops killed in action against the Germans and another 50,000 against the Russians. At least 133,000 were wounded fighting the Germans; the number of casualties inflicted by the Russians is unknown. The Germans captured nearly 700,000 Polish prisoners and the Russians 300,000. German losses were 11,000 killed, 30,000 wounded and a further 3,400 missing in action.

Such losses did not concern Hitler. On August 27, he had told his generals that the Poles "had to be subjugated with the utmost ruthlessness. Our strength," he said, "lies in our speed and our brutality ... the aim of the war lies not in reaching particular lines but in the physical annihilation of the enemy." He was on the spot to see his orders being carried out. Immediately after the British and French declaration of war, he left Berlin for the front. His headquarters was an armored train, stationed first in Pomerania, and then in Upper Silesia, from where he motored to view the fighting from a safe distance. On September 19, he visited Danzig, where he was greeted by ecstatic crowds of ethnic Germans, and then, after the fall of the city, he flew to Warsaw to inspect the devastation inflicted on the capital by his armies and airplanes. He then returned to

German infantry tackle a strongpoint in an unnamed village during the April 1940 Norwegian campaign. Signal followed the official line that the Germans had invaded Norway to protect the Norwegians against imminent Allied aggression.

Berlin, where, in early October, he promulgated a peace offer to France and Britain. Though this was rejected by both countries, little or no fighting subsequently took place. The months of "phoney war"—or Sitzkrieg as the Germans called it—now began.

Scandinavian invasions

It was not until April 1940 that Hitler was ready to make his next move. He had postponed his projected offensive in the west due to constant bad weather, and the crash-landing of a Luftwaffe courier airplane in neutral Belgium. The staff officer who was a passenger in the airplane failed to destroy the attack plans he was carrying and they fell into Belgian hands. Now, the Fuehrer's attention shifted north to Scandinavia, and to Norway in particular. Admiral Raeder, commander-in-chief of the Kriegsmarine, had been pressing

There has been shooting...

A special correspondent in Norway describes the fight for a burning village occupied by the enemy:

A German tank halts at the entrance to the village . . .

Its advance covered by a tank, an infantry detachment proceeds Toward the suspected village. There has been some shooting. Houses are burning, having been set on fire by Norwegian troops. Every nerve is strained. Have enemy forces established themselves here for defence? The detachment halts, and gets well under cover . . .

The advance becomes more cautious . . .

The men jump from fence to fence, from yard to yard, with their fingers continually on the triggers of their guns. Apart from the collapsing of the red walls and roofs and from the crackling of the fire, there is nothing to be heard . . .

Then there is more shooting . . .

Enemy machine-guns are shooting out of a half collapsed barn. The detachment immediately gets into position, and its leader sights the enemy gives an abrupt signal and . . .

for a pre-emptive invasion since the previous October. Worried that the British themselves were planning some course of action that would sever the vital supply routes by which Swedish iron ore reached the Reich's hungry armaments plants, Hitler was ready to listen.

On March 1, Hitler ordered his generals to start preparations for Operation Weserubung. Norway and Denmark were both to be invaded. The Wehrmacht was given just over a month to plan the entire attack. Early in the morning of April 9, German land forces crossed the Danish border from the south. Paratroops secured the airfields at Aalborg in north Jutland, while seaborne forces landed at Copenhagen and four other points along the Danish coast. Less than two hours later, the Danish government ordered all resistance to cease.

Norway was a different matter. Here, the Germans, commanded by Colonel General Niklaus von Falkenhorst, were divided into five invading groups. Group One landed at Narvik in the north, Group Two at Trondheim, Group Three at Bergen, and Group Four at Kristiansand. Group Five was tasked with capturing Oslo. These landings did not go unopposed. The Norwegians put up a stout resistance, their coastal batteries sinking the German heavy cruiser *Blucher* as it attempted to steam up the fjord to the capital. Two attacks by units of the British Home Fleet on April 10 and 13 sank ten German destroyers anchored in and around Narvik. The Germans also lost fifteen troop transport vessels, delaying the arrival of reinforcements. Though they swiftly succeeded in capturing all the major Norwegian towns and cities, Hitler's troops found it difficult to deal with the country's mountainous terrain, which gave the Norwegians the chance to put up a fight against the invaders.

The Allied debacle

By April 16, the Germans had secured their position in southern Norway. A few days earlier, however, British troops, supported by French Chasseurs Alpines and a number of Polish units, had landed at the tiny ports of Adalsnes and Namsos. A further landing to attack the Germans garrisoning Narvik followed on April 17.

Things went badly for the Allies from the start. The British troops were ill-equipped for winter fighting. Even more to the point, they were bombed mercilessly by the Luftwaffe from the moment they landed, which enjoyed total air superiority. Soon, the British at Namsos and Adalsnes had to be humiliatingly evacuated. Though, after much dithering and delay, Narvik was finally taken on May 29, events in France, following the German breakthrough there, forced a further Allied withdrawal. After blowing up the harbor, the occupying force sailed for home on 8 June. The day before, King Haakon VII and his government had sailed into exile on the cruiser *Devonshire* leaving orders for a ceasefire.

The conquest had cost Hitler 5,500 men and more than 200 airplanes. It had secured total German control of Sweden's iron ore exports and given the Kriegsmarine valuable bases from which to intensify its submarine war. Even more significantly, though, a number of its most modern warships had been sunk or put out of action. The consequences for the Kriegsmarine were to be serious, especially when it came to planning the projected invasion of Britain following the fall of France in June 1940.

Scapa Flow and the River Plate

Of the three German fighting services, it was the Kriegsmarine that was the most active during the long months of the "phoney war." On October 14, 1939, the submarine *U-47*, commanded by Gunther Priem, succeeded in penetrating the great British naval base of Scapa Flow in the heart of the Orkney Islands, and sinking the battleship *Royal Oak* as she lay at anchor. Meanwhile, the pocket battleship *Admiral Graf Spee*, which had sailed from her home port of Wilhelmshaven for the South Atlantic in the last week of peace, had started to hunt down British merchant ships there and in the Indian Ocean.

By early December, the *Graf Spee* had sunk nine such vessels unchallenged. Then a Royal Navy task force, consisting of three cruisers commanded by Commodore Henry Harwood, caught up with her and brought her to battle off the River Plate. Though she inflicted heavy damage on her attackers, the pocket battleship herself was damaged and forced to seek refuge in Montevideo harbor in neutral Uruguay. Believing mistakenly that the British had been reinforced, and told by the Uruguayan government that he had to sail within seventy-two hours or face internment, Hans Langsdorff, the *Graf Spee's* commander, signaled Berlin, saying that an "escape into open sea and breakthrough to home waters" was "impossible" and requesting a decision as to whether his ship should be "scuttled in the Plate estuary or whether internment is preferable." The answer—according to the official German News Agency, and sent by Hitler himself—was short and to the point. "No internment in Uruguay. Attempt effective destruction if ship is scuttled." On the evening of Sunday December 17, Langsdorff obeyed this order to the letter. He scuttled the *Graf Spee.* A few days later, he killed himself. According to some reports, he was sitting on his ship's battle ensign when he fired the fatal shot.

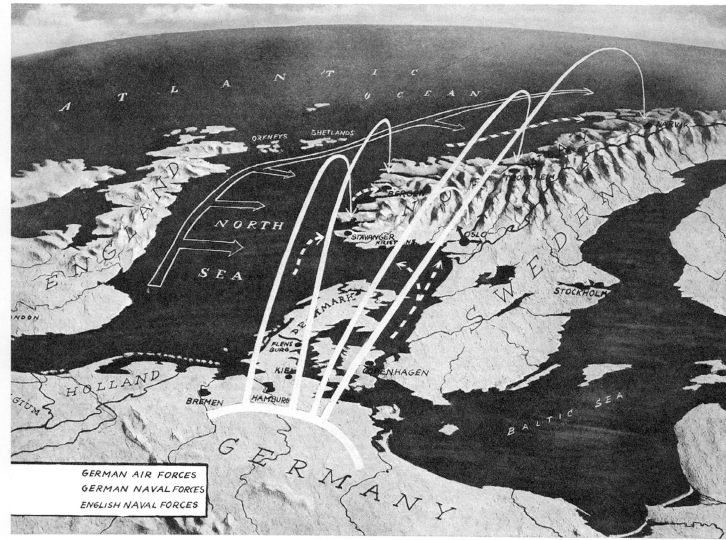

This was the course of our lightning expedition to Denmark and Norway which was too quick for the British invasion

Long before the 9th April English freighters had been bringing war material to Norwegian harbours. After that England proceeded to lay mines in Norwegian territorial waters and on the 9th April English troopships accompanied by units of the Royal Navy were already on their way to land in Norway. Then there was the sudden roar of German fighter machines over Norwegian aerodromes, and German war- ships appeared suddenly in the entrances of the harbours of Oslo, Bergen and Narvik, being followed by troopships. The most important points were occupied like lightning by German troops. At the same time German forces also took over the defence of Denmark against any attempts at invasion by the English. The map shows the progress already made in occupying the country immediately after the 9th Apri

Ten hours too soon

The last parade before the enterprise

The officers and men of a German landing party have their tasks exactly explained to them before going into action; their eyes eagerly follow every movement of the officer's lips

German flying units arrive

Units of the German air force appeared at dawn on the 9th April over Norwegian territory; they came to reconnoitre, and to transport material, and to employ force in the event of resistance

In Denmark also

Bodies of troops were landed from troopships, and co-operated with the detachments, which marched in from the south. The troops were ready in field-service order for landing

Marines to the front!

The advance detachments of marines in their blue uniforms were the first to land, and began with the systematic occupation

At 3,30 a. m. on the 9th April in the office of the German Embassy in Oslo, the First Secretary von Neuhaus was awaiting the Ambassador Dr. Bräuer. He entered the room with instructions that had been brought from Berlin by special courier

At 5 a. m. acting according to these instructions the German Ambassador proceeded as plenipotentiary of the Reich to the Norwegian Foreign Office, to hand over the memorandum of the German Government

The first German aeroplanes having appeared over Oslo and landed at 10 a. m., the first troops arrived about 2 p. m. before the premises of the German Embassy, and mounted guard there

OSLO
9th April

The new German military plenipotentiary for Norway, General von Falkenhorst, discussed with the German Ambassador and plenipotentiary of the Reich the measures to be taken for the defence of Norway

At 3 p. m. the main body of the German troops marched into Oslo. At the same time other Norwegian towns such as Bergen, Trondheim, and Kristiansand were occupied. The German soldiers systematically advanced into the country from the towns

On 10th April, one day after the German army had taken over the defence of Norway against the intended aggression of the Western Powers, complete quiet reigned in the capital of the country. Life went on in the usual manner, and in the parks the inhabitants were enjoying their spring sunshine

On the way over
Mountain riflemen detailed for service in Norway being instructed in the use of swimming-jackets

Hastening towards the destination
A divine fighter machine flying to Hamar

A centre of interest
Here we see a motorised unit resting and how heartily the German troops and Danish population are associating together

Photographed on April 12 in the morning
King Christian of Denmark enjoying his usual morning ride in the streets of Copenhagen

IN COPENHAGEN

A familiar sight these days in Oslo: German infantry is landed
Large German troop-ships arrive in the Norwegian harbours in a ceaseless stream. Soldiers, arms, and ammunition pour forth from the ships. For the first time German troops land on Norwegian soil; they are on guard against England as far as the Arctic Circle

England's Plans Frustrated

Pictures of the Occupation of Norway

Crowds line the roads to see . . .
German troops march through the Norwegian capital. New weapons, German songs and unfamiliar music arouse their interest. They know now that these well-disciplined colums have not come to oppress and besiege them, and that a great power is behind them

All coastal batteries are surrendered
Coastal defence against attacks by English air and naval forces is taken over by the Germans in systematic cooperaration with Norwegian military officials

At army headquarters

Here the Commander is explaining plans to his staff with the aid of a map. He gives the orders for the advance towards the west and north. Messages come and go. Orders are given—in short, headquarters are the brains of the army

With his automatic pistol cocked . . .

A soldier on the lorry guards his comrades on the march. The enemy lurks on the roads, in the dense woods and on the steep rocks. Isolated Norwegian groups, uninformed of the political situation, continued to resist the Germans

High above the reefs and fjords:

A German sentry before a Norwegian coastal fort

Tanks thundering forward

On the road from Oslo to Sönefoss they light on battlements and trenches, and meet with resistance . . .

In Norway's fjords, on rocky coast and islands:
Everywhere German soldiers are on guard, all coast batteries, even beyond the Northern Polar Circle, are fully manned and ready for the enemy

German anti-aircraft guards the air regions over Norway
The eyes of the men at the fast-firing guns follow the horizon tirelessly from West to North, peering through the breaks in the clouds — ready day and night for enemy flyers

Under the German war flag
The crews of the coast fortifications communicate constantly by means of safety signs, blinklights or radio

On guard
in the North

When evening falls on Norway's fjords...

*comes the most dangerous hour of the day. The attentiveness of the men at the guns
becomes still sharper, for this is just the time when enemy flyers often attempt an attack*

Onslaught in the West

In the Polish and Norwegian campaigns, *Signal* played catch-up. The magazine did not begin publishing until late April 1940, so both attacks were covered retrospectively. When Hitler invaded the Low Countries and France that May, it was a different story. *Signal* photographers were on hand from the start to record key moments in the six-week campaign, from the initial invasion of Holland and Belgium, to the breakthrough at Sedan, the triumphal entry into Paris and France's capitulation, which most Germans believed would lead to the end of the war.

Fall Gelb (Case Yellow), the codename for the invasion of Belgium, Holland, Luxembourg, and France in May 1940, was long in the planning. Originally, the idea had been to employ a variant of the Schlieffen Plan, which the German General Staff had put into action in August 1914 at the start of the First World War. It had concluded with the German advance being checked at the battle of the River Marne, ending their hopes of knocking out the French in a short, sharp war.

When Hitler's attack was launched on May 10, it seemed as if the Germans were following much the same plan, though this time they struck at Holland as well as Belgium. Certainly Maurice Gamelin, the Allied commander, had no doubt this was Hitler's intention. He flung his best-mechanized troops—the British Expeditionary Force (BEF) and the French 7th and 1st Armies—across the Franco-Belgian frontier. Gamelin's plan was for the BEF to race to the River Dyle and take up position along its banks, while elements of the Seventh Army pushed on toward Breda and link-up with the Dutch. Not all the Allied commanders favored the Breda part of the plan; General Georges, the commander-in-chief in the northeast, had warned that it was "in the nature of an adventure." Gamelin was not to be deterred. The three armies moved forward swiftly into Belgium in accordance with their orders.

Surprise in the Ardennes

Had Hitler attacked in 1939 as he had originally intended, this indeed would have been the plan of attack the Wehrmacht would have followed. Unfortunately for Gamelin, the Fuehrer changed his mind. Bad weather had already forced the postponement of the attack on several occasions when, in January 1940, the pilot of a Luftwaffe reconnaissance airplane, who had foolishly offered a staff officer friend a lift, lost his way in foggy flying conditions and crash-landed just across the Belgian frontier. The staff officer had a copy of the attack orders with him on board. Believing that security had been fatally compromised, Hitler ordered the General Staff to devise a new plan.

Fortunately for the Fuehrer, General Erich von Manstein had already set to work. He was something of a maverick, who had fallen out of favor with General Franz Halder, the German Army's Chief of Staff, for criticizing the original attack plan. Instead, Manstein argued for a bold new redistribution of German forces. General Fedor von Bock's Army Group B, consisting of twenty-nine divisions, would still attack first, swinging down through Holland and Belgium to ensure that Allied attention would be focused on that part of the front. However, the Schwerpunkt (thrust) of the main attack would be farther to the south through the hilly and heavily forested Ardennes.

The French General Staff considered the Ardennes impassable for tanks. Nevertheless, this was where Manstein proposed concentrating the forty-five divisions of General Gerd von Rundstedt's Army Group A, including 1,222 of Hitler's available panzers. When Manstein met Hitler on February 17, he assured the Fuehrer that the lightning assault, backed by the Luftwaffe's dive bombers, would disorientate the Allies and disrupt all their efforts to launch effective counter-attacks. Hitler ordered the adoption of the new plan.

Everything went as Manstein had predicted. While the Allies were mesmerized by von Bock's thrust in the north, Army Group B bored its way unnoticed through the Ardennes to emerge near Sedan on the River Meuse on May 12. They faced the French 9th Army, commanded by General Andre Corap and one of Gamelin's weakest formations. In a fierce two-day battle, the panzers forced their way across the river and opened up a 50 mile (80km) gap in the Allied line as French resistance collapsed before them.

M. g. to the front
It will be quickly sending its steel greetings to the enemy

Infantry creeping forward

Zzzzz . . . with eyes like a lynx,
it is possible at any minute to light on the enemy

There was little or no co-ordination between the various Allied fighting forces: confusion—and sometimes panic—reigned as the Luftwaffe began strafing the roads, which soon became clogged with fleeing refugees and retreating soldiers.

The question facing the Allies was in which direction the panzers would turn once they had broken out of their bridgeheads. Gamelin believed that they would either turn east to attack the French fortifications along the Maginot Line from the rear, or head straight for Paris. He was again mistaken. Instead, the panzers moved west, sweeping up the valley of the River Somme. On May 20, the first German tanks reached the English Channel. Gamelin had been fired by Paul Reynaud, the French premier, the day before. His replacement was the seventy-three-year-old General Maxime Weygand, who had been hastily recalled from Beirut to take over as supreme commander of the faltering Allied forces.

Attack at Arras

The new commander warned Reynaud that the odds were now stacked against the Allies. He told the premier bluntly: "You will not be surprised if I cannot answer for victory, nor even give you the hope of victory." In just ten days of fighting, fifteen French divisions had been totally destroyed: another forty-five in the north were in imminent danger of being encircled. The Dutch had already capitulated following a savage air attack on Rotterdam. Crack German paratroops had taken Fort Eben Emael, and the Belgians had been thrown back over the Albert Canal. The BEF and the French 1st Army Group, threatened by the Wehrmacht on three sides, were in danger of complete encirclement.

Gamelin had already issued orders for a counterattack before he was dismissed, but Weygand promptly canceled them, saying that he needed time to assess the situation for himself. Eventually, he came to much the same conclusions as his luckless predecessor. His idea was to launch a powerful pincer movement to cut through the panzer corridor, with the BEF and the French 1st Army Group attacking from around Cambrai in the north, and the other French armies advancing northward from the Somme. The two thrusts were to meet in the neighborhood of Bapaume.

Even before Weygand had promulgated his orders, the British had anticipated him. Urged on by General Sir Edmund Ironside, the Chief of the Imperial General Staff, Lord Gort, commander-in-chief of the BEF, attacked west of Arras on May 21. Though it was not the massive counterblow Ironside had called for—instead of four French and four British divisions attacking simultaneously, only the British took part—the assault initially took the Germans by surprise.

Major-General Harold Franklyn was in overall command of the attack, with Major-General Giffard Le Quesne Martel leading the British armor. Tanks of the 4th and 7th Royal Tank regiments, supported by the 6th and 8th Durham Light Infantry, advanced in two columns from the west of Arras. The right-hand column found itself confronting elements of the Waffen-SS Totenkopf motorized infantry division. The left-hand one struck at General Erwin Rommel's 7th Panzers in the village of Wailly.

At first, the Germans were thrown into confusion by Martel's spirited attack. Rommel, who was quickly on the spot, recorded: "the enemy tank fire had created chaos and confusion among our troops in the village and they were jamming up the roads and yards with their vehicles instead of going into action with every available weapon to fight off the oncoming enemy." Rommel reacted instantly. "With Lieutenant Most's help," he wrote, "I brought every available gun into action at top speed against the tanks. Every gun, both anti-tank and anti-aircraft, was ordered to open rapid fire immediately." The British eventually were forced to retreat. Out of the seventy-four tanks that had started the attack, only thirty-one were fit to go into action the following day.

A fractured relationship

In the meantime, Weygand flew north. At Ypres, he met the King of the Belgians and General Gaston-Henri Billotte, commander of the 1st Army Group. However, he missed meeting Gort, who, thanks to a communications breakdown, arrived an hour after Weygand had left for Paris. It was Billotte who had to put Gort in the picture. Gort agreed to the attack, though, according to King Leopold, "he considers the chances of the maneuver in which he is going to take part succeeding are practically nil." Then, disaster struck. On his way to brief General Georges Blanchard, commander of the 1st Army, Billotte was injured in a car crash. He died two days later without regaining consciousness

The consequences were catastrophic. Not only was Billotte the only Allied commander in the north to have been briefed by Weygand at first hand; he was the only French commander in whom both Gort and King Leopold retained some confidence. In any event, time was rapidly running out. After a brief pause, Hitler's panzers resumed their drive up the Channel coast, capturing Boulogne and Calais and trapping the BEF, the French 1st Army, and the Belgians in a pocket. Initially, this stretched from Gravelines on the coast in the west, to beyond Ostend in the east, and as far as Valenciennes in the south. After Belgium's surrender on May 28, it shrunk rapidly to an area only about 32 miles (50km)

Taking cover as a French shell falls near them – "a damned near miss" according to the original Signal *caption. It is likely this photograph was taken on the Western Front before the blitzkrieg started in earnest in May 1940.*

square around Dunkirk.

Gort was faced with a dilemma. He could either attack southward or fall back on Dunkirk and try to evacuate his army from there. He chose the latter course. He had already told London that "any advance by us will be in the nature of a sortie and relief must come from the south as we have not, repeat not, ammunition for a serious attack." When Weygand's promised counter-attack failed to materialize, Gort abandoned Arras and began falling back toward Dunkirk and the Channel coast.

The last battles

With the evacuation from Dunkirk underway, Weygand and his severely depleted forces readied themselves to resist the inevitable German thrusts across the Somme and Aisne, and on towards Paris and south and west deep into the French heartland. Against the 104 divisions the Germans mustered, the French could field only forty-three infantry divisions, the remnants of their three armored divisions and three similarly weakened DLMs (Light Mechanized Divisions). In addition, there were the British 51st Highland Division and 1st Armoured Division—the latter reduced to a third of its original strength—plus seventeen divisions tied down holding the Maginot Line.

As Weygand feared, it was not enough. Von Bock opened the German attack on June 5, with von Rundstedt joining in four days later. The French put up a spirited resistance until Rommel's 7th Panzer Division broke through west of Amiens and swept forward southward before turning northwest, swinging around Rouen and heading for the sea to cut off Weygand's now isolated left wing. Meanwhile, Von Rundstedt was making equally speedy progress. General Heinz Guderian, the architect of the Blitzkrieg, flung his panzers across the Aisne. Soon, an irresistible mass of armor was thrusting southward.

With the fall of Rouen to the west, and the crossing of the River Marne to the east, Paris itself came under immediate threat. On June 10, the government fled the capital—first to Tours and then to Bordeaux; the next day, Paris was declared an "open city." The Germans marched into it unopposed on June 14.

As disaster followed disaster, the peace party in the French cabinet gained increasing strength. Weygand himself was in favor of asking Hitler for an armistice. So, too, was Marshal Philippe Petain, the hero of the battle of Verdun in the First World War. Reynaud had recalled him from the ambassadorship to Spain to join the cabinet. Pouring scorn on Reynaud's suggestion that the French fight on from North Africa, he told him that "the armistice is in my eyes the necessary condition of the durability of eternal France." On June 16, exhausted and isolated, Reynaud resigned and Petain took over. As France descended into almost total chaos, the new French leader broadcast to the nation, saying it was time to stop fighting and sue for peace. On June 24, the armistice came into effect. Hitler could celebrate the triumphant conclusion of the greatest military encirclement in history.

Is your office still keeping pace?

Is all work attended to in due time? You can improve efficiency using machines to help your office staff. CONTINENTAL SILENTA is a noiseless writing machine which obviates nervous strain and allows quick and undisturbed typing. The CONTINENTAL bookkeeping machine, Class 300, does prompt and reliable posting and relieves you of irksome additions. The CONTINENTAL automatic bookkeeping machine, Class 700, handles all kinds of accountancy work practically automatic, thus setting capable employees free for more difficult tasks.

WANDERER-WERKE

AKTIENGESELLSCHAFT SIEGMAR-SCHÖNAU

Holland

The German march over the Dutch, Belgian and Luxemburg frontiers began along a wide front on May 10 in order to forestall England and France. The first decisive breach was made with the storming of Fort Eben Emael. Holland capitulated after 5 days. The Maginot Line was pierced along a front of 100 kilometers in length. German tank divisions thrust through France rapidly as far as Abbéville, Boulogne and Calais and then turned East. In the North the Shelde River positions were overpowered. The Belgian army capitulated on the 18th day. Just as in the case of Poland, a new type of weapon and corresponding tactics decided the outcome.

The flying artillery completed its task: *On May 10, the German Air Force systematically destroyed 72 Dutch, Belgian and French airports, and demolished several hundred enemy planes on the ground (picture above) thus assuring German supremacy in the air from the first day of the campaign. This air supremacy is the preliminary condition for the ensuing air attacks on the enemy's reinforcements, and for successful reconnaissance work*

Lightening action of parachute troops. *They occupy important airports and make it possible for air units to land. They also prevent the destruction of bridges and railway junctions on the German roads of advance. They interfere and confuse the enemy forces behind the front*

and Belginm in 18 days

Man after man they fall out of the thundering machines ... *The planes fly in close formation, engines throttled, over the jumping place. The men jump in quick succession so that the group reaches the ground in as close a formation as possible*

Head first toward the ground. *The planes are especially equipped for parachute jumping (picture at right). The body has only one wide door opening without doors. The parachutist uses the handles to give himself more clearanc in making the jump. The first few seconds of the jump are a free drop — then the parachute opens*

Buildings of tactical importance *at road crossings are at once occupied by the parachutists and taken under fire from vantage points*

On a bridge in Rotterdam. *A parachute with ammunition is salvaged*

In a Rotterdam street: *Reinforcement material has been landed by parachute*

Rotterdam on fire: *Sections of the retiring Dutch army erected barricades all over the city, making it a stronghold of resistance. German "stukas" therefore attacked the city and broke down all resistance*

On a roof in Rotterdam: *A parachute sharpshooter levelling his gun*

An emissary arrives: *Rotterdam has surrendered*

The tanks roll on. *Skirmishing tanks and light armoured units are already on the other side. The heavy tanks follow on ferries built by the engineers*

In five days:
Advance to the Belgian-French frontier

Strong armoured units gather on May 14 at the Maas River crossings while the infantry is still engaged in widening the bridgeheads. The tank battle begins — the greatest in the history of this modern weapon. Between the 14th and the 28th of May the towns of Dinant, Givet, Valenciennes, St. Quentin and Abbéville fell in rapid succession. The shores of the Channel were reached

The great tank battle in France

For the first time in this war *strong units of German and French tanks meet. The German attack is assisted by the "stuka" planes (diving fighters). Heavy anti-aircraft is also put into action and subdues the enemy by direct firing*

Sedan in flames

After the German occupation French artillery bombarded the town setting whole streets on fire

The first coloured photographs
of the
great battle in the west

**The enemy's
lines of retreat — Germany's lines of advance**

Burnt-out motor-cars, abandoned equipment, broken glass and rags . . . . On the roadside thousands of French prisoners, an assortment of the coloured races of the earth

above: **Way for the storming party**

A passage has been made in the wire closure by a concentric charge. At the same moment when it explodes the German skirmishing party charges forwards, and before the enemy realizes what has happened hand-grenades are already bursting in the enemy position

below: **There is no means of coping with the flame**

The sapper has worked his way right up to the wire obstacles protecting the m. g. position. A few spurs of flame and the deadly stream of burning oil has put the adversary out of action. The flame throwers must be fearless men with nerves of steel

The German air patrols advance over ńo man's land far into the enemy country

Quick fighter planes guard them in their flight over the enemy positions, and keep the enemy quick fighters at a distance; these reconnaissance machinés then advance further alone, making use of every means of cover in the sky, and generally succeeding in flying without being observed right up to the prescribed targets. Their return over the fortresses of the Maginot Line, and the flying stations of the French quick fighters is again guarded by our own quick fighters who fly out to meet them

Booty of the reconnaissance machine:
A photograph from the Maginot Line with bunkers and holes caused by German shells

Before the
No Man's Land

"Day by day
we experience the same thing again and again",
writes our special reporter Kenneweg as text for this sketch of Hans Liska. "At a great altitude and always just under the clouds the heavy reconnaissance machines, underneath and beside them formed in twos and threes the little silvery quick fighters: and thus they disappear on the other side of no man's land. Then the quick fighters come back. We count them: 1, 2, 3 . . . 8, 9. They are all there, and then we know that the reconnaissance machines have got through. A few hours later

we see them, but now in inverted order: First the quick fighters alone advancing from Germany towards the west and disappearing in the blue sky far off. Then one hears again the sound of the engines. Thousands of eyes from the forefield search the sky, and then one sees them again and counts again 1, 2, 3 . . . 8 and 9 . . . 12, 13. They are all there. "Have you seen them, old chap?" ask those on the ground. "They are back again" and they smile at one another.

The soldier in the forefield has a special liking for his comrades in the air; he knows the individual types of machines,

and their tasks, and he knows also how important it is for him and for them to be successful. We shall soon get to know them closely for we are leaving the forefield, and the bunker zone in a few days to be attached to the flying stations and anti-aircraft batteries of the air defence zone.

We have to-day entrusted to the military post a result of our work during the last fourteen days, that is to say, films, drawings and sketches of the "land that belongs to no one", out of the forefield, out of the chief fighting line, and out of the bunker zone. Our report from the air defence zone will soon follow.

No man's land

Forbach, a district and industrial town in Lorraine, since 1918 in possession of the French. Population = zero

The windows were smashed, furniture broken into pieces, books and papers torn up and thrown into the street, this work of destruction having been committed by the French on their retreat. This was the condition in which our reporters found the place when visiting it with a patrol

Silence on the wine road, German frontier place, known for its wine gate, which was also called "The gate of peace". Number of inhabitants = zero

Amidst the ruins of this town which had been senselessly destroyed by the fire of the enemy there is a German m.g. position for covering the advance of a patrol

Street battle in Forbach

By our artist in accordance with statements made to him by the German officer who led the action. A German patrol, which had been attacked by the surprise fire of the enemy out of several houses of this town in no man's land, succeeded in defeating the enemy who was in superior numbers and in making prisoners

In the far north *an aeroplane is circling above the snow-covered landscape. Men jump from the machine, parachutes open — reinforcements for the brave men in Narvik* P. K. Böttcher

The soldier with the camera

Unexampled documents from the Propaganda Companies

II. The unknown P. C. man

Many people will have wondered how it is possible that detailed P. C. reports can be read or vivid eye-witness accounts can be heard on the wireless on the day following an event which has occured several hundred miles inside enemy country.

The deeds of the men who make these things possible deserve to be recounted. One example may serve for many:

A mixed reporter unit belonging to a Propaganda Company had been detailed for duty with an advancing tank division. The open, unprotected cars contrasted strangely with the armoured reconnaissance cars and tanks, but the unit, in spite of the fact that its cars were by no means meant for cross-country driving, kept well up with the foremost troops. The French front had been successfully penetrated. The advance into the hinterland was proceeding rapidly. In the evening, the division was more than 60 miles ahead of the old front.

The oral reporter belonging to the unit had taken advantage of a short halt to describe the manner in which the line had been penetrated and to outline the victorious events of the day. The two photographers had "shot" 15 spools of Leica films, and 8 spoken folios by the wireless reporter were also ready, descriptions of the course of the battle and the questioning of prisoners which provided much useful information. All that remained to do now was to convey this material to the rear. Eightly miies back through the darkness!

. . . advancing into France! *Columns of German troops marching along the roads of Artois, Burgundy and the Ile de France . . . pictures as such as this one, which in itself has no tense dramatic element, nevertheless convey the swinging rhythm of the great historical event* P. K. Huschke

The war is over for him. *The poilu has left his giant of steel and goes towards the German infantrymen with upraised arms. They have silenced his "firebreathing fortress". Human courage is harder than steel—the picture convincingly symbolizes this truth   P. K. Utecht*

Everything goes well for the first few miles. Now and again the motorcyclist despatch rider encounters supporting units belonging to his division and piquets from his own troop. After half an hour he is alone: There is no sound but the roar of his engine. A village is burning a long way off. For miles the road runs straight as a die towards it. The leaping flames throw a ghostly light across the road.

He has now reached the entrance to the village. The heat is tremendous. He must make his way, through. Part of the village is still undamaged. An ambulance car is drawn up in front of a small farm. He stops and asks for water. He is given a glass of wine. He asks if there are any French in the neighbourhood. None have been seen. He sets off again along the straight road! Suddenly an invisible power knocks the handle-bars out of his hands. He is thrown from the cycle. His machine lands in a ditch. He slowly pulls himself together, quite shaken by his fall. His hands are bleeding. His machine is undamaged as is also the courier's bag with the reports. He switches on his torch. He had crashed into a dead horse.

After another three miles, he is subjected to fire from the left. Lights out and full throttle! Suddenly he hears a huge crashing and rending a few hundred yards in front of him. The French have just blown up the bridge. He jams on the brake, leaps from his machine which he pushes up to a brush by the side of the road and takes cover. He hears voices. He releases the saftey-catch of his rifle. The voices die away in the distance.

With his courier's bag across his shoulder, he resumes his road after half an hour's wait. He leaves his motorcycle behind for the time being, and goes reconnoitring. The bridge has been completely demolished. The river is more than thirty yards wide. He tests how deep it is with a plank which he makes loose. It is impossible to wade through. He creeps under

Britain's departure from the Continent. *The roads along which the British retreated towards the Channel ports were lined by tall pillars of smoke; towns and villages belonging to their "Allies" were pillaged and set on fire*
P. K. Schmidt

Rouen in flames. *The French fought desperately to hold the opposite bank of the Seine at Rouen, but the bastions were forced and the burning town was captured*
P. K. Wehlan

The spectacle of "total" war. *After Warsaw, it was Rotterdam that, issuing a challenge, learned how hopeless it was to resist the German Luftwaffe —and paid for the lesson by the destruction of the centre of the city* P. K. Carstensen

The tanks storm forward: *The streets of Orleans are cleared of the enemy* P. K. Kipper

He starts his engine and drives off. He reaches the next bridge in a quarter of an hour. It is undamaged, sentries are posted on the other side of the bridge. He is just about to shout to them, when he sees that they are French. Without increasing his speed he drives on through the village. It is occupied by the enemy, but nobody recognizes him. He turns off the left and comes on to the main road. There is movement here: a column on the march, pushing its way forward. German soldiers! He is safe. He makes his report to the first officer whom he encounters and an hour later he has reached the information centre of his company. He has carried out his instructions . . .

The hand of death. *A German bomber has challenged a British motor torpedoboat. The crew has left the ship after a number of M. G. bursts. Their boat is heading towards the coast which lies at a distance of six miles. Bombs now rain down—the next, a direct hit amidships, sends the vessel to the bottom of the sea. P. K. Wundshammer*

Captured in the inferno of Dunkerque. *Exhaustion and hopelessness have furrowed the face of this British soldier P. K. Titz*

Compiègne — the last act! *At the spot where in November 1918 the conditions of a humiliating armistice were dictated to Germany in a most offensive manner, the German guard of honour parades in June 1940 at the commencement of the historic ceremony which for ever obliterated the "crime of Compiègne"* P. K. Borchardt

The roads of the vanquished. *Who could look at this scene in a mighty tragedy without feeling deeply moved? Refugees making their way homewards hurry past the never-ending columns of prisoners. The boy on the perambulator who is tired to death causes the prisoners to forget for a moment their own fate* P. K. Weber

a bush behind the embankment of the bridge and gets out his map and his torch. The nearest bridge is five miles away. It lies to the right of the road. The voices which he had just heard had gone off towards the left . . .

The magic of weapons. *A huge mortar during the battle. It towers up in the smoke of the battle-field like some prehistoric monster* P. K. Bauer

Back to the motor cycle. He stows the bag away in the side-car. But he does not dare to start the engine. He is afraid of betraying his whereabouts. The French cannot be very far as yet. So he pushes his machine the 300 yards down to the blown-up bridge. Then he turns to the right and follows the course of the river. The dawn is beginning to break in the east.

A frightful moment? No: psychological moment. *As the German troops reach an enemy cupola a shell bursts. The P K man—takes first his photo and then cover* P. K. Grimm

Historical Hours Around Paris

In his book "Foch, the Man of Orleans", the famous English author Liddel Hart describes the decisive hours in the Wood of Compiègne in November 1918 in following words

The first half-hour of the 7th November had barely elapsed when Foch received a radio message from the German High Army Command giving the names of the negotiators and requesting that a meeting-place should be named. The message went on: "The German Government would be pleased if the arrival of the German Delegation could be made the occasion of a temporary cessation of hostilities, in the interests of humanity." Foch disregarded this request and simply invited the Germans to come to the outposts of the Debeneys front.

July 14, 1919: The Triumph of France

The victors of the World War 1914/18 march under the Arc de Triomphe. On top, the "Conqueror of the Marne". General Joffre and Commander-in-Chief Foch

June 14, 1940: Marching-in of the Germans in Paris
A German train section crosses the Place de l'Etoile in front of the Arc de Triomphe. On the foreground an anti-tank gun

March 1, 1871: The Victorious German Troops Marching into Paris

Bismarck ordered that most of the troops should not march under the Arc de Triomphe but besides of it. An armistice was stated under the condition that the town of Paris was to be occupied by German forces until the conditions of peace were accepted by the National Assembly

The Marshal took Wemyss and Weygand aside for a moment to examine the credentials, signed by Prince Max of Baden, by which Erzberger, Count Oberndorff, Major-General von Winterfeldt and Captain Vanselow were given full powers to negotiate an armistice, and to arrive at an agreement subject to the assent of German Government. Two somewhat younger officers completed the deputation.

After the papers had been inspected the Marshal took his place at the table, with Weygand on his right, Wemyss on his left. Erzberger sat opposite Wemyss and Winterfeldt opposite Foch. True to his principles, Foch took the initiative by asking: "What is the purpose of your visit? What do you want from me?" Erzberger replied politely that he had come to receive proposals from the Allied Forces regarding the signing of an armistice. "I have no proposals to make."

Taken aback by such an answer, the Germans maintained silence. Finally Count Oberndorff asked: "How shall we express ourselves? We are not bound to observe any particular form. We are ready to say that we wish to learn the conditions of an armistice." "I can name no conditions."

Erzberger now began to read out the note of President Wilson. Foch quickly interrupted him: "Do you wish to request an armistice? If so, please say so . . . formally." "Yes, that is so, we desire an armistice." „Very well, then we will read out to you the conditions under which it may be granted."

Weygand now read the chief clauses out, and they were translated one after another. Grave and immobile, Foch sat there listening. Now and again he tugged sharply at his moustache. Wemyss toyed with his monocle. Winterfeldt's face revealed increasing dismay.

When Weygand had finished, Erzberger proposed that military operations might cease immediately. The revolution had broken out, and the soldiers would no longer obey. He feared that Bolshevism would overrun Central Europe, and should that occur, it would be very difficult for Western Europe to avoid being affected. The German Government needed to be relieved of the pressure of the Allies, in order to restore discipline in the Army and order in the land.

At 5 p. m. Foch, accompanied by Admiral Wemyss, left Senlis in a special train for Rethondes which lies in the Forest of Compiègne. The train was shunted on to a siding which had been built for the heaviest rail artillery. Foch retired into his sleeping-car. It was not until 7 a. m. the following morning that the other train slowly glided up alongside. The Germans had been held up by barriers after emerging from their own lines. Weygand climbed up on to the train and informed them that Foch would receive them at 9 o'clock or shortly afterwards.

When the Delegation appeared at the appointed time in the saloon car, they were received by Weygand and Admiral Hope stiffly but politely. Weygand said that he would inform the Marshal. A few minutes later Foch appeared, accompanied by Admiral Wemyss. The officers saluted one another. The stern face of the Generalissimo betrayed no sympathy for the humiliated enemy. Erzberger received from him the impression of a small man, full of vitality, whose first glance revealed that he was accustomed to command. Erzberger, speaking in low tones, presented his suite. upon which Foch remarked briefly: "Have you any papers, gentlemen? We must verify your credentials."

Sixty-Nine Years Ago
Barricades on the Grand Boulevard. To day the Parisians had prepared entirely for street-fights against the German troops. In 1871 these sort of barricaeds were erected by the Government against the Parisian mob

Twenty-two Years Ago
"What's the purpose of your visit?" "What do you want of me?" With this words general Foch and his staff received the German delegation in his Pullman Car in the Forest of Compiègne. General Weygand (second from left) read aloud the conditions of the Armistice of the Allies

This reference to the internal conditions in Germany came as a revelation to Foch. Facts began to give support to his belief . . . and his bluff. Harshly he rejected Erzberger's proposal. "You suffer from an illness which only attacks the loser. I am not afraid of it. Western Europe will find ways and means of averting the danger."

Winterfeldt now produced a paper and declared that he had been charged by the Government and the High Army Command with a special duty. He read out the paper, the wording of which was: "The armistice conditions of which we have just learnt, require careful consideration. In view of the fact that it is our intention to arrive at an understanding, this examination of the conditions will be completed as soon as possible; nevertheless, this will require a certain time. During this time hostilities between our Armies will continue and many victims will be claimed as much amongst the soldiers as amongst the civil population. They would fall needlessly at the last minute, although their lives could be spared for the benefit of their families." In short, the German Government and the Army Command repeated the proposal that hostilities should cease.

Awaiting the Parade on the Avenue Foch
A mounted-band in front of the Arc de Triomphe, awaiting the beginning of the march

Burning Oil Tanks in the Northern Paris
Heavy smoke clouds witness the activity of German Dive bombers still after the marching in of the German Forces

Life in Paris Is Going On
The day after the capitulation of the city. Parisians at the Champs Elysées are observing the approaching cars of the German reinforcements

Compiègne in June 1940
German soldiers in the Memory Hall, looking into the Pullman car of generalissimo Foch. In this car the German negotiators got the conditions-of-armistice on November 7, 1918

Foch replied inexorably: "No. I represent here the Allied Governments, who have laid down their conditions. Hostilities cannot cease before the armistice has been signed."

"Would it be at least possible to prolong the present truce by twenty-four hours? We need time to communicate with our Government."

"We will grant you facilities as regards contact with your government, but the time has been decided upon by our Governments and cannot be prolonged. It amounts to 72 hours and will expire on Monday, 11th November at 11 a. m."

Defenders of —

French culture

Even during the war of 1914—18 France used coloured troops to defend her interests. The continual annual decrease of population of the country was at that time such that the French Army could not be kept up to strength. Even for the occupation of the Rhineland black troops had to be called upon. And again today France confronts German soldiers with her coloured troops: Berbers, Moroccans, Arabs, Senegalese and Bantu negroes, Cingalese — a variegated mixture of peoples and races

A view across the Avenue Foch during the parade on the occasion of the troops' entry into Paris

These poor old women, driven from hearth and home by ruthless propaganda, haunt the highways of France

Just as in times of absolute peace *the Parisians are sitting in front of the cafés in the Champs-Elysées drinking their apéritifs. Among them are German soldiers, and the population of the capital of France seems to have become accustomed to seeing them*

PARIS,
24 hour after
the
occupation

Regiments of Poilus and their coloured auxiliaries *proceeding between the famous arcades in the Rue de Rivoli and the Louvre on their way to the prisoners of war camp*

A Mars-la-Tour veteran *this old Parisian who fought in the war of 1870 is conversing with a German corporal*

An experience which many Parisians have not had: ascending the Eiffel Tower
German soldiers taking the first opportunity of getting a bird's eye view of Paris, which has been left intact

Poilus who have been taken prisoner — at liberty
The German speaking Alsatians taken prisoner in Paris have received permission from the German command to proceed alone to the rallying camps. Their relatives accompany them on the way

Paris policemen and German military
The unaccustomed sight in their streets causes the Parisian policemen controlling the traffic to have a good look at the German soldiers

Somewhere in France: the end of a defended town . . .

The enemy had converted this town into a fortification, and one morning the German advance was held up; for every house was a fortified position bristling with machine-guns and cram-full of men pouring a murderous fire into the streets. Then amidst the howling of sirens, swarms of dive-bombers suddenly swooped down from the sky, dropping in all directions death-bringing bombs of every calibre. Roofs and walls were torn to pieces and *the resistance of the enemy broken. Flames burst forth from the empty window frames, debris piled up in great mounds, and the roads became blocked with charred beams. The Germans had beaten the enemy and taken possession of the town. The illustration over-leaf shows evidently that the war only roared along the strongly defended retreat-highways of the enemy. Homesteads in the vicinity of these roads remained absolutely undamaged*

Here the German troops broke their way trough:

An armoured turret in the area of the Maginot Line Extension was smashed by German guns. The fire from this turret dominated a wide stretch of the foreground

Dunkirk

With the military situation in northern France and Belgium deteriorating into near chaos as the Allies fell back, the Wehrmacht continued its onslaught confident of victory. Despairing of French inability to mount any effective counter-offensive, Lord Gort, commander-in-chief of the BEF, ordered his weary troops to fall back toward Dunkirk and the Channel coast, and to prepare for evacuation by sea. Few gave Operation Dynamo, as it was christened, much chance of success; it was estimated that the British would be lucky to evacuate 45,000 troops from Dunkirk's harbor and surrounding beaches.

Sunday May 19 was a momentous day in the story of the 1940 Blitzkrieg in the west. Not only was General Maurice Gamelin sacked as Allied commander to be replaced by General Maxine Weygand, it was also the day when Lord Gort, the BEF's commander-in-chief, concluded that, despite the wishes of the French, his army might have no alternative but to fall back toward the Channel ports. If it came to the worst, Gort thought, it was from there that the BEF would have to be evacuated. Concurrently in London, the Admiralty was already starting to make plans for just such an eventuality. Operation Dynamo, the codename for the evacuation, was placed under the command of Vice-Admiral Sir Bertrand Ramsey, Flag Officer Dover, who immediately began the immense task of assembling suitable shipping in the Thames estuary and the harbors in the south of England.

The panzers halt

As the BEF slowly yielded ground, fighting its way toward the coast, the situation worsened rapidly. By May 22, Guderian's panzers were already at the gates of Boulogne and Calais. The former surrendered on May 25 and the latter fell late the following day. Then, as Guderian prepared for a final drive on Dunkirk, he received an amazing Fuehrer directive. "Hitler," he wrote after the war, "ordered the left wing to stop on the Aa. It was forbidden to cross that stream. We were not informed of the reasons for this. The order contained the words: 'Dunkirk is to be left to the Luftwaffe'...We were utterly speechless."

The order could have been issued for a variety of reasons. It may have been that Hitler was worried about the terrain, which he feared was unsuitable for armor. He may have decided to husband his panzers for a final decisive stroke against the French. Or, as some have speculated, he may even have been willing to let the BEF escape—after all, it would have to leave all its heavy equipment behind—to make it easier to force peace terms upon Churchill and his new government.

As chief of the Luftwaffe, Goering may well have played a part in the decision. He pleaded with the Fuehrer to give him a free hand over Dunkirk, assuring Hitler of his confidence that his airmen could finish the job singlehanded. What is known for certain is that General Gerd Von Rundstedt, who had already tried to slow down the panzer advance, strongly advocated halting them completely.

The evacuation begins

Hitler took three precious days before finally deciding to rescind the order. This gave Gort and the BEF what they most needed—time. By the time the panzers were ready to resume their advance, he had managed to throw up a strong defensive shield around the Dunkirk bridgehead. The BEF now stood at least a chance of survival.

The evacuation began on 26–27 May with the arrival at the port of the troop transport Mona's Isle. That first night, only 7,669 men were evacuated. The next day, however, a Royal Navy shore party, led by Captain William Tennant, arrived. He had been tasked with coordinating what was to become a massive rescue effort. At the start, Tennant faced substantial difficulties. Thanks to heavy German shelling, and relentless bombing by the Luftwaffe, the entire dock network had been put out of action. Only the East and West Moles protecting the harbor entrance were still intact. They could not accommodate big ships. Nor would they be sufficient on their own for the navy's purposes.

Tennant decided that the broad, flat beaches stretching north from the battered port would have to be pressed into service for embarkation, as well as the East Mole. Accordingly, he signaled the Admiralty, asking for as many small boats as possible to be sent across the Channel to ferry the waiting troops on the beaches to the bigger ships lying offshore. The first of these "little ships" arrived off the French coast on the night of May 29. Before the evacuation was finally concluded, nearly 300 of them were engaged in this perilous task.

The numbers rise

Both the vessels engaged in the evacuation and the men on the beaches faced almost constant Luftwaffe bombardment. On May 29, no fewer than ten destroyers, eight personnel carriers and paddle-steamers, and an assortment of smaller craft were put out of action by German bombs. The ships that suffered the most were the ones moored around the Eastern Mole. That afternoon, three air raids in quick succession heavily damaged seven out of ten of them. Then, the weather came to the aid of the British. Heavy mist shrouded the airfields from which the Luftwaffe was operating and grounded many of its airplanes. Despite the best efforts of its aircrew, it was forced to moderate the ferocity of its attacks.

The number of rescued troops rose. By May 30, 125,000 men of the BEF had made it back to Britain; the following day, a further 68,014 were taken off, the largest daily total of the entire evacuation. That day, Gort himself sailed for

Signal surveys the scene after the BEF's forced evacuation from Dunkirk. Signal gloried in the fact that the British had been forced to leave all their heavy equipment behind. It ignored the fact that more than 300,000 British and French troops had got away.

home, having been ordered to hand over command to General Sir Harold Alexander, one of his Corps commanders.

The great evacuation was nearing its end. By the morning of June 3, the last British troops had been embarked, but the navy were now occupied in trying to evacuate the French. At dawn on June 4, the last ship left Dunkirk with a final contingent of French soldiers on board. In total, 337,000 men, of whom 110,000 were French, had been saved to fight another day.

The last resistance is broken!

On the beach at Dunkirk: loaded guns, tanks ready to move off, coastal forts, these are all put out of action, deserted by their crews and demolished by the force of German arms

Tanks versus warship

English warships and transport vessels were fired on and damaged by tanks unexpectedly arriving on the scene

On England's threshold

Pictures of the great battle of annihilation

This is what was left

As yet huge quantities of war materials were abandoned by the British in their hurried flight

It would not . . .

explodde. An unexploded shell on the embankment near a French fort

At the last moment

The British attempted to make an improvised jetty to their ships by driving long rows of lorries into the water at low tide. But all in vain!

Direct hits

A large unit of German fighting planes carried out an attack off Dunkirk, during which 18 warships and 49 transport steamers were either sunk or severely damaged by bombs

The last phase of the great annihilating battle in the West once more demonstrates the irresistible power of the combined German arms. The English had desperately attempted to hold the French coast lying opposite their island. They were unsuccessful. Protected by the French, they desperately attempted to reach their island and safety. This also was a failure. The élite of the British Expeditionary Force was annihilated and vast quantities as yet still unascertained, of war materials fell into German hands. The German army stands on England's threshold.

Many thousands . . .

The remnants of the British army defeated at Dunkirk, which were unable to reach the ship, were captured by the Germans. Endless columns march towards the collecting buses behind the front

The Lull Before the Storm

When a jubilant Hitler received news of the fall of Dunkirk at his battle headquarters, he immediately ordered that bells throughout the Reich should be tolled for three days. The Wehrmacht now moved swiftly to finish off the hapless French, whose remaining armies soon collapsed into total disorder. France sued for peace and signed an armistice on June 22; all fighting ceased shortly after midnight three days later. "There are no Allies anymore," the final Wehrmacht communiqué exulted. "There remains only one enemy—England!"

In common with the vast majority of Germans, Hitler was confident that, with the fall of France, the war was as good as over. No sooner had he presided over the start of the armistice negotiations at Compiegne, he set off on a tour of First World War battlefields, taking with him three old comrades from the company in which he had served as a corporal. He also managed to fit in a day-trip to Paris—the only time he visited the French capital. Together with Albert Speer, his personal architect, and the sculptor Arno Breker, he arrived there shortly before dawn on June 28 and embarked on a lightning sightseeing tour. He and his companions visited the Opera, which was specially illuminated for the occasion, the Eiffel Tower, the Invalides and the artistic quarter of Montmartre. "It was the dream of my life to see Paris," the Fuehrer enthused to Speer, "I cannot say how happy I am to have that dream fulfilled today."

Hitler was not the only German to be in holiday mood. Thousands upon thousands of his victorious troops were enjoying their well-earned rest in the hot summer sun. Swarms of them, following in their leader's footsteps, descended on Paris, seeing the sights and, plentifully supplied with so-called Occupation Marks, indulging in an orgy of shopping. On the wreckage-strewn beaches of northern France, they kicked off their jackboots to paddle in the warm water and gaze across the Channel towards the white cliffs of Dover. General Fedor von Bock, the commander of Army Group A, paid a visit to Dunkirk to inspect what the BEF had been forced to leave behind in and around the town and on the beaches. "The English line of retreat presents an indescribable appearance," he wrote. "Quantities of vehicles, artillery pieces, armored cars and military equipment beyond estimation are piled up and driven into each other in the smallest possible space. The English have tried to burn everything, but in their haste have only succeeded here and there."

Celebrating victory

On July 6, Hitler arrived back in Berlin, ready for the victory parade that was scheduled to take place on July 16. Vast cheering crowds took to the streets to greet him; a carpet of flowers covered the route he drove from the station to the Chancellery, where he repeatedly appeared on the balcony to acknowledge the plaudits of the thousands gathered below. The parade itself was even more spectacular as contingent after contingent of handpicked troops marched through the Brandenburger Tor for the first time since 1871. Two days later, in a special ceremony convened at the Kroll Opera House, the Fuehrer promoted twelve of his triumphant generals to the rank of field marshal. The feverish celebrations were mirrored by others in cities and towns throughout a triumphant Reich.

It seemed that peace with Britain must lie just around the corner. Certainly, Hitler was prepared to offer terms. On July 19, in a speech he delivered to an expectant Reichstag, he made what he termed "a last appeal to reason" to the British government and people. "I can see no reason," the Fuehrer concluded at the end of a two-hour oration, "why this war must go on." The British response was immediate. The offer was rejected within an hour.

Planning the invasion

Like most of his countrymen, Hitler could not believe that the British had stubbornly turned down his offer to negotiate. "The Germans I talk to," wrote William Shirer, an American correspondent in Berlin, "simply cannot understand it." However, there was no alternative to preparing to launch an invasion. This was easier said than done.

The German fleet had suffered

substantial losses during the Norwegian campaign. Three cruisers and ten destroyers had been sunk, and two heavy cruisers and one old battleship put out of action. This left Grand Admiral Raeder, commander-in-chief of the Kriegsmarine, with only one heavy and two light cruisers plus four destroyers available for deployment in the English Channel. Nor could the navy be ready to launch the invasion until mid-September. Raeder argued that the best course of action was to postpone it until the following May.

The army had its problems as well. Most of the 2,000 or so invasion barges that were soon slowly massing in the Channel and North Sea ports were unsuited to making a sea-crossing in anything other than a

total calm. The General Staff wanted to land on a broad front stretching from Portland Bill to Dover, but Raeder, mindful of the risk of attack by the vastly superior British fleet, refused to countenance anything but a less ambitious plan.

One thing everyone from the Fuehrer downward recognized was the vital importance of the Luftwaffe destroying the RAF, and so winning total air supremacy. Without air cover, the ships of the Royal Navy would be an easy target for German dive bombers should they try to intervene. The British Chiefs of Staff were of the same mind. "The crux of the matter," they reported to Churchill and his War Cabinet, "is air superiority." Lose it and it was more than likely

Hitler, together with Rudolf Hess, salutes the Reichstag's deputies in July 1940. Signal *linked the picture to a story about the opening of the Bayreuth Wagner Festival to back up the official belief that peace with Britain was just around the corner.*

that Operation Sea Lion, as the invasion plan was codenamed, would succeed.

The bombastic Goering, newly promoted to the rank of Reichsmarschal, was totally confident that his Luftwaffe was more than equal to the task. The RAF, he assured Hitler, would be driven out of the skies in a matter of days. What his aircrews christened the Kanalkampf, and the British the Battle of Britain, was shortly to begin.

Just as in peacetime

A day's racing in Berlin

Europe's most beautiful steeple-chasing track. *This year's great day on the Berlin race track at Karlshorst was a warm Sunday in late autumn. There were eight races on the programme including the "Grand Prix of Karlshorst" with a stake of 65,000 marks, the highest in Germany*

Just as in peacetime, *the spectators thronged the stands and the grass along the course. The fast electric trains left Berlin every three minutes. Programmes and racing papers were sold out ten minutes after the meeting began*

Whose money is on the right horse? *The young lady's tip seems to have been a good one. Her horse is the first to come round the bend into the straight. But the winning post is still a long way off. The two wounded officers favour the stable of the Army School of Riding and Driving. Their horse is Tootish, a fleet chestnut with legs of steel. But its rider broke his collarbone the last time he rode and today he is riding with his arm in a sling. Will he manage it?*

Coming round the bend. *A photograph showing the beauty of racing and riding. The horses' hoofs thunder over the green turf. The jockeys shorten the reins. Now for the last jump!*

Photographs:
Diedrich Kenneweg

He has done it! *Wolf, the jockey, rode the race with one arm. A fall would have been very serious. But he and Tootish won the Grand Prix in spite of everything. The jockey's face as he goes off with the saddle to be weighed-in shows the strain it cost him*

Happy Interlude
in Wartime

A true little story in pictures,
photographed by Hanns Hubmann

1. Hanns Hubmann, our Berlin photographer, attends a dress rehearsal in a Berlin cabaret, for the purpose of collecting a few good pictures. One of the dancers takes his eye — she looks very familiar to me, he thinks, and speaks to her. Sure enough, it is Gerda Kurz . . .

2. Gerda Kurz, for four years "second from the left"
in the chorus of the Metropol Theater in Berlin. She is no longer "second from the left" in the chorus. Although she was not at all badly off there—she earned 250 marks a month— she was ambitious and wanted to get ahead; Hans Hubmann decided to picturize her story

5. I was lucky in being able to live at home with my parents
I helped wherever I could, lent a hand in the kitchen and kept a watchful eye on the kid brother's school work . . .

3. HIS picture occupied the place of honor before her mirror in the dressing-room
"How did you manage it all, anyway?" asked Hubmann. Said Gerda, "Hard work. Sometimes very hard work, but we wanted to get married and Peter's earnings stopped of course when he was called to service, at the very beginning of the war. (He's in a town on the border, you know.) We'll be needing so many things when we marry that I decided something had to be done about it"

4.
Gerda went on with her story:
"I prepared myself for every possible development.
I took vocal lessons twice a week. I went in hard for acrobatics and sports. Training is everything in our profession . . . Of course all this cost a lot of money, but .."

6. "Fetching rations" was also part of my job!

7. "When I thought I was ready to take the jump,
I went to the Reich Theatrical Chamber. They at once sent me here to the Kabarett der Komiker (Comedians' Cabaret), under Willi Schaeffer's direction. They said Mr. Schaeffer needed new talent. Competition was hard but I made the grade. Now I'm . . ."

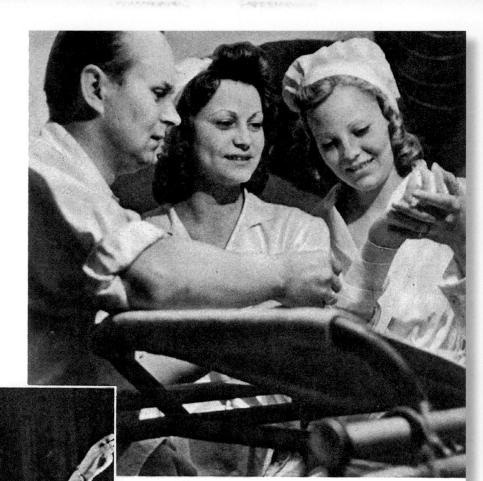

9. Hanns Hubmann photographed her there, and not only on the stage
Gerda is doing her bit on the Home Front. She is a nurse in her theater's air protection organization. She has learned all about bandaging and the treatment of poison gas victims

10. A few weeks later . . .
Hanns Hubmann is best man — and official reporter — at a proxy marriage. Peter thought the German victory offered a good opportunity to slip into the matrimonial yoke. As his troop is expected to go into action soon, he applied to his company commander for permission to marry. Hanns Hubmann had him send a picture of the "wedding without a bride". (Above) At the "wedding without a groom" Hubmann was present himself, as best man. (Right) Gerda Kurz says "yes" and signs her name in the registrar's office of her district in Berlin . . . A happy little interlude in times of war

8. " . . . solo dancer at the Comedians Cabaret."

That's how we work

SIGNAL interviews five film composers about their art and technique

"I very seldom compose at the piano, admitted Theo Mackeben. "It is a delusion of the layman that the composer is continually strumming on the keys. He doesn't strum at all. In the same way, the popular song is not the main thing. The importance of the popular song in the film is almost negligible from the musical point of view. It is an inspiration, the fruit of two minutes—or no inspiration at all. It is quite a different thing if a chanson has to play a dramatic rôle, as in "Bel ami" when the aim was to explain the leitmotiv of the film. The text was to be a clear indication of the hero's character."

"Often enough night is turned into day," says Harald Böhmelt. "But that is what I need: everything must be quiet round about. Over and over again I have to work with the stopwatch in my hand, for on one occasion they need music for 30 metres of film and on another occasion the music may only last 58 seconds. And then the transitions! The honourable audience, once it has left the cinema, rarely has any recollection of the "incidental music" and this incidental music is just as difficult if not more difficult to compose than the so-called 'hits.'"

"How is it that both the Zarah Leander song 'Es wird einmal ein Wunder geschehen?' and my 'Seemann' became famous so quickly?" asks Michael Jary. "I can't tell you. Perhaps the word 'sailor' calls up a special picture. It is a fact that the song became popular much more quickly along the German coast than anywhere inland. But then... I could almost sing another song about what used to happen in the beginning wherever I appeared when there was a musical instrument within reach!"

"I swear by my sound projector," says Werner Bochmann. "I have a copy of the sound film made for me and then I play it through again so that I can do better next time I am passionately interested in the technics of sound films. So much depends on the grouping of the musicians in front of the microphone. You often hear of an 'unfortunate mixture' of music and dialogue in films. And people complain that the simultaneous projection often results in the dialogue being indistinct. There are certain facts that one must know: a star's voice is recorded on a certain frequency and you must know this if the music is not to encroach. If this is taken into consideration and if instrumentation and composition are separated as far as possible from the frequency zone of the human voice then the simultaneous projection of music and dialogue cannot have a disturbing effect."

"A popular song cannot be composed to order," says Franz Grothe. "It is not a matter of thought. The easier and more effortlessly the musical inspiration comes, the greater is the prospect of success. And then chance, how the song is put over in the film or in the theatre for the first time, all plays an important part. In the cinema it is already clear whether the song has really got home or not. The wireless sometimes gives a finishing touch."

"Heimat, deine Sterne" from the Terra film "Quax, der Bruchpilot"

"Wenn ein junger Mann kommt" from the Ufa film "Frauen sind doch bessere Diplomaten"

Werner Bochmann. He inherited his serene smile from his native Meerane where he was born at the turn of the century. While studying chemistry, he went in for music as a sideline. When he finally chose music for his profession, he recognized that here, too, he had to earn a living. He made this discovery while sitting in a café where an Argentinian band was playing. The band needed a temporary pianist, so Bochmann slipped on the gaucho's costume. In his spare time he composed and sat about in the waiting-rooms of film agencies. One day... He was especially interested in the technical side of the film and developed into a specialist on sound projection. His songs have since gone round the world, for example, "Heimat, Deine Sterne", "Abends in der Taverne" and "Gute Nacht, Mutter!"

Franz Grothe. The fact that his father was agent for a well-known piano factory is said to have had only an indirect influence on his talent for composing. That of his mother, a singer, was considerably greater. This hundred per cent Berliner, Franz Grothe, was lucky enough to be able to devote himself entirely to the study of music. His activity as conductor and regulator for a gramophone record factory was excellent practice. After that he made rapid progress, and when one has the help of a beautiful woman ... The composer's wife is the film star Kirsten Heiberg, who is a particularly good interpreter of his song hits. The experience gathered while working with orchestras fitted him for the position of co-founder of the "Deutschen Tanz- und Unterhaltungsorchester" of the German Radio which has since become world famous. As a composer, Grothe has a special talent for songs so that his popular hits have a permanent appeal

MELODIES FOR EUROPE

"War" in U.S.A. but no enemy. *Soldiers of the American Army in heroic pose on guard before a factory making aeroplane parts in New Jersey*

Photographs: PK. Meinhold, A. P., PK. Hochscheidt

Roosevelt, "the father of war", *at the daily conference during breakfast in bed. Seated on the right is his adviser Hopkins, on the extreme left his family doctor, and in the centre a wise-cracker*

Home Guards *practising the defence of London against the "Fifth Column" and parachutists. A "nursemaid" belonging to the Fifth Column" surprises a sentry* ▼ The last. Bolshevist *"graves" in a "cemetery" in the Soviet Union*

A soldiers' song conquers the air and the hearts of all

...with you, Lili Marleen!

About four years ago in a Berlin café a certain song was sung for the first time. The audience liked it, but it did not make a very lasting impression. Lale Andersen, the cabaret singer, however, recorded it for the gramophone. In spite of all, it was just another song among millions. It was called "Lili Marleen." The words were taken from the volume of poetry "The little harbour organ" by the Hamburg poet Hans Leip, the music is by Norbert Schultze.

Three years later, in summer 1941, the German soldiers' radio station Belgrade was put on the air. Everything happened rather suddenly: among the hastily assembled equipment was a case of more or less (chiefly less) up-to-date records including "Lili Mar-

Lale Andersen emphazises with her hands the rhythm of the opening bars of "The Lamp-post Serenade"

The first bars of the most popular soldiers' song

By permission of the Apollo Verlag Paul Lincke, Berlin SW 68   Photographs: Hedda Walther

leen." The song was broadcast. After a few days dozens of letters came from soldiers asking for the "song with something about a lamp-post in it." Then came a regular deluge of field-post letters from France, Norway, Crete and the Ukraine: "Broadcast 'Lili Marleen'." Now for many months, at 10 p. m. every evening, the Belgrade station has been broadcasting to all fronts the "Sentry Serenade", or the "Lamp-post Serenade", to quote two of the many names by which the song is known, and hundreds of thousands of German soldiers are never tired of hearing it. All over Europe people are whistling it and humming it and Lale Andersen has to sing it at least twice wherever she appears:

"Vor der Kaserne, vor dem grossen Tor
stand eine Laterne, und steht sie noch
davor.

So woll'n wir uns da wiedersehn,
bei der Laterne woll'n wir steh'n
wie einst.

Lili Marleen!"

Literal translation of the above verse:

In front of the barracks, in front of the big gates stood a lamp-post and it is still standing there. Let us meet there again, let us stand by the lamp-post as we used to, Lili Marleen.

What is the secret of its success? Lale Andersen's voice? But she has sung many other songs. The song itself? It had been known for years before it became famous.

Only Lili Marleen could tell us its secret, Lili Marleen whom no one ever saw. . . .

The last verse . . . ,,Out of the silent past, Out of the land of my dreams, your loving lips call to me . . ."

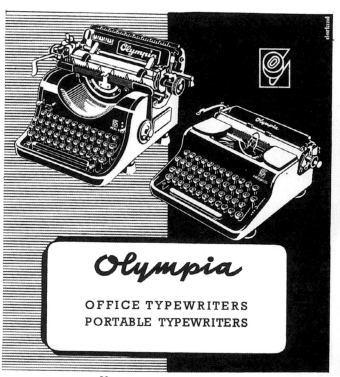

"Du hast Glück bei den Frauen, bel ami," from the Tobis film "Bel ami"

Theo Mackeben. "Film music should be an integral part of the action. The less the spectators can remember of the music in a film, the better it was!" It was Theo Mackeben who uttered this sarcastic pronouncement. Born in Preussisch-Stargard in 1897, he began to play the piano at the early age of five and at fifteen he had made enough progress to perform at concerts. Then the World War broke out. Mackeben was called up and served in a regimental band. Later on, he realized that it was his mission not to interpret but to create. After working for the wireless and the theatre, he began to compose for the cinema. "Bel ami," "Pygmalion," "Heimat," "Das Herz der Königin" are milestones in his film career. His name is linked up with many of Zarah Leander's successes. His operetta "Der goldene Käfig" has just been put on the stage in the Admiralstheater and now the Ufa is enticing him to collaborate

MELODIES

s dreht sich alles nur im Leben um die Liebe," from the Ufa film "Liebe und die erste Eisenbahn"

"Es wird einmal ein Wunder geschehen," from the Ufa film "Die grosse Liebe"

Harald Böhmelt. A glimpse of Harald Böhmelt's home immediately reveals him as an art collector. He has a special weakness for Eastern Asia which could easily explain the mysticism in his music. Born in Halle, he studied the history of art and philosophy in his native city. Then, however, his musical talent took the upper hand and sent him from Nordhausen to Halberstadt and back to Halle where he acted as conductor at the municipal theatres. He became known in Berlin as the conductor of the concerts in Monbijou Palace. Then he received offers from the wireless and later from the films. The cinema world appreciates above all in Böhmelt his folk music, works full of a tender, captivating charm. At first, his film career with all its intrigues and international tendencies was not always easy. But "Was man vergessen kann, lohnt keine Tränen," as he says in one of his songs

Michael Jary. That this former monastery pupil conducted a church choir while still a schoolboy is not a fact which would appear immediately obvious. But bearing this fact in mind, it is difficult to believe that Michael Jary is the composer of "Davon geht die Welt nicht unter" and "Ich weiss, es wird einmal ein Wunder geschehn," the two biggest hits ever scored by Zarah Leander in the whole of her career. This musician's path has taken many a turn, from the municipal theatre in Beuthen through many night clubs in Berlin, until at last his "day's work" was crowned with a scholarship awarded to him by the city of Berlin. This gave him the opportunity to compose "serious pieces." Decisive for Jary's film career was the sailor's song which the Rühmann-Sieber-Brausewetter trio sang with such gusto. Since then he has been a made man

FOR EUROPE

Even in wartime German popular music is diffused throughout the world by the cinema and the wireless. SIGNAL selects a few outstanding examples

The Battle of Britain

As the preparations for what became known as the Battle of Britain intensified, Goering boasted that his Luftwaffe, given four days of clear flying weather, would sweep the RAF out of the skies. "The German air force," Hitler proclaimed, "is to overpower the English air force with all the forces at its command in the shortest possible time." Goering was quick to obey. Telling his commanders that "everything depends on using all possible means to defeat the enemy's air force," he ordered the Luftwaffe into all-out attack. The resulting battle was one the RAF could not afford to lose. It would determine the future course of the war.

Goering's airplanes were deployed in three air fleets—Luftflotte 3 in Normandy, Luftflotte 2 in northern France and the Low Countries, and Luftflotte 5 in Denmark and Norway. These were commanded by Field Marshal Hugo Sperrle, Field Marshal Albert Kesselring, and General Hans-Jurgen Stumpf. To defend Britain, Air Chief Marshal Sir Hugh Dowding, who had been commander-in-chief of RAF Fighter Command since 1936, had 700 modern fighters available. He divided them between four groups—10 Group covering southwest England, 11 Group the southeast, 12 Group the Midlands and 13 Group the north of England, Scotland, and Northern Ireland. It was 11 Group, led by Air Vice-Marshal Keith Park, a 44-year-old New Zealander and expert fighter tactician, which was to bear the main brunt of the great air battle.

On the face of it, the portly Reichsmarschal and his subordinate commanders had every reason to feel confident. They had 2,422 aircraft at their disposal, 949 of which were Heinkel He 111, Dornier Do 17 and Junkers Ju 88 bombers, 336 Ju 87 dive bombers, 869 Messerschmitt Me 109 fighters, and 268 Me 110 twin-engine Zerstorers. The Luftwaffe's

aircrews, battle-hardened by their combat experiences over Poland, Norway, and France, were spoiling for the fight. The veterans had also flown for Franco in the Condor Legion during the Spanish Civil War. Though they recognized that taking on the RAF would not necessarily be a pushover, they were certain that ultimately they would score yet another speedy victory.

In some ways, however, the Luftwaffe's superiority was less marked than comparing numbers of aircraft might imply. Though the Me 109, its mainstay fighter, was as good as the Spitfires and better than the Hurricanes with which Fighter Command was equipped, its limited endurance meant that it could spend only minutes in British airspace before being forced to turn for home to refuel. British aircraft production was also outstripping that of Germany. Driven on by the dynamic Lord Beaverbrook, Churchill's newly-appointed Minister for Aircraft Production, the British aircraft industry was working flat out seven days a week. In just a few weeks, the production of new aircraft rose by 62 per cent, new engines by 33 per cent, repaired aircraft by 186 per cent, and repaired engines by 159 per cent. This meant that nearly 300 new

aircraft a week were pouring off the production lines; in addition, in the last two weeks of June alone, more than 250 damaged aircraft were repaired and sent back to squadron service. By contrast, German aircraft production was falling way behind that of Britain. In June, only 220 fighters were built, and 344 bombers. The following month, these figures fell again. Repair figures were even worse. During the whole of 1940, only just over 1,000 damaged Me 109s, and a paltry 59 Ju 88s, were made airworthy.

Above all, Fighter Command had radar to give it early warning of approaching German attacks. Dotted along the British coast in a vast arc, a series of twenty-one gigantic long-range radar masts—they were as much as 360 feet tall—stood looking out to sea. They worked in tandem with thirty shorter, more squat shorter-range radar stations and were supported by 30,000 volunteer members of the Observer Corps, who manned 1,000 observation points further inland. The plots were fed through to Fighter Command headquarters at Stanmore, Middlesex, to the four Group headquarters around the country, and to any sectors under specific threat of attack. The sector

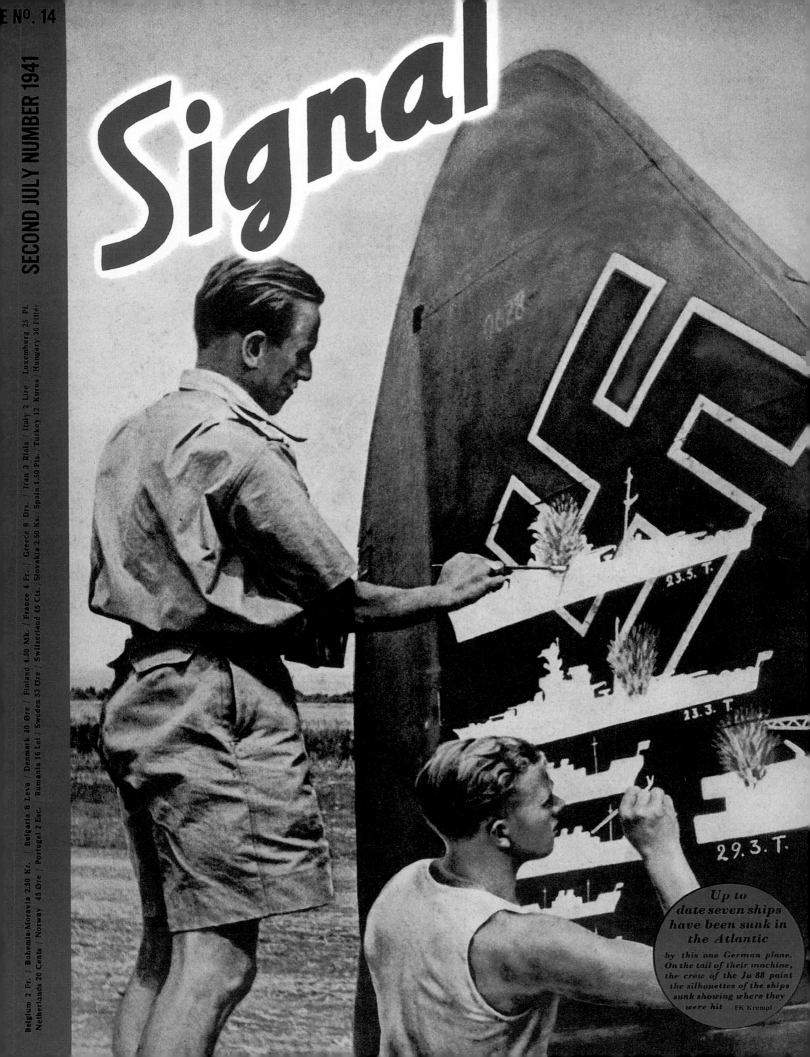

controllers ordered the fighters into the air, and then used radio to help to guide them to their targets. Luftwaffe intelligence had no clear idea of what these strange masts were for, and totally failed to appreciate what a vital role they played in Britain's air defense system.

Adlertag and after

Goering chose August 13 as Adlertag (Eagle Day), when the massed might of his air fleets would be turned against the RAF to begin the process of pounding it into submission. The day, however, started badly for the Luftwaffe, as Colonel Johannes Fink, commander of KG 2 was to discover. His Do 17 bombers took off at 7.30am, climbing high over northern France towards Cap Gris Nez, where they were supposed to rendezvous with their fighter escort. No fighters, however, appeared; instead, an unexpected cloud bank loomed ahead. Fink nevertheless decided to press on with the attack.

As they approached the airfield that was their target, Fink's aircrews prepared to drop their bombs. Suddenly, the rearmost Dorniers were set upon by Spitfires from 74 Squadron, diving down out of the morning sun. Fink lost one Do 17 in this first attack, and most of the others were damaged. Then, as the battered bombers flew over the Thames estuary on their way back to their base near Cambrai, they came under attack again—this time from 111 Squadron's Hurricanes. Four Dorniers were shot down in flames; a further four managed to limp home, trailing clouds of smoke and riddled with bullet holes. Speechless with fury, Fink telephoned Kesselring himself to complain. The field marshal told him that, because of the change in the weather, Goering had ordered the attack postponed until the afternoon. The decision had been made in time to stop the fighters taking off, but not the bombers. Apparently, there was no means of contacting them directly to order them to turn back once they were in the air.

Things went from bad to worse. When twenty-three Me 110s from Caen arrived over the Dorset coast, they were promptly engaged by three Hurricane squadrons waiting in the sky above them. By the time the Me 110s managed to break off the action and turn for home, one had been shot down over the land, six more had crashed into the sea, and a further seven had been damaged. Just nine of the Me 110s made it back to base unscathed. Two groups of Ju 87s heading for Middle Wallop in Hampshire were, despite their fighter escort, equally roughly received. Around a third of the dive bombers were shot down; nearly all the survivors suffered some degree of damage.

The battle intensifies

Though the Luftwaffe managed to mount an impressive total of 1,485 sorties that day, they lost thirty-nine airplanes as opposed to only fifteen RAF fighters. When the attacks were renewed two days later, they lost another seventy-six machines; the RAF twenty-nine. The JU 87s were suffering so badly that soon they were to be withdrawn from the battle entirely.

Goering was nonplussed by the losses, even though the egregious colonel Beppo Schmid, who combined being a member of his personal staff with playing a leading light in Luftwaffe air intelligence, convinced him that the Luftwaffe was destroying many more RAF fighters than actually was the case. On August 16, Schmid told the credulous Reichsmarschal that Fight Command had just 430 aircraft left, of which only 300 could be considered serviceable. In fact, Dowding still had 653 airworthy fighters ready for action.

The Reichsmarschal decided that a change of tactics was required. Instead of allowing his fighters to roam freely above the aerial battlefield so that they could engage Fighter Command's Spitfires and Hurricanes on the most favorable terms, he ordered them to stay close to the vulnerable bombers and protect them at all costs. Arithmetically, what this meant was that three fighters were now committed to defending each bomber. He also decided to concentrate on knocking out Fighter Command's ground bases, though paradoxically he also told his airmen to stop wasting their time attacking the RAF's vital radar stations, because, as he put it, "not one of those attacked has so far been put out of action." Luftwaffe air intelligence had completely failed to detect their true significance.

Crisis point

As August drew toward a close, the battle intensified farther. Every clear day saw more mass Luftwaffe attacks. The RAF began to give under the strain. Not only were its fighters now being shot down in increasing numbers as they sought to decimate Goering's bombers, but it was also losing pilots at an unsustainable rate. Then, the Luftwaffe changed tactics again.

Hitler had given strict orders that London was not to be bombed, but, on the night of August 24, several German bombers, aiming for an aircraft factory at Rochester, mistook the River Thames for the Medway and accidentally dropped their bombs on Millwall, Tottenham, and Islington instead. The British response was immediate. The following night, around fifty Bomber Command aircraft were despatched to bomb Berlin. They bombed the German capital again on the night of 28 August.

Both raids did little actual damage. Only a handful of bombs actually

In the cloud-covered sky over England The same spectacle every day: A Messerschmitt fighter has discovered a Spitfire and steers towards it. The British plane, from being the pursuer, now becomes the pursued. The R.A.F. pilot dives in an attempt to escape, but the Messerschmitt follows, hurtles towards him, spraying him with machine-gun fire until the enemy plane crashes to the ground

fell within the city during the first attack. The second was slightly more successful, with twelve Berliners being killed and twenty-nine wounded. Nevertheless, the moral impact was considerable. Goering himself had assured the Berliners that their city would never be bombed.

Two nights later, the RAF was back again, targeting Tempelhof, the city's main airfield. Another air raid followed on September 3. Hitler had had enough. In a speech he delivered at the Sportsplatz the following day, he vowed revenge. "If the British air force drops two, three or four thousand kilos of bombs," he raged, "then we will now drop 150,000, 180,000, 230,000, 300,000 or 400,000 kilos, or more, in one night. If they declare that they will attack our cities on a large scale, we will erase theirs. We will put a stop to the game of these night-pirates, as God is our witness. The hour is coming when one or the other of us will break, and it will not be National Socialist Germany!"

The tide turns

The vengeful Fuehrer despatched Goering to take over personal command of the battle. London was now to be subject to mass attack. On the afternoon of September 7, the Reichsmarschal stood on the cliffs of Cap Gris Nez with his staff and assembled commanders watching the largest Luftwaffe formation yet assembled thunder over his head. It consisted of 900 aircraft—300 bombers and 600 fighters. The sky was thick with German aircraft, stacked up at various levels one upon another as far as the eye could see. As the bombers battered London's docklands—they returned that night to continue the work—the British sent out the codeword that indicated invasion was considered imminent.

The Luftwaffe struck at London the next day, and again the following one, this time targeting the City and the West End. With the pressure mounting to fix a date for the launching of the invasion, or postpone it until a later date, the pressure on Goering to achieve a decisive result mounted almost by the hour. On September 15, he accordingly launched what he intended to be a knockout blow.

The Germans attacked in two

A Messerschmitt Me 109 stalks an unsuspecting Spitfire. The photograph was probably faked. As far as Signal was concerned, the Luftwaffe was winning the Battle of Britain. In reality, the opposite was the case.

waves—one in the morning and the other in the afternoon. Kesselring, in charge of the operation, put all the airplanes he could into the skies; the RAF, similarly at full stretch, claimed to have destroyed 185 of them for the loss of only twenty-five aircraft and eleven pilots. The real figure for Luftwaffe losses were sixty-one aircraft destroyed with another twenty so badly damaged that they had to be written off.

It was not the decisive victory Goering had expected. Two days later, Hitler postponed Operation Sealion again; on October 12, he ordered the invasion canceled until the following spring. The Fuehrer was now set on another course of action. Turning his back on Britain as Napoleon had before him, he began speeding preparations for an all-out attack on the Soviet Union.

"It's time now, Max..."

Before the night-raid on London

At a night-flying base somewhere on the coast. It is raining in torrents and the night is as black as pitch. The aerodrome is far away and in the distance green and red positional lights blink. Suddenly there is the flash of a torch-lamp. Dangerous reddish blue sparks are emitted out of the exhaust pipe of an aeroplane. Further off there is a jet of flame. There is everywhere the roaring of engines from different parts of the big aerodrome, it is a continuously vibrating noise; that is the music of the flying base. In the midst of all this can be heard the sound of hushed human voices, then the rattling of bombs and machines being handled, that is all.

"Be careful with the bomb. Push it and let us have a little more light. Now you can heave it up. Steady on. Come more this way."

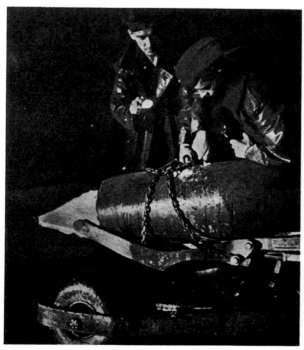

"This one is also to go, but must first have the fuse put in. That's how it's done, do you see? Bring your torch-lamp nearer. Can you hear how the storm is beginning to rage out there? All the same it won't disturb us. What time is it? Almost midnight?"

"Well, gentlemen, it is now just 12 o'clock. Are there any more questions? There are not any? Very good, then be at your machines in ten minutes, please. Good luck."

The Squadron leader: "You're lucky boys, it's moonlight. Everyone get to his bus and start off. I'll follow you, and we'll meet over London. Get a move on, old chap"

"Is everything all correct, Max, and everyone at his post? You're doing the bombing, Max. Have you looked to see if the bombs have been attached?"

"Don't you worry. The bombs we've got with us are plenty. Well, what are we waiting for? Are we going to make a start or not?"

"Another minute and a half. It's time now, Max"

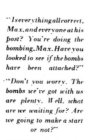

"Get into the machine, Max. Have you got the log book and maps?" "Of course I've got them both, and also picture postcards, if that's what you mean." "Get a move on, Max, it's time"

An old soldier of the ground personnel to a young one: — "Look out, you're getting into the runway again. Just look at it. isn't it like a huge and dangerous beast being hurled into the night? Like a beast with flaming eyes? Look after your cap. You see, it's been blown off, you must also beware of the wash from the prop. Do you see how the machine is rising, it's now away from the ground. Silence. Why are you stumbling? Can't you yet see at night? You'll learn how to do so. Did you ask what kind of wind that is? It's the storm, lad. the storm of the Atlantic. Did you ask where the moon is? Well, it's disappeared again. old son."

Left:

The pilot: — "Do you see how they're searching for us, Max? They've been waiting for us, Max, and now they're sending their regards up to us. What they'd best like would be to burn us up with their beams. What do you say? They're getting at us? No, they're not, but we're getting at them. Are they still disturbing you? I've already got used to them. And, even if they find us, they can't hurt us. Why not? Because we're convinced that they can't. They only give light, but they don't bite"

At the flying base: "Wireless message from the Squadron leader!"

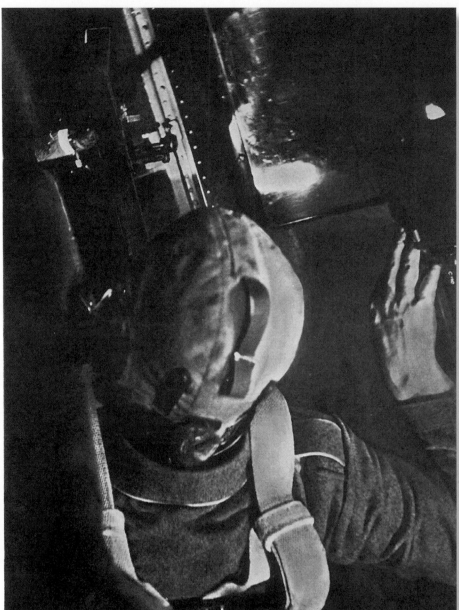

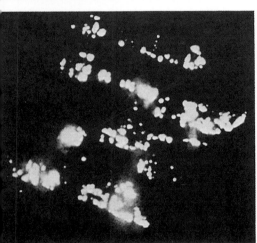

"Do you see London burning underneath us? I should hardly think the Englishmen are now singing their soldier song "The bells of hell go tingelingeling, for you and not for me". "Do you think they're singing that now?"

"Are you ready, Max? Have you got your finger on the button and the target sighted? You have, well drop the bombs".

Left:
"All machines on their way back from London undamaged, boys"

Right:
The soldier, showing the machine its place at the air base, shouts up to it as soon as the propellers stop: — "What's it look like in London?" A voice from the plane answers: — "In London did you say? Well, the bells of hell are tingelingeling-ing The bells of hell!"

THE END

We are flying across the Channel in a formation of dive-bombers consisting of three machines. We are flying above the clouds. I photograph our two companions

With the pilot's eyes...

and the long-distance camera in a dive-bomber

by PK. A. Grimm

The first dive-bomber in our formation, dips to the right and prepares to dive

And now the second

And now we too dip our wing

I am a "Special Leader" in the Propaganda Company. But not in the Air Force. It is true I have often flown, but never in war time. But it is my great desire to take part in an attack on the enemy in a dive-bomber and at last I have received permission to do so. As far as cameras are concerned, I take my Leica with the long-distance lens with me.

I arrive about midday at the flying field from which we are to start. I immediately realize the difficulties of my whole situation: I cannot put on flying-kit, I cannot put on a parachute and above all, what is most important, I cannot be strapped in. I must be able to move, I must be able to stand and I must be able to take photographs across the pilot's shoulder. For this purpose the section between the two seats must be removed. This all comes to light whilst I am standing near a machine the engines of which are already warming up. The pilot, a lieutenant, smiles indulgently and says: "I don't think you will be successful in what you want to do. You see, you will no longer be able to tell what is above and what is below you and you will only have very vague ideas about your own person."

Of course, it is possible things will turn out that way. In any case, I climb up across the aeroplane wings to my seat behind the pilot. I am holding my camera, the best one I possess at the moment, tightly in my hand, and I am just about to arrange myself in my seat when the signal to start is given. We are off.

Everything now takes place incredibly quickly. In a very short time the aeroplane is flying at a height of 2500 metres. The Channel is already lying below us. We have penetrated a bank of clouds and climbed still higher. I now notice for the first time that we are not alone, but that we are flying in formation. Two dive-bombers are ahead of us. We are all at the same height. Beneath us, clouds. We sometimes catch a glimpse of the Channel through a gap in the clouds. Above us is the sun, below us snow white clouds and through the gaps patches of blue, the Channel. I know that our objective is a steamer which the reconnaissance planes have reported. The lieutenant flies on in silence. I hold my camera on my knees, consider my situation and come to the conclusion that at the moment, I am still in good form. I try myself out, I stand up and experiment to see in what attitude I shall best be able to take photographs during the dive which we are to make.

And now the moment has come when it seems that the adventure is to begin. I have as yet seen absolutely nothing on the surface of the Channel, but the lieutenant shouts through his microphone: "All clear for the attack!" I stand up.

I see the first machine in our formation plunge down to the left.

I see the second machine in our formation plunge down to the left.

Both machines are swallowed up by the clouds. Something is happening to my body. It changes place. Now I know what is happening to it. I am now really standing on my head, yet I do not fall. By a tremendous effort of will I hold my camera and like a flash of lightning the thought crosses my mind that I am after all able to hold it in such a way that at the critical moment I shall be able to take my photographs across the pilot's shoulder. I suddenly consider my position and discover that with a few fingers grasping some object or other I am in a position to steady my whole body and my camera. My will seems to triumph over the laws of gravity. Now, however, something happened which at the moment seemed so terrible to me that I shall never forget it. Until now it had naturally been light here. We are plunging in sunshine. All at once darkness surrounds me. Nothing is visible any longer. What has happened to me? Has some accident happened to us? — I must say that I find it very difficult to relate at all what occurred to me at this moment. A frightful depression swept over me which was all the more severe as I had previously been as it were in a state of happiness. I shouted aloud. I no longer have any idea of what I shouted. And the reason will also never be known. Or will it perhaps? The whole world beneath me had disappeared. It was completely erased. Nothing real existed any longer to form a hold for my sensations. We pierced the bank of clouds.

There is our objective: the ship

Immediately a most extreme happiness overwhelms me: still hurtling downwards and as though liberated from my body and released from all material things I recognized the sunshine, the sea, the coast and also the objective. We have not flown straight down into hell, into grey oblivion, no, we are diving down to attack a ship. I have regained control over myself. Once more I am alive in the world of our war — and with a feeling of happiness I immediately realize that I have been successful in screwing up my concentration to the highest pitch. Below us is the steamer, our objective, my camera is in my hands and I am making one exposure after another. Uncanny, but very oppressive too; the ship continually grows bigger, it is rushing towards me.

Then — a wrench passes through the whole plane, my body is convulsed for

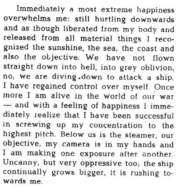

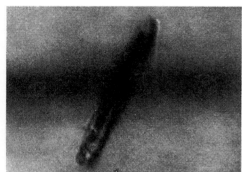
Fast as lightning we shoot towards the objective. The ship grows larger

When we land, a comrade comes and says to me: "Just show us how you stood in the dive-bomber to take the photographs". I demonstrate how I did it and my comrade photographs me. The lieutenant, the pilot of the plane, smiles

the fraction of a second: the bomb has been released. I take another photograph, but a superhuman strength, an iron hand presses me downwards. I drop to my knees, I fall across the wireless apparatus, I am a worm, crushed and trampled upon, a being incapable of making the slightest movement and all my mental strength is just sufficient to enable me to realize that in this second the pilot arrested the dive.

I have already come to myself again. Below me lies our objective and I photograph the ship which has been struck and is belching forth a pillar of smoke.

And still larger. Another 1200 metres to the objective

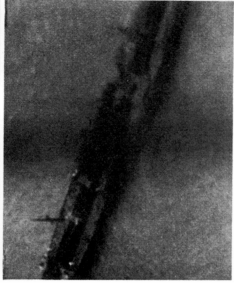
400 metres distance. Another photograph. The bomb will be released in another second

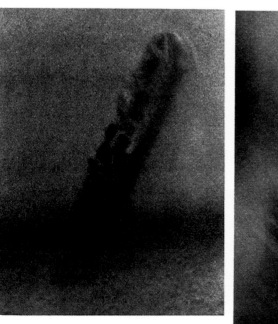
800 metres distance. The ship grows larger

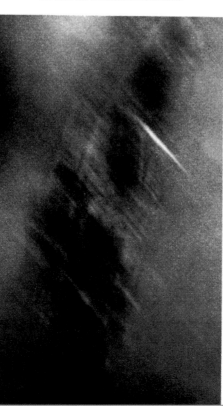
The ship suddenly disappears from the view-finder. The plane has finished its dive

The plane is once more flying horizontally. I photograph the hit

... and how it appears to his "victim"

I stand on the ship which the dive-bomber is going to approach. A plane plunges out of the clouds at a height of 2500 metres

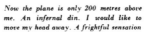

The machine is only 400 metres distant now. It is plunging vertically at us. It is a terrible sight

Now the plane is only 200 metres above me. An infernal din. I would like to move my head away. A frightful sensation

It hurtles towards me from a height of 1500 metres

800 metres! The sirens of the falling machine sound uncanny

A hundred metres above me the plane straightens out and flies away over my head

I turn and see a weird animal soaring upwards

I have also taken photographs from on board a ship of what an attack by a dive-bomber on a ship looks like. This was not during the course of a real engagement, but I asked the pilot of a dive-bomber to fly down in the direction of the ship on which I was. He did so. What such an attack looks like when seen from the ship is shown by the pictures on the following pages

The dive-bomber is moving away . . .

. . . and regains the clouds

The End

"I flew with them..."

Our photographer-correspondent, Hans Schaller, takes the first coloured photographs of an attack by German dive-bombers

Ready to start
Our fine planes, of the Ju 87 type, says Schaller, take their grim load on board from the long row of bombs (right)

Five hands grasp the crank
One engine after another begins to roar. In the meantime the commander has given . . .

. . . his last instructions
to the crews. Two minutes later our flight begins. We speedily gain height and lay our course for X.

1

2

3

... flying towards the enemy

The first row of planes (left above) is flying next to my machine, our correspondent continues. I have been allowed to follow them with my camera until the bombs fall. We are already high above the clouds and "my" planes are below me. They are just changing their course. I cannot hear them above the noise of my own machine; they seem to be flying quietly and noiselessly above the landscape like sharp-eyed birds of prey, eager to claim their victim, thirsting to attack (above). We shall soon reach our objective — one of the dive-bombers is already leaving the formation! The machine tilts to one side (left), begins to dive ...

FROM BLITZKRIEG TO BARBAROSSA

Though the Luftwaffe had been defeated in the Battle of Britain—a fact naturally never admitted by *Signal*—Hitler was still completely confident of ultimate victory. Immediately after the French capitulation, he ordered his military chiefs to begin planning a surprise attack on the USSR. The Fuehrer no longer feared a war on two fronts; he assured his generals that, in comparison to the invasion of France, crushing the Red Army would be child's play.

War in the Balkans

While the Luftwaffe's bombers attempted to blitz Britain into submission, Italy, which had entered the war on Hitler's side in June 1940, looked to expand in the Balkans as part of Mussolini's efforts to build a new Roman Empire. On October 25, without telling Hitler of his plans, the Duce invaded Greece. Within weeks, the Italians were being driven back all along the line, and were repulsed in North Africa the following month. Hitler saw no alternative but to intervene himself. His Balkan incursion was quickly successful, but it cost the Fuehrer valuable time. It delayed the launch of Operation Barbarossa—the German attack on the USSR—by a crucial six weeks.

In June 1940, after nine months of non-belligerency, Mussolini declared war on Britain and France. It was, the Duce declared, a "revolutionary" war—one that would result in a fundamental redistribution of territory and resources, and the final realization of the Fascist aspiration to dominate the Mediterranean. The reality was somewhat different. When Mussolini told Marshal Pietro Badoglio, the chief of the Italian General Staff, of his decision to go to war, Badoglio, according to his own later account, told the Duce that, given Italian lack of military preparedness, this would be "suicide." Mussolini brushed aside the protest. The war would be over in weeks, he assured his worried generals. "I only need a few thousand dead so that I can sit at the peace conference as a man who has fought."

Though *Signal* welcomed the Reich's new ally with open arms, it soon looked as though Italy might prove a military liability rather than an asset. The Italians totally failed to break through France's Alpine defense system when, at Mussolini's insistence, they struck at the already-defeated French. Only Marshal Petain's decision to ask Hitler for an armistice saved them from probable humiliation. In North Africa, despite the Duce's urgings, Marshal Rodolfo Graziani stubbornly put off attacking the British. After much prodding, his army finally lurched across the Libyan border and into Egypt on September 13. The Italians got as far as Sidi Barrani, a desolate outpost 54 miles (87 km) inside the country. Then they stopped and dug in.

The Italians in Greece

This was not what Mussolini had expected. He had gambled everything on securing a quick, spectacular, cheap victory. Back in April, he had told Count Galeazzo Ciano, his playboy Foreign Minister and son-in-law, "to make a people great, it is necessary to send them into battle even if you have to kick them in the pants." If Graziani would not oblige him, he would look elsewhere for the military success he craved.

Accordingly, the Duce switched his attention from North Africa to the Balkans. In March 1939, his forces had marched into and annexed Albania. He now had his greedy eyes on a bigger prize—Greece. Paradoxically, the actual decision to attack the Greeks was provoked by the actions of his Axis partner. Hitler, without prior consultation, had prevailed upon Marshal Ion Antonescu, Romania's newly-appointed prime minister, to allow the Germans to take control of the vital Romanian oil fields. The infuriated Duce decided to retaliate. "Hitler keeps confronting me with a fait accompli," he complained to Ciano. "This time, I shall pay him back in his own coin. He will learn from the newspapers that I have occupied Greece. The equilibrium will be restored." The Fuehrer was aware his ally was up to something, but was not completely sure what the Duce intended. Hastily, he arranged to meet Mussolini in Florence to warn him against launching any Balkan military adventure. He was too late. On his arrival on October 28, Mussolini gleefully greeted him with the worlds "Fuehrer, we are on the march." Italian troops had crossed the Albanian border into Greece earlier that morning.

Having made his decision, Mussolini gave his General Staff just a fortnight to prepare for the invasion, as opposed to the three months Badoglio initially advised him would be needed. General Sebastiano Visconti Prasca, the commander-in-chief in Albania, was put in charge of the initial attack. He planned to take the Greeks by surprise. But,

Hell in a Serbian village

"A short distance from a village," reports our correspondent, "we received the message that we were about to encounter the main body of the Morava Division. Immediately afterwards heavy enemy artillery fire rained down on our tanks. Enemy anti-tank guns were in position near the church. We had to break through. My tank rattled down the slightly curved street past the enemy gun emplacement. The shells burst right and left of the tank but the firing was very inaccurate. We stopped near the village school. Then suddenly we got a wireless message from the tank behind us: "Tank 'Schimmelmann' to tank 'Erika'. Enemy artillery left is using your tank to get the range. Change your position at once and take cover." Without delay the tank turned on harshly grating tracks. A moment later a shell from the artillery transformed the spot where it had been stationed into a crater. At top speed we drove on. Our artillery and tank artillery prepared the next village for the approaching storm. We could observe the hits re gistered. Then our tanks attacked, every gun spat fire, but even before we reached the street barricade at the entrance to the village the resistance had been broken. Tanks and artillery lay shot to pieces, guns of the most modern pattern stood abandoned, and munition columns were on fire. The whole street was lost in haze and smoke. Suddenly a Serbian soldier, his face distorted with fright, ran up to our tank. He had left his post and had only one thought: to escape from this hell unfortunately for the Italians, the Greek army had already established strong defenses in the invasion area before the Italians were ready to cross the frontier. When they did so, heavy rain slowed their progress and also deprived them of air cover. The attack was soon bogged down in the mountains and the mud.

Visconti Prasca had expected the Greeks to stay on the defensive. They did not. Much to his surprise, they counter-attacked and rapidly forced the Italians back. Mussolini replaced Visconti Prasca with General Ubaldo Soddu, but the new commander failed to check what looked like becoming a complete rout. Mussolini got rid of the exasperating Badoglio next, forcing him to resign and ordering General Ugo Cavallero to take over as head of the General Staff. Soddu, too, was sacked. Rumors had reached Mussolini that, even in Albania, he was devoting his evenings to composing film music.

The Germans intervene

As the dispirited Italians fell back farther and farther, Mussolini came close to despair. "Every great man makes one mistake," he told Ciano, "and mine was when I believed General Visconti Prasca. He was so confident. The human material I have to work with is worthless, quite worthless." The crestfallen Duce was left with no alternative but to go cap in hand to Hitler and beg him for military assistance.

Hitler realized that the Italians could not cope unaided. On January 19, 1941, he summoned Mussolini to the Berghof, his Bavarian mountain retreat, and told him he would send his troops into Greece as early as possible that spring. He had already authorized planning to start for Operation Marita, the code name for their invasion. He had also persuaded Hungary to join the Tripartite Pact. Romania

and Bulgaria followed. The Fuehrer had two main aims. The first was to protect the Romanian oil fields, which produced the fuel on which his panzers relied, from possible air attack by RAF bombers flying from Greek airfields. The second was to stop the British from using Greece as a forward base from which to threaten his southern flank when he launched Operation Barbarossa, the attack he was readying against the Soviet Union.

Neighbouring Yugoslavia presented Hitler with a further problem. Deeply divided politically— the Serbs and Croats leading the quarrelling—it seemed that the only thing holding the country together was the Karadjorvevic monarchy and this, too, was losing grip. Ever since Alexander I, the last Karadjorvevic strongman, had been assassinated by a Croat separatist during a state visit to France in 1934, Prince Paul, his agreeable but less capable brother, had acted as regent for the infant Peter I. Hitler now put ever-increasing pressure on the vacillating Paul to follow in the footsteps of the other Balkan states and adhere to the Tripartite Pact. Paul held out until March 25. Then he caved in and signed.

The consequences were certainly not what Hitler had anticipated. Slovenes and Serbs took to the streets in mass protests. Two days later, a coup staged by anti-German Serb officers in Belgrade ousted Paul and put Peter, now aged 17, on the throne. The Fuehrer's reaction was predictably violent. He summoned his generals and declared that, in view of the Yugoslav betrayal, the country must be invaded at the same time the Wehrmacht struck at Greece. It would be "a lightning operation;" any resistance was to be crushed "with merciless harshness." Italy, Hungary, and Bulgaria would all gain Yugoslav territory, while the

Croats would be granted their long-sought independence. Like Poland, Yugoslavia would be erased from the map.

Blitzing Belgrade

The attack on Yugoslavia began on April 6. Waves of Luftwaffe bombers plastered Belgrade as the prelude to what had been aptly named Operation Punishment. Some 5,000 Yugoslavs were killed in the attack. The German 12th Army, stationed in Bulgaria and commanded by General Wilhelm von List, simultaneously invaded southern Yugoslavia and northern Greece. In Yugoslavia, it drove directly towards the capital. Other German, Hungarian, and Italian forces poured across the country's northern border two days later.

The Yugoslav army, though a million strong on paper, was poorly equipped, badly trained, and suffered from the same ethnic divisions as the country itself. While its Serbian soldiers were eager to fight, the Croatians and Macedonians unwillingly conscripted into its ranks were quick to surrender. On April 10, Germany recognized Croatia's independence; on April 13, Belgrade was occupied by motorcycle reconnaissance troops of the Waffen-SS Division Das Reich. The Yugoslav government capitulated five days later.

The Greek collapse

Even as Hitler's armies readied themselves for their assault, the Greeks tried to avoid war with Germany. British offers to send an expeditionary force to help them were stalled until the last minute. When the first elements of it, docked in Piraeus, arrived, the disembarking troops were astounded to find the local German consul and military attaché on the quayside, brazenly recording their arrival. Athens still had not broken off

Prompt German reaction frustrated British efforts to spread the war to the Balkans, according to this Signal *map. In fact, a reluctant Hitler was forced to intervene to save his Italian ally from disaster after Mussolini's ill-advised Greek invasion.*

diplomatic relations with the Reich.

More crucially, instead of the nine divisions the Greeks considered the minimum credible deterrent, the British initially managed to muster only two, plus a single armored brigade. The Germans were ready to put eight infantry divisions, three motorized divisions, and two panzer formations with a combined strength of 200 tanks into the field against them. The RAF, for its part, could spare only eighty aircraft for Greece, which meant that it was outnumbered ten to one by the Luftwaffe.

The Germans struck first in Macedonia. Though the Greeks, holding the fortifications along the Metaxas Line, put up a tenacious resistance, sheer weight of numbers forced them to retreat. The withdrawal gathered pace when the 2nd Panzer Division, advancing from Yugoslavia, outflanked the Greek defenses near Lake Dojran and pushed forward to Salonika, which fell on April 8. The 60,000 Greek troops trapped in Macedonia capitulated. Almost simultaneously, the Germans thrust through the Monastir gap toward Florina, capturing the town and then cutting behind the Greek positions keeping the Italians pinned down in Albania. Though the Greeks attempted to fall back to the Aliakmon Valley, they, too, were forced to surrender.

With the Greek army seemingly disintegrating and his own forces threatened with encirclement, General Sir Henry Maitland Wilson, the British commander-in-chief, ordered his troops to fall back and be ready for evacuation. The Greeks were not sorry to see them go; on April 16, General Alexandros Papagos, the Greek supreme commander, urged Wilson to withdraw from Greece to save the country from further devastation. Two days later, Alexandros Koryzis, the Greek Prime Minister, killed himself, leaving the nation leaderless. General Georgios Tsolakoslou, commander of the Army of Epirus, asked the Germans for an armistice the following day.

Fall of Crete

Wilson's evacuation started on April 24, the day after King George II and his government fled to Crete. It lasted a week. By April 30, when, having marched into Athens three days before, German forces reached the southern tip of the Greek mainland, it was estimated that more than 50,000 soldiers, including a number of Greeks and Yugoslavs, had got away.

It was the end of the mainland battle, but not of the Greek campaign. Its final stage started on May 20, when Crete was invaded. The Germans committed 17,530 men by glider, transport plane, and parachute to the capture of the island. Against the advice of his service chiefs, Churchill ordered New Zealander Major-General Bernard Freyberg and the 35,000-strong garrison to hold Crete regardless of cost.

Though the British, through decoding enemy signals, knew where the proposed German drop zones were located, Freyberg failed to realize that keeping control of Maleme and its airfield was the key to the entire battle. When, late on May 21, the airfield fell to the Germans, the British position swiftly became untenable. On 27 May, Canea was overrun with Suda Bay falling the following day.

Freyberg ordered as many of his soldiers as possible to trek south over the mountains to Sphakia, from which it was hoped they could be evacuated. The Royal Navy was able to evacuate 13,000 of them, plus a further 4,000 from Heraklion before heavy shipping losses forced the evacuation to be ended on June 1. Almost 12,000 British and Commonwealth troops were left behind on the beaches together with several thousand Greeks.

For the Germans, however, Crete proved to be a pyrrhic victory. It was, said General Kurt Student, the commander of the assault, the "grave of the German paratrooper." Hitler's faith in the offensive power of airborne forces was broken; German losses were so severe that they never attempted a major airborne operation again.

Aircraft carrier Italy

Italy requires no aircraft carriers. The whole of the Apennine Peninsula is the natural taking-off ground for a strong air force such as Italy has developed. Numerous bases on the islands in the eastern and western Mediterranean make it possible to carry out air attacks even on the enemy's most distant positions. The straits between Sicily and Tunis, Crete and Cyrenaica (in the middle of our picture) and also the waters round Gibraltar (front) which are more than 930 miles from Rome, and the vicinity of the Suez Canal (right, in the background) are daily and nightly the scene of conflicts in which the Italian Air Force, thanks to the central position of its base, plays a decisive part

PK. drawing:
Front Correspondent Hans Liska

On the balcony of the Palazzo Vecchio in Florence

The appearance on the balcony of the Führer and the Duce is preceded by a fanfare of trumpets. The crowd greets these two men, the founders of a new and happier Europe, with tempestuous enthusiasm

The Italian Army

Ready to fight — Prepared for war

The Italians are a young nation. Although the Roman Empire lays claim to being the oldest in Europe, Italy is a new state. This probably explains the spirit of the Italian army. A youthful spirit pervades this great machine, a latent power can be felt in its fever for action. The standard of motorization is high. The doctrine of Italian military science, which endorses

**"The force of our arms is undoubtedly great,
but greater still is the firmness of our hearts"**

These were Mussolini's words at one of the great parades on one of the traditional national holidays showing the force and efficiency of the Italian army. Beside Mussolini the Crown Prince: Fascism hand in hand with the Crown, fighting for the right to live of the Italian people

Badoglio in conversation: —

An attentive listener

Pietro Badoglio, Chief of the General Staff, and Duke of Addis Ababa, is not only a splendid narrator but also an attentive listener

Badoglio cuts in

Whenever the conversation touches the sphere in which he is the first expert of the nation, he likes to take part in the debate

The narrator on the defence

A fighting method upon which he frowns, and for which he is temperamentally unfitted: long discussions

. . . and attacking

Just as he defeated the enemy in battle, so he now puts an end to objections thanks to his exact military knowledge

132 militia battalions of blackshirts

132 militia battalions were incorporated in the Italian army, one blackshirt legion for each infantry division. Thus the greyish green regiments of the army and the legions of blackshirts form from henceforth one single bulwark

mobile warfare and frowns upon a "war of nerves" or of defense, appeals to the youthful spirit of the nation. But on the other hand— Rome was a world empire 2000 years ago. So this vigorous, potent young army has the advantages of a glorious national history, and the experience gathered in 2000 years. It also knows the value of organization, and every young Italian soldier today considers himself the apostle of Roman civilization, just as his ancestors did 2000 years ago. Graziano, 20th century Scipio Africanus, not only conquered Libya, but immediately began its colonization. His soldiers built military roads through the deserts, founded cities and reclaimed sand-buried oases. The "Cittadino soldato", the soldierly citizen, has been molded by today's training into a type which also existed

The Song of Victory

flows from his lips. The great victories that Italy gained in Libya, Abyssinia, Spain, and Albania

2000 years ago. The Italian army has two problems to solve. The first is in the Mediterranean, the European Mediterranean area. The second, and more complicated, is on the "fourth coast", the African side of the Mediterranean. From the first day of his rise to power, Mussolini has equipped, organized and trained his armies for these tasks. The Italian army has already proved itself equal to the burden on four battlefields: Graziani's conquest of the Fezzan and the Senussi oases of Kufra were the first feelers extended on African soil, which incidentally still bears the columns, fortresses, temple ruins and graves of ancient Rome. Then came Abyssinia, a colonial war won by Badoglio in record time, another triumph of mature organizing ability and youthful enterprise. Then Spain and Albania . . . new victories which brought new experience. It may well be said that the Spanish war formed the Italian army as we know it today. The mixed divisions of General Roatta, second in command of the Italian General Staff, were here put to the test for the first time. The air force too had excellent opportunity to try out new types of machines in Spain — planes which now play the most important role in the Italian Air Force. This is Italy's army! Rich in experience — spendidly equipped and burning for action, highly alert to its great aims in Europe and abroad. Not a neutral army, but one belonging to a non-combatant power, ready to fight.

"The pilot Mussolini has created one of the strongest airforces of the world," *said General Pricolo, Secretary of State in the Ministry of Air a short time ago before the Fascist parliament. The efficiency and experience of our pilots, the genius of our inventors and engineers are materials of which Italy will never run short*

Tested in Spain
The small two-men tanks, the employment of which decided many battles in the Spanish War

Ubaldo Soddu
Secretary of State in the Ministry of War, which Mussolini personally directs

Rudolfo Graziani
the conqueror of the Fezzan and Harar, the Scipio Africanus of the 20th century, chief of the General Staff of the Italian army

Mario Roatta
head of the Intelligence Department in the Abyssinian War, commander in Spain, now vice-chief of the General Staff

Stood the test in Abyssinia and Albania
Every Italian infantry division has besides the usual infantry, machine-gun and motorized troops also an artillery regiment

Thermo-pylæ

During the hard fighting in the Greek mountains, heavy German artillery continually had to be employed in order to force a breakthrough by the Germans. Above the flash of the guns and the smoke, the white peaks of Olympus rise in eternal peace

The main resistance of the enemy has been broken at Thermopylæ. Mechanized columns follow the rapid advance of the tanks. Enemy fire is still occasionally directed against the line of advance. The crew leap from the lorry and take cover. But the advance can no longer be held up

After days of fighting and marching: the warm springs of Thermopylæ! Uniforms are stripped off in a moment, and the marching troops have soon become a jolly group of bathers

Photographs:
P.K. Müller

This is how the German troops were greeted in most places in Greece
At the head of the population, the Greek Orthodox Archbishop and the Mayor of a small town greet the commander of the troops just marching in

A memorable sight:
The flag of the young and victorious German Army waves above the centuries old pillars of the Acropolis

To the Führer of the German people

The entry of the German troops has once more brought law and order to Greece. A letter addressed to the Führer by the People's Commission of Alexandropolis (formerly Dedeagach), the capital of the Greek district of Ebros, provides especial confirmation of this fact:

"The population of Alexandropolis, who for three days have now lived in the territory occupied by the glorious German troops, have today voluntarily gathered together in order to express their heartfelt thanks to Your Excellency as Supreme Commander of the glorious German army. They promise always to give testimony to their unalterable gratitude for the great civility and true chivalry shown by the courageous troops of occupation to the population. Life, honour, property as well as customs and national tradition have remained untouched. This is already demonstrated by the fact that life is continuing just as before along the same paths."

Alexandropolis, 10th April 1941
The People's Commission of Alexandropolis wishes to convey to your Excellency its gratitude and admiration.

Bishop   President
Pataron Heletios *Anas. Pentzos*
Members
Nic. Stiropoulos Konst. Saridis
General Secretary Manganaris

The capitulation
The agreements are signed. Left: General Jodl from the Führer's Headquarters; behind (standing): The Chief of Staff of the South-East Army, General Greiffenberg; in the middle (seated): The representative of the Greek Army, General Tsolacoglu who later formed the new Greek Government
Photograph: Schlickum (P. Com.)

Above the Acropolis

The engines hum as the German machines sweep across the deep blue skies of Greece. Below them in the landscape they see the red-brown earth, the cypress hedges, the white walls, and the marble stones. classical land greets them with its pillared halls and temples. A new epic is sounding over th

mmortal Athens of Pericles. The buildings he created in spite
i the Peloponnesian War and which still today are a testi-
ony to the superior spirit that animated the Greek ideal
of beauty, are witnesses of the glorious events of our time.
The engines hum — and far below the unforgettable pano-
rama unfolds and fades away once more for an iron will is
driving them on. But the dazzling fame that clings to
their wings and the victory that accompanies them are
lasting things.
Photograph: Roder (P. Com.)

The Axis in North Africa

At the same time as he was preparing to come to the aid of the Italians in Greece, Hitler also agreed to send an expeditionary force to North Africa to bolster up the faltering Italians there. He chose General Erwin Rommel to command the newly formed Afrika Korps. Within weeks of Rommel's arrival in Tripoli, his troops were pushing the over-extended British back. Over the next year the battle see-sawed back and forth until, in June 1942, Rommel was within striking distance of Cairo and the Suez Canal. Finally, the British found the man to stop him. General Sir Bernard Montgomery, the 8th Army's new commander; would "hit Rommel for six" and drive him out of North Africa.

When Rommel arrived in Tripoli on February 12, 1941, the military situation in North Africa would have daunted a less self-confident general. In December 1940, General Sir Archibald Wavell, British commander-in-chief in the Middle East, had launched a major offensive, which drove the Italians out of the chain of fortresses they had constructed around Sidi Barrani, and threw them back in disorder out of Egypt.

Wavell quickly followed up his success. Marshal Rodolfo Graziani, his Italian opposite number, ordered his troops to make a stand at Bardia. General Annibale Bergonzoli, nicknamed "Electric Whiskers" by the British, felt confident that his 45,000-strong garrison, backed by 400 guns, and huddled behind newly-constructed defenses and a massive minefield, could hold out indefinitely. Events were to prove him wrong.

Wavell's men launched their assault early on January 3, 1942. By 8.00am, crocodiles of Italian prisoners were already trudging disconsolately through the British lines. By 3.00pm, the battle was over. Around 40,000 Italians surrendered. The Australians, who had borne the brunt of the attack, lost a grand total of 456 men.

There was no stopping Wavell now. Tobruk fell to the Australians on January 22, and Benghazi a few days later (the Italians had already evacuated the port). On February 1, Graziani signaled Mussolini that he intended to abandon Cyrenaica completely, and fall back farther west into Tripolitania. As the surviving Italians streamed towards Tripoli, their retreat was cut off at Beda Fomm. On February 7, they surrendered. It was the end of one of the most one-sided campaigns in modern military history.

Rommel takes the offensive

Initially, Hitler decided to minimize his North African exposure. Libya, he told his generals, was militarily insignificant, but its loss might jeopardize Mussolini's hold on power. It might also free British forces for action elsewhere. Rommel was told firmly that his job was to bolster up the Italians, and confine himself to protecting Tripolitania against any renewed British attack.

The 5th Light Motorized Division, a force put together from elements of the 3rd Panzer Division, was the first German formation to arrive in Tripolitania; 15th Panzer followed. This meant that Rommel had 31,000 men at his disposal. Immediately, he began complaining that it was not enough. Nor was he happy at having to answer to the Italian supreme command. He flew back to Germany to appeal to Hitler to be allowed to launch an offensive of his own into Cyrenaica. The Fuehrer turned him down flat.

Rommel pressed ahead regardless. When Luftwaffe aerial reconnaissance revealed that the British seemed to be pulling back from their forward positions, he ordered his troops to advance. Supported by two Italian divisions—the Ariete and Brescia—the 5th Light pushed forward to El Agheila, and then on to Mersa Brega without meeting significant resistance. It was the start of an offensive that would see the British driven out of the whole of Cyrenaica in little more than a week.

If truth be told, Rommel had more than his fair share of luck. Churchill had insisted that many of Wavell's best troops be withdrawn and sent to support the Greeks. Nor was the attack expected; Wavell believed that the Axis forces would not be in a position to challenge the British in Cyrenaica before May at the earliest. If Rommel did attack,

Soldiers of the Afrika Korps take a break from the battle and the heat in the remains of a Roman temple. The picture essay from which this photograph comes praises German ability to adapt to weather conditions on all fronts.

the British commander was certain the farthest he could possibly advance was to Benghazi, after which supply difficulties would force the Germans to halt.

Wavell had miscalculated. Instead of halting, Rommel divided his troops into four columns and pressed farther and farther forwards. Three of the four columns cut overland through the hump of Cyrenaica to converge on Meehili, while the other pursued the British down the coastal road. This was the Via Balbia, soon to be renamed the Rommelstrasse by the Afrika Korps. Benghazi fell on April 4, and Derna on April 7. Tobruk was cut off on April 10, and Bardia captured two days later. By April 25, Rommel had reached the Egyptian frontier.

Desert stalemate

Not everything was going Rommel's way. Despite repeated attacks, the garrison in besieged Tobruk held out. The Germans needed to

take the port to ensure that they would receive sufficient supplies to maintain the momentum of their advance. Rommel's repeated failure to force Tobruk to surrender meant that his forces had to halt at the Halfaya Pass and at Sollum, not far across the Egyptian border. Shortage of supplies meant that Rommel now could neither advance nor retreat.

Wavell launched his first attempt to relieve Tobruk on May 15. Aptly named Operation Brevity, it was a complete failure. A month later, he tried again with Operation Battleaxe. But, though this time he did manage to recapture Sollum, he got no farther. After three days of inconclusive fighting, he called off the attack.

For Churchill, this was one failure too many. He despatched Wavell to India, where the luckless general took over from General Sit Claude Auchinleck as commander-in-chief. The latter shifted to the Middle East to take over from Wavell. Like his predecessor, Auchinleck was under almost constant pressure from London to attack. Like Wavell, too, he resisted it stubbornly until he judged he

could go over to the offensive with a fair chance of success.

Operation Crusader

Auchinleck launched Operation Crusader on November 18, 1941. On paper, he had all the advantages; the 8th Army, as the Western Desert Force had been renamed, could field over 700 tanks, while the Afrika Korps had only 320, of which nearly half were Italian. Rommel's forces were also hampered by a shortage of gasoline and lack of ammunition.

Rommel dismissed the attack as no more than a large-scale raid, but soon the Afrika Korps was fighting for its life. Tobruk's garrison smashed through the German siege lines, and began to push east to link up with the New Zealanders advancing along the coastal road. Rommel reacted by thrusting southeast with his two panzer divisions, aiming to reach the Egyptian frontier and relieve the garrisons at Bardia, Sollum, and his troops holding the Halfaya Pass. For three days, confusion raged as both sides maneuvred to gain a decisive advantage. Eventually, it was Rommel who was compelled to order a withdrawal. His ill-advised raid had scattered his forces and exhausted his meager fuel reserves. He was now trapped in a battle of attrition he could not hope to win.

On December 4, the 8th Army relieved Tobruk; three days later, Rommel ordered his troops to fall back to Ain el Gazala about 50 miles west of the port. The forces the retreat left stranded at the Halfaya Pass and Bardia were forced to surrender. Then, as the British attacked his defenses at Gazala on December 15, Rommel ordered a further retreat right back to Tripolitania.

On the surface, Crusader appeared to be a great British victory. Rommel had lost 340 tanks, 332 planes, 2,300 killed, 6,000 wounded, and 30,000 missing or captured. But the Afrika

Through clouds of water and sand

Through the foaming spray of the wave breaking over the bows of the troopships, through the dust of the African desert sand rising round the armoured reconnaissance car ... two photographs of the way which lead General Rommel's mobile troops to victory in Africa. Photographs : Mahlo and Schultz

Korps had not been eliminated and the price the British had paid for victory was a heavy one. Resupplied with tanks and fuel, Rommel struck back on January 21, 1942. Like Wavell, Auchinleck was taken by surprise. Benghazi fell on January 29 as the resurgent Afrika Korps drove the British back in confusion. Rommel cleared Cyrenaica of British troops in just 15 days.

From Gazala to El Alamein

Auchinleck ordered 8th Army to dig in along a north to south line running from Gazala on the coast to Bir Hacheim, a small desert outpost about 50 miles (80 km) inland. General Neil Ritchie, in field command, split his troops between seven defensive boxes behind which were smaller defensive positions placed to block the obvious lines of advance towards Tobruk. The gaps between the defensive positions were patrolled by 849 tanks. Rommel had 340 German and 225 Italian tanks at his disposal.

The British position looked strong, but it had weaknesses which Rommel was quick to exploit when the battle opened on May 26. He ordered most of his Italian divisions to distract the British by attacking them head-on, while his panzer divisions swung round the southernmost box at Bir Hacheim, and the Trieste Division penetrated the gap between Bir Hacheim and the next box 13 miles to the north. Though the Italians got bogged down in the minefields the British had laid to the south of the Gazala Line, the rest of the attack went according to plan. After two days of fighting, Rommel's forces had bypassed the key boxes, and penetrated to the heart of the British defensive triangle.

Nevertheless, Knightsbridge, the box held by the Guards Brigade, withstood everything Rommel could throw at it, while the Free French garrison at Bir Hacheim repulsed the Italians. It looked as though Rommel's attack was running out of steam, but, instead of launching a counter-attack, Ritchie ordered his troops to stick to their boxes. It proved to be a fatal mistake.

Rommel sensed that he had a chance of snatching victory from the jaws of defeat. Concentrating his forces in an area the British called the Cauldron, a depression in the middle of their positions, he readied himself to attack the box to his east, at the same time renewing the attack on Bir Hacheim. The box fell on June 1; the Free French were finally forced out of Bir Hacheim ten days later.

In theory, the British still should have been able to hold on, but, in practice, they were on the verge of being defeated heavily. On June 12, Rommel attacked northwards; the following evening, Ritchie realized that his tank losses were such that his armor could no longer protect his southern flank. The next morning, he ordered the Gazala Line to be evacuated. "The battle has been won and the enemy is breaking up," Rommel noted laconically in his diary. The surrender of Tobruk on June 21 was the icing on the cake.

News of the collapse reached Churchill while he was conferring with President Roosevelt in Washington. It reduced him to near-despair. Mussolini flew to prepare for a triumphal entry into Cairo, while Hitler promoted Rommel to field marshal, the youngest German general ever to hold the rank. He also authorized him to drive forward into Egypt with the command "Onward to Cairo!" For his part, Auchinleck resolved to make a last-ditch stand against the triumphant Axis forces. He chose El Alamein, less than 100 miles from Alexandria, as his battleground.

The tide turns

Rommel crossed the Egyptian frontier on June 23; on June 30, he reached El Alamein. Unable to outflank the British position, he decided on an immediate frontal assault. It was unsuccessful. Auchinleck fought him to a standstill. On July 3, Rommel abandoned the attack and went over to the defensive.

A disappointed Mussolini flew back to Rome, just as Churchill arrived in Cairo to review the situation. He had lost faith in Auchinleck's ability to win a decisive victory and now brought in General Sir Harold Alexander to replace him as commander-in-chief. Command of 8th Army was given to General Sir Bernard Montgomery. The latter was not the premier's first choice. General William Gott had been selected for the job, but he was shot down and killed on his way to taking up his appointment.

Montgomery proved an inspired selection, quickly enthusing his new command with his own self-confidence. Having beaten off Rommel's last attempt at a breakthrough in a two-day battle at Alam Halfa starting on August 30, he patiently readied 8th Army to launch its own offensive. By the time he was ready to give battle on October 23, he had 230,000 men and 1,200 tanks ready for action. The British also enjoyed total air superiority.

The resulting battle turned into a slogging match as 8th Army attempted to break through Rommel's defenses. The end came on November 4, when, with only thirty tanks capable of further action, Rommel, despite Hitler's orders to stand fast and fight to the last man, ordered a retreat which soon degenerated into full-scale flight.

Four days later, an Anglo-American expeditionary force landed in Morocco and Algeria and, having come to terms with the Vichy French, began to roll eastwards. The Germans and Italians were caught between two vastly-superior armies. Though they held on in Tunisia until the following May, the end for the Axis in North Africa was clearly in sight.

The desert sand flies up...

A German fighter breaks its journey at an Italian aerodrome at the front in Africa

Desert sand and palm-trees...

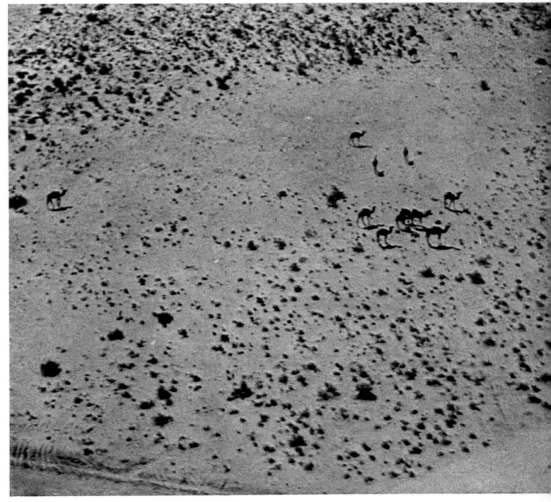

A picture brought back from a reconnaissance flight . . .

The camels belong to a British convoy, the movements of which it was the duty of the German machine to observe

A battle-plane setting out from Sicily on an air raid in the direction of Malta

THE
AIR FORCE EMBLEM
on the Southern Front

Shot down by German anti-aircraft guns

The wreckage of a British plane which attacked an aerodrome in Sicily. On the right: Battle-planes on an aerodrome in Sicily

A sandstorm at Sollum. *The guard of a tank regiment has taken up its position on a hill in front of the camp. The first gust of wind comes, at about 11 a.m. It whirls the loose sand into the air. Each sentry puts on his goggles, binds a cloth round his mouth and nose, and ties his scarf tightly round his neck. Until about four in the afternoon, the world around them will be a raging inferno of sand and yellow light which the eye cannot penetrate. Photographs: PK. Kenneweg (2)*

The watch in the desert

It has stood the test on all fronts. *This A.A. gun was in Poland, accompanied the advance through Belgium and France and is now in one of the advance bases in Africa on the Halfaya Pass. It has travelled more than 6,000 miles and has experienced snow, rain and heat. Shell after shell has gone through the barrel. The last examination showed, however, that no measurable wear and tear could be found at any spot. Both barrel and gun carriage are still in the best of health and the sureness of aim of this old warrior is as good as it was on the very first day*

Between Libya and Egypt

A stretch of country about 625 miles wide, without roads or tracks, the Libyan desert, separates the chief centres of Libya from those of Egypt. Only at two places, at the oases of Siwa Jarabub and 125 miles north, at Sollum on the Mediterranean coast, does the terrain allow military operations of any size to be carried out. Sollum and the bay which stretches as far as the desolate sand and granite hills in the desert had been converted by the British into a strong fortress to which they attached the importance of a miniature Gibraltar

The victor "without experience of the tropics" General Rommel, the Commander-in-Chief of the German Africa Corps, together with officers of his staff, visits the scene of the Battle of Sollum. British military experts had predicted a rapid victory for the British Commander-in-Chief, General Wavell, whom Churchill has since transferred in disgrace to India, because General Rommel had had no experience of the tropics

A cool bathe after a hard battle The counter-attacks of the German tanks during the Battle of Sollum, during which such heavy losses were inflicted on the British, were carried out with the thermometer at more than 120 degrees Fahrenheit. After the enemy's retreat the crews of the German tank refresh themselves in the waters the Mediterranean *Photographs: PK. Moosmüller*

The Germans in Tripoli

German sentry in the harbour of Tripoli. *It was here that the German troops landed on African soil for the first time*

Parade beneath the palms. *One of the German tanks which soon afterwards were victorious in their first engagement with British troops in the desert*

Wearing pith helmets in the streets of Tripoli. *Dense crowds of Italians and natives line the streets of Tripoli through which the German troops are marching for the first time*

The commander of the German forces in Africa inspecting the troops

Photographs: H. Schneider, PK

His first flight in Africa

An American airman tells his story

PK. Photographs: War Correspondens Friedrich, Wagner

A German war correspondent in Africa photographs an American bomber as it crashes some distance away on the horizon. The cloud caused by the impact becomes visible first and then . . .

. . . there is an explosion followed by a dense black cloud which rises steeply into the air and—picture below—slowly disperses. Another front correspondent, however, spots the American pilot descending by parachute

Dragging his parachute along behind him, the shot down American flying officer approaches with his hands raised in surrender. He is eager to talk, a natural reaction after the mental strain of the air engagement and being shot down. The American lieutenant says that he is 24 years of age, a native of Philadelphia and had volunteered for service in Africa. The journey had been deured unpleasant. His ship had made long detours and had finally sailed close in along the coast of Africa being menaced all the time by U-boats. At long last he had reached the front but had been brought down on his very first flight . . .

A little later the American met his vanquisher, a sergeant-major who has been awarded the Knight's Insignia to the Iron Cross. Their encounter took place at an altitude of 18,000 feet. The American lieutenant admits that he was extremely surprised to find himself suddenly attacked by a German machine in spite of the security provided him by the large bomber unit in which he was flying. He had then tried all the usual tricks in order to shake of his antagonist who had nevertheless forced him to go down to 3,000 feet and scored many direct hits on his plane so that finally he had no other alternative but to bale out . . . The American was quite obviously pleased to have 'escaped so lightly. His machine (picture below) is a complete wreck

A reconnaissance party returns. At dawn the party had left the advance position on the Halfaya Pass and marched towards the British lines, eight miles there and eight miles back. They penetrated behind the British outposts and made important sketches of the positions. They are now returning along the shore of the Mediterranean from their dangerous enterprise

Seven men return to their quarters. They are passing through apparently untouched desert empty of human beings

Refreshment after a sixteen mile march. A cool drink and a piece of good wholesome bread

The desert sand has now swallowed up four of them. This photograph was taken a few seconds later from the same spot

Camouflage and deception

On the left: **The last one disappears here.** The whole country is cut by trenches miles long and spreading to a depth of several hundred yards. These positions are so well situated and camouflaged that they cannot be recognized even only a few yards off

On the right: **What the reconnaissance party discovered.** The salt lake between the German and British positions described by a previous patrol has again been seen today and a photograph has even been taken of it. It does not, however, actually exist. The reconnaissance party marched through it. It consisted of sand like everything else all around and was only a mirage

Photographs: PK. Kenneweg (7)

An M.G. nest in the very front line. Only the mouth of the barrel peeps above the ground. The hand grenades are lying ready for use on the protecting sandbags. Since June of this year when the British were defeated at the battle of Capuzzo, they have avoided this invisible position and not attempted another attack

The four plagues of the desert

PK. Kenneweg, "Signal's" reporter who is at present with the German and Italian troops fighting in North Africa writes to us: "I don't know which of the plagues is the worst. Like misfortunes, they seldom come singly. Dripping with perspiration, tortured by thirst and flies, and almost suffocated by dust, we curse every desert on the face of the earth"

Sand *Our faces are caked with dust. We are driving along the 40-mile road that runs through the desert round Tobruk. The car can only do 5 miles an hour here. It rocks like a ship in a storm, jolts along the uneven road surface, and runs up against boulders. The sand rises, smothering both car and man. It fills our eyes, our mouths, our nostrils, our sleeves, and our caps, and trickles down our backs. The journey lasts eight hours. When we arrive at our destination, we are all entirely beyond recognition. There are many such roads in Africa*

Mosquitoes *Thank heaven we are equipped with efficient mosquito nets! They are easy to set up, and when we make a halt or in our quarters, they afford good protection. The rest of the time the mosquitoes reign supreme. We have given up trying to fight against them. We have abandoned our hands, arms and faces to them and only beat them off when we want to take a bite. Now and then one of us jumps up and dances about cursing. A cloud of flies rises, but it helps only for a few seconds*

Thirst *We have to get accustomed to the water here. It has a salt content of 5 to 13 per thousand We use the least salty for making tea. The water cans are all marked, and woe to the man who uses good water for washing on a journey through the desert. As long as the tea is hot, the salt taste is unnoticeable; cold tea, on the other hand, is very salty. But whether hot or cold, it is a bad thirst quencher; it might even be said to aggravate it. In the evening in sheer desperation we swallow the contents of our mineral water bottles in a few gulps. "Do you remember the water we had at Derna?" the soldiers exclaim almost lyrically. "That was real water, wasn't it?" The water in every well here differs. The company that is lucky enough to have sweet water within reach is the envy of the whole front*

Heat

"How hot is it there really?", people often ask me in letters. Soldiers have a habit of exaggerating, for they are not too particular about a matter of ten degrees or so. Here are the facts: On the coast at midday the thermometer measures 104 to 122 degrees F., inland it is 9 degrees hotter. And in the shade? There is no shade. A soldier can make himself a kind of tent with stones and blankets and so enjoy a little shade, but it is not advisable to lie in it for long during the day-time. It gets hotter and hotter there, so that it is like lying in a Turkish bath. One could also spread a tent-cover as a kind of roof and sit under it, but a soldier has not much time to spare for lounging around. The best solution is to get accustomed to going about in a bathing costume and a topee and to take advantage of the breaths of wind that come in from the sea now and then. At night it is considerably cooler, sometimes the thermometer sinks 36 degrees, so that one can sleep quite soundly. If one is lucky, one may find one of the old water holes in one's sector. (Picture below) They are 5 to 6 yards deep: the cover, pierced with a little hole, is about one yard thick. They are deliciously cool, free from mosquitoes, and sand-proof. These are the only places where, enjoying a cool drink, one is free from the four greatest plagues of the desert   Photographs: PK. Kenneweg

Operation Barbarossa

At dawn on June 22, 1941, Germany launched 3.5 million men, 3,500 tanks and nearly 2,700 aircraft in an all out assault on the Soviet Union. Operation Barbarossa was underway. Hitler was supremely confident that the new campaign would be won in no more than two months. "We only have to kick in the door," he assured his field commanders, "and the whole rotten structure will come crashing down." Certainly, the Russians were taken by surprise. Stalin had refused to listen to warnings that the Nazis were on the brink of attacking him. Even when he received news of the invasion, he clung to the belief that it was a "provocation" launched without Hitler's knowledge by the German generals.

Hitler had brought together the largest invasion force ever assembled in human history. Field Marshal Walther von Brauschitsch, the commander-in-chief, could pit three massive army groups, each supported by a Luftwaffe air fleet, against the USSR. Army Group North, commanded by Field Marshal Wilhelm von Leeb, consisted of seven divisions and three panzer divisions. Field Marshal Fedor von Bock's Army Group Center had 42 divisions and nine panzer divisions; Field Marshal Gerd von Rundstedt's Army Group south, fielded 52 divisions, of which fifteen were Romanian, two Hungarian, and two Italian, plus five panzer divisions. It was an awesome display of firepower that the Russians could not come close to matching. Hitler was moved to comment "the world will hold its breath."

Surprise and speed were the two crucial elements the Germans employed to throw the Soviet forces opposing their thrusts into disarray. On the first day of the offensive alone, Luftwaffe airstrikes against Soviet airfields destroyed more than 1,200 Russian aircraft, many of them caught on the ground before they had the chance to take to the air. By the end of the week, the figure had risen to more than 4,000. On the ground, German panzers and mechanized infantry raced forward, their aim being to trap the Soviet frontier armies in a series of encircling movements, ultimately pinning them back against the line of the rivers Dnieper and Don.

The initial breakthrough

In the early stages of the great offensive, German armored forces moved forward far and fast, cutting off and capturing huge numbers of Soviet troops and their equipment. It took Army Group Center under a week to break through the Soviet defenses; by the end of the second week of July, it had already taken 600,000 prisoners as it powered forward inexorably towards Smolensk. By the end of July 16, it had taken the city. The road to Moscow lay open before it. Not to be outdone, Army Group North smashed its way through Latvia, Lithuania, and much of Estonia, and was soon well on its way to Leningrad. Though somewhat slower to get off the mark, Army Group South was penetrating into the Ukraine and advancing on Kiev.

There was understandable jubilation in the German camp at such astonishing successes along so broad a front, but stiffening and ever more determined Soviet resistance led to a brake being put on the advance. On July 30, the army supreme command ordered the troops in the east to pause and regroup before resuming operations. Little more than a month after it had begun, Operation Barbarossa had started to lose its initial momentum.

Hitler now made what proved to be a singularly unfortunate intervention. He decided to cut short von Bock's drive on the Russian capital and instead pursue other objectives in the north and south. He ordered General Herman Hoth's 3rd Panzer Group to turn north to support von Leeb's assault on Leningrad, and General Heinz Guderian's 2nd Panzer Group to move south to help von Rundstedt to take Kiev. Having secured the Ukraine, Army Group South would head for the Crimea to deprive the Soviet air force of a possible base for bombing attacks on the Romanian oil fields.

Von Bock protested that the decision to weaken his army group was ill-timed and misconceived. "The War Directives are always saying that the point is not to capture Moscow!", he told General

In the granary of the Soviet Union

Infantry combing a field of maize, a type of terrain just as treacherous as woodland

PK. Photographs: Front Correspondent A. Grimm

Franz von Halder, chief of the Army General Staff. "I don't want to capture Moscow! I want to destroy the enemy army and the mass of this army is standing in front of me! The turn away towards the south is a sideshow, however large it may be, through which a question mark is placed over the execution of the main operation, namely the destruction of the Russian armed forces before the winter. It does not help at all!" Halder sympathized, but failed to get the Fuehrer to change his mind.

Operation Typhoon

After the war, with the advantage of hindsight, many German generals blamed Hitler for the enforced change of strategy which, so they argued, threw the entire assault plan out of kilter. Instead of following the classic Prussian military doctrine of focusing on the enemy's center of gravity, the Fuehrer had taken his eye off the ball and, in all probability, cost Germany victory in the east.

At the time, Hitler's decision to weaken his forces in the center did not seem to pose any immediate problems. Guderian's transferred panzers broke through the Soviet positions in the south, repelled a last-ditch counter-offensive and captured Kiev, taking a further 665,000 prisoners together with 884 tanks and more than 3,000 guns. Subsequently, Kharkov and most of central and eastern Ukraine were occupied. By November 21, Army Group South had pushed as far forward as Rostov-on-Don, opening up the prospect of cutting off Soviet oil supplies from the Caucasus, and taking control of the industrial resources of the Donets Basin. Even von Bock hailed the operation as "a brilliant success."

Guderian and his fellow commanders had scored some of the greatest German military victories of the entire war. By the end of September, the Soviet army had lost in excess of 2,100,000 men, of whom 430,000 had been killed. The rest had either been taken prisoner or gone missing, while a 688,000 more had been wounded badly enough to require hospitalization. German losses amount to 551,000 killed, wounded, and missing in action.

Hitler believed that no army could stand such casualties. On September 23, he told propaganda minister Joseph Goebbels that the Wehrmacht had achieved a decisive breakthrough. The Fuehrer predicted confidently that Moscow would soon be encircled, and that Stalin then would be bound to sue for peace. He authorized von Bock to go ahead and resume his march on the Russian capital.

Operation Typhoon was launched on September 30. Three German armies, fielding 2,000,000 men and 2,000 tanks between them, and backed by massive Luftwaffe air support, moved eastward on a 300-mile-wide front. Their aim was to envelop the Soviet formations opposing them around Vyazma, about 125 miles south of Moscow. The town fell on October 7; the Germans took 673,000 prisoners, and captured 1,242 tanks and 5,412 guns. The following day, addressing the annual gathering marking the anniversary of the abortive 1923 Nazi beer-hall putsch, Hitler declared in Munich: "Never before has a giant empire been smashed and struck down in a shorter time."

The German advance continued. On October 14, General Herman Hoth's panzers captured Kalinin to the northwest of Moscow, so breaking the northern wing of the Soviet front. For the Russians, the threat of encirclement loomed yet again as Guderian's five panzer divisions launched a pincer movement from the southwest. Then the weather broke. Continuous heavy rain turned the Russian roads to sludge. The panzers slowed to a crawl and then a halt. They remained bogged down in the mud for three crucial weeks.

The enforced delay gave Marshal Georgi Zhukov, the ablest of Stalin's generals who now had been put in command of the capital's defenses, the vital time he needed to prepare. Some 900,000 reinforcements were positioned behind the River Volga. Even more crucially, Soviet intelligence reported that the Japanese had decided against attacking Russia in the east. Accordingly, on October 12, Stalin ordered 400,000 well-equipped troops, 1,000 tanks, and 1,000 aircraft westward from Siberia to take up position behind Moscow, ready not just to check any further German attempt to advance, but to launch a devastating counter-offensive when the time came.

Zhukov attacks

By November 14, as winter began to set in, the ground had hardened enough for von Bock to resume his advance. His panzers rolled forward once more; by December 2, some of his advanced fighting patrols were within sight of the suburbs of the capital. The Germans were to get no further.

On the night of December 4, the temperature plummeted to well below freezing and the snow began to fall. The Russian winter had arrived. The German troops, ill-prepared for its rigors, began to freeze. "The wind," wrote General Gotthard Heinrici "stabs you in the face with needles and blasts through your protective headgear and your gloves. Your eyes are streaming so much you can hardly see a thing." Tanks and other vehicles were immobilized by the cold. The Luftwaffe was grounded by the driving snow.

The moment had come for Zhukov to launch his carefully-prepared counter-offensive. On December

5, his Siberian divisions attacked along a 200-mile (320 km) front, concentrating initially on pinching out the German salients north and south of the capital. Von Bock was unable to decide whether to try to continue with his advance or call it off. It was Hitler who intervened to call a halt. However, he simultaneously ordered von Bock to hold his ground at all costs.

Issuing such an order was one thing. Implementing it was quite another. As the Soviet pressure increased, confusion began to set in on von Bock's battered forces. On December 16, having dealt with the German salients, Zhukov ordered a full-scale advance westward. The Soviet thrusts seemed unstoppable. "They are everywhere pushing through the wide gaps that have opened up in our front," Heinrici recorded. "The retreat in snow and ice is absolutely Napoleonic in its manner. The losses are the same."

Hitler reacts

Hitler acted brutally to try to resolve the situation. He had already sacked von Rundstedt, who had allowed his troops to withdraw from the outskirts of Rostov to avoid encirclement on December 1. On December 16, he replaced von Bock with Field Marshal Gunther von Kluge—the official story was that von Bock had asked to be relieved of his command for reasons of ill health. The same day, the Fuehrer fired von Brauschitsch. He took over supreme command himself. The upheaval continued. On December 26, Guderian himself was dismissed. General Erich Hoepner and Field Marshal von Leeb followed.

Having established complete domination over his army commanders, Hitler finally decided to relax his hitherto rigid insistence on holding onto conquered ground at all costs. Von Kluge was given permission to carry out a series of tactical retreats and to establish a chain of fortified forward supply bases. The German soldiers nicknamed these all-round defensive positions "hedgehogs." The Soviet offensive

Andrei Vlasov, pictured here with a volunteer machine-gunner, was a Soviet general who defected to the Germans after his capture and formed the so-called Vlasov Army to fight on their side. Signal's point was that Stalin's Soviet Union was obviously falling apart.

continued until, with the spring thaw, it ran out of steam. Stalin himself had contributed to this by insisting stubbornly on continuing to attack along the whole front, rather than concentrating all his forces against Army Group Center.

Stalin's decision prevented the disaster from becoming even worse. Nevertheless, its scale was apparent to all. Zhukov had pushed the Germans back to the point from which they had launched Operation Typhoon. He had also proved decisively that the Wehrmacht was not invincible. For all their advances, the Germans in the east had failed to achieve their objectives. Operation Barbarossa, though initially an enormous tactical success, had turned into a strategic failure.

Infantry and artillery storm the citadel of Brest-Litovsk

Special report by PK. Grimm II and PK. Müller-Waldeck

10.00 a. m. : *The German infantry men are lying in their positions among the barbed wire before the citadel of Brest-Litovsk. They are supported by grenade throwers*

M. G.'s join in the attack

Light trench mortars of the German infantry do their bit

At 11 a. m. there is a pause in the fighting for the infantry. For the next half-hour the artillery is concentrated on the citadel which is to be stormed. The infantry captain takes advantage of the short interval granted to him and his men to have a refreshing drink

On the morning of 24th June 1941, German artillery and German bombers have prepared Brest-Litovsk for the attack. Our infantry has been lying on the ramparts in front of the fortress for the last three days. It is 10 a. m. — the last act of the drama is about to begin and it is at this point that "Signal's" report commences. In the casemates and barracks, several thousand Soviet troops are fighting desperately against the Germans. The surrounding houses are on fire, and acrid smoke billows over the scene of battle. Soviet snipers fire from the roofs; the Soviet troops show the white flag, but then shoot at the German spokesmen and at ambulance men, and send Russians forward in German uniforms.

11.30 a. m. the German artillery once more intervenes. Fire simultaneously belches from the barrels of guns and howitzers. An extremely heavy cannonade now begins. The infernal din is dominated by the deep roar of a gigantic mortar. Tremendous columns of smoke rise into the air, powder magazines explode. The earth trembles.

"Signal's" correspondents are lying entrenched about 300 yards from the wall of the citadel and watch the terrific effect of the artillery fire from close quarters. One of them describes it as follows: "We continually take cover from the shrapnel, in order not to be within range of that of our heavy guns which is very wide. The explosions tear asunder the earth on the ramparts. The guns suddenly cease firing. After the cannonade which lasted 30 minutes, a complete cessation of firing has been ordered. We are not allowed to fire a shot, not even at the armed enemy, unless fire is first opened on us. The minutes of sudden calm after the infernal din pass in an atmosphere of tense expectancy. A pall of smoke hangs in the air.

There! The first Russians come running over without their weapons. Larger groups are already beginning to appear. The first of them have now reached the ramparts where we are lying. They are searched for arms. Now they are standing with us on the rampart and shout across to their comrades: "Priditje, priditje!" Other groups, with their arms raised, come running across, some of them still without their boots. The terror of the last half hour still shows in their features. They also drag their wounded with them, who are immediately tended by the German ambulance men. Ten minutes later, our flag is flying over the citadel. The Germans have occupied Brest-Litovsk."

11.35 a. m.

The artillery observer lies far in front. It is just five minutes since the German artillery joined in the storming attack. The first powder magazine has been set on fire. A few seconds later it explodes. The citadel's last hour has come. — During the last 25 years the German soldier has fought for Brest-Litovsk three times. This strong fortress surrounded by water, dug-outs, and concrete fortifications has been called the "Verdun of the east." In the Great War, in the Polish campaign and once more in the war against the Soviets, the field-grey of the German uniforms is seething round the walls of this fateful city. And for the third time Brest-Litovsk is stormed

→

In a race for mercy, *immediately after the artillery had finished the bombardment, the defenders of Brest-Litovsk run towards the German soldiers in the forefield of the citadel*

12.05 a. m.:
The first Soviet soldiers surrende

With their hands up and carrying white cloths the last Russians leave the citadel. They are not allowed to lower their hands until they have been disarmed in the forefield. This precaution was introduced because Soviet soldiers often waved white cloths — the sign of surrender — but on being allowed to approach nearer they shot at the German soldiers

The timid behaviour of this Sovie Russian is testimony to the effect of Moscow's infamous propaganda. H does not believe that the German do not fight against defenceles prisoners. Meanwhile his comrad is beckoning to other Soviet soldier in their hiding-place to surrende

Storming into the citadel. *The smoke of the artillery is still hanging over the scene of the fighting when the first German soldier storms into the citadel. Have the Soviet Russians really abandoned the powerful fortress?*

12.10 a. m.:

The citadel has fallen

Every projecting part of the walls of the riddled fortress, *through which the Bug flows, is carefully guarded. Every step forward in the fallen citadel could mean death: the Soviet troops who have been incited against the Germans, take refuge from them in the cellars of the barracks*

3 p. m.: *The struggle for Brest-Litovsk is over. Through the streets that have been taken by the victorious Germans, the disarmed columns of the Soviet army are marching into captivity*

The flag of victory
German infantry hoist the Swastika on the citadel of Brest-Litovsk. For the third time in 25 years the "Verdun of the east" has been stormed by German soldiers

1939/40

Bolshevism takes up new positions of attack

In September 1939 Soviet soldiers marched into Eastern Poland, in March 1940 Finland was compelled to surrender parts of her territory, in June 1940 the Soviet Union forced Rumania to give up Bessarabia and Northern Bukovina, and in July 1940 the three Baltic states were occupied. In this way the Soviet made preparations for military operations against the German Reich and against Europe

The meaning of the struggle

For the freedom and unity of Europe

It was an important hour in the history of the world when Germany decided to take up the struggle against the Soviet Union and Bolshevism. For a quarter of a century the whole of humanity had been oppressed by the menace of Bolshevism. Yes, it seemed that there was no remedy against the preparations which for years were being made in this vast state for a world revolution. And in Moscow the lives and the happiness of millions of people were hazarded in order to be prepared for the day when Communism could commence its campaign of world conquest. The masses, the millions of people in this tremendous state, were deprived of shoes, clothing and all other necessities of life in order to be able to build factories for the manufacture of guns and aeroplanes.

This state of affairs was still unchanged when the new British war broke out in the autumn of 1939. Only for Moscow it commenced too early. Their preparations were as yet not complete and they did not feel strong enough to take part in the big game from the very outset. Stalin concluded a pact of friendship with Germany and waited. On the western frontier of Germany both the French and the Germans had a rampart built of steel and concrete. At that time everybody still believed that such a means of defence would prove impenetrable against any means of attack. Therefore, if a war was to be waged on this frontier, it would last a very long time and this would naturally lead to the exhaustion of both Germany and the Western Powers. In the meantime the Soviet Union could continue to increase its armaments so as to be able, as the last powerful nation, finally to fall upon the other countries now exhausted by the war.

Stalin's calculations were wrong

But it turned out differently. The war in the West lasted only a very short time. It did not even last one year. France was overrun. Stalin's calculations had proved to be wrong. In order nevertheless to reach his old aim he had now to prevent Germany from finishing the war. On account of continued extortions and increasing concentration of troops on the Russian western frontier, through the occupation of positions from which Germany could be more conveniently attacked in the rear, the Reich was prevented from employing its full might against Britain.

It commenced with Russia's attack on Finland. There followed the complete absorption of Lithuania, Latvia and Esthonia. From this example the

world could judge what it would mean for Europe if the Bolshevists had succeeded in overthrowing Germany and in dealing with all the other European states as they had in the case of the Baltic States. The occupation of these states brought the Soviet Union considerably further forward on the Baltic; the Baltic, however, is of the greatest importance for the existence of the German Reich as it is indeed for all the Northern European countries.

Rumania was to take the lead

The Bolshevists' plan became still more evident when they marched into Rumania. In Moscow it was probably hoped that the invasion would cause general confusion in Rumania and would cripple the entire life of the country, so that it would then be an easy matter to carry the Red Revolution into the neighbouring countries. In this case also Germany was to have been dealt a mortal blow. For it was essential for supplying Central Europe with food products and raw materials that peace should reign in the whole of the South-East, on the Danube and in the Balkans, so that land could be cultivated and mines could be worked. They did not succeed in disturbing this peace. On the contrary, Bulgaria, which had always been the favourite aim of Soviet Russian policy, entered into closer relations with Germany. For this, as will be recalled, she was reproached by Russia, although Stalin had undertaken, in the pact with Germany, to observe a certain line of demarcation in regard to Europe, which he had already encroached upon in the case of Rumania. When finally the Yugoslav coup d'état government applied to Moscow, the Soviet Union concluded a treaty with this government, which, having regard to the situation at that time, could mean nothing other than a grave provocation of the Greater German Reich. Probably at this moment it was recognized in Moscow that they had gone too far. They consequently let it appear, outwardly, as if great value were attached to friendly relations with Germany, but it was impossible to deceive the Reich Government any further. On the occasion of the visit of M. Molotow to Berlin at the end of last year, the Bolshevists had already demanded the abandonment of Finland and Bulgaria and also the sacrifice of Turkey. Apart from this, the Reich Government received an increasing number of reports about the activity, which was becoming more intense, of Communist centres and also sabotage and espionage which was being carried on with renewed zeal in Germany and other European countries.

And at the same time they concentrated the main body of their forces on Germany's eastern frontier.

The concentration of the Red Army

The more it became apparent that Germany was likely to defeat Britain, the more energetically did the Soviet Union adopt measures which resulted in the military forces of the Reich being tied up in the East and consequently kept back from the decisive tasks before them. The Union became a true ally of Britain, who for years had been seeking the friendship of the Soviets.

On 1st May, 118 infantry divisions, 20 cavalry divisions and 40 mechanized and tank brigades were concentrated on the eastern frontier of Germany. This represented:

70 % of all infantry divisions,
60 % of all cavalry divisions, and
85 % of all mechanized and tank brigades.

The frontier aerodromes had their full complement of bombers and fighter planes. Parachute formations and innumerable transport planes were ready for immediate action.

The troops stationed in the close vicinity of the frontier were intended purely for attack: — tank units, mechanized infantry, heavy mechanized artillery, parachute troops and bombing squadrons.

Four army groups were formed.

The most northerly, between Memel and Suwalki, directly threatened East Prussia. It consisted of about 70 % infantry and 30 % tank and mechanized units.

South of this, several armies had marched up in the territory around Białystok which forms a salient projecting into Germany. Eastwards, a reserve army was standing by. Of these forces, about 35 % were tank or high-speed mobile troops.

In the area surrounding Lwów, which also projects into Reich territory, there was stationed a further particularly powerful Red Army group. The tank, mechanized and cavalry divisions amounted in this case to about 40 %.

A further army group directly threatened Rumania and the other Balkan States from Bessarabia.

This was no movement of troops for guarding the frontier; it was, on the contrary, a preparatory step in view of a large-scale offensive operation with important objectives. These facts in themselves sufficed to show only too plainly what the plans of the Soviet Union were; actual confirmation was afforded by the discovery of secret Communist instructions and the finding of important documents and maps on which the zones of action and objectives far into German territory are marked. For example, the report of the Yugoslav Military Attaché in Moscow, dated 17th December 1940, contains the following words: "According to statements made in Soviet circles, the arming of the Air Force, the tank arm and the artillery is in full progress according to the experiences of the present war, and in the main will be concluded by August 1941. This is probably the extreme time-limit up to which no perceptible changes in Soviet foreign policy need be anticipated."

The whole of
Europe was suddenly awake

It was evident that this development had been clearly recognized in the whole world and that it was realized what would happen if the attack on Germany succeeded. It was then that the Führer's decision enabled the German Reich to anticipate the attack in the rear which had been prepared In all the countries of the world, even in the broad masses of Britain and America, the news was received with joy that Germany had summoned the strength and the boldness to settle accounts with Europe's ancient enemy in the East before finally dealing with Britain. Germany's Allies, headed by Italy, Rumania, Slovakia and Hungary declared war on Soviet Russia. Finland also fell in with Germany. Sweden allowed the passage of German troops. Volunteer armies were formed everywhere. First in Spain, still suffering from the bleeding wounds received in the struggle against Communism, then in Denmark, Norway and Holland, even in France, who also broke off relations with Moscow. In short, the whole of Europe was suddenly up in arms against Bolshevist Russia. Never since time immemorial had the people of Europe been so united; for upon victory over the Soviet Union depends the destiny of all nations, the fate of the whole world.

But it is not only a matter of destroying Bolshevism for ever, it is also a question of release from that other menace which up to now has only manifested itself from the West, that is to say, where Britain and the United States are trying to cut off the entire European Continent from oversea supplies. In the Great War of 1914 to 1918 the cutting off of the Continent by Britain from the sea would never have led to the desired result, that is to say, to the starving of Europe, if Russia had not at the same time closed the doors against Europe from the East. Certainly it was found possible at that time to defeat Russia, but it was too late, nor was there any way of utilizing the conquered territories for supplying Central Europe. Just as Britain is protected by the surrounding seas, so was Russia protected then and earlier still by her gigantic dimensions which made it impossible for armies to occupy the whole country.

The pincers will break

Today it is different. The battles which have been won up to the present in this war have proved that it is now possible with the aid of mechanization to cover enormous distances with great rapidity. Europe today is in a far better position than the exhausted Germany of 1917 to make the most of such an advantage, not only for itself but also for all those countries which are prevented by Britain and America from receiving necessary supplies from overseas. By reason of the German victories in Russia before which the whole world stands breathless, the cutting off of oversea supplies will remain ineffective in the long run for the whole of Europe. The pincers in which Europe was to be gripped will break. Europe, which on account of over-population was always anxious whether sufficient to eat and sufficient raw materials for industry would be received from overseas would be freed not only today but also tomorrow and for all time from the tyranny of those who were in a position to curtail vital supplies whenever they thought fit.

Europe will not only be free but will also endeavour to maintain her unity and the co-operation of all the countries within her boundaries which enables her to take preventive measures against the threats from outside. That is the meaning of the struggle which Germany has now undertaken on behalf of the interests of all the people of Europe.

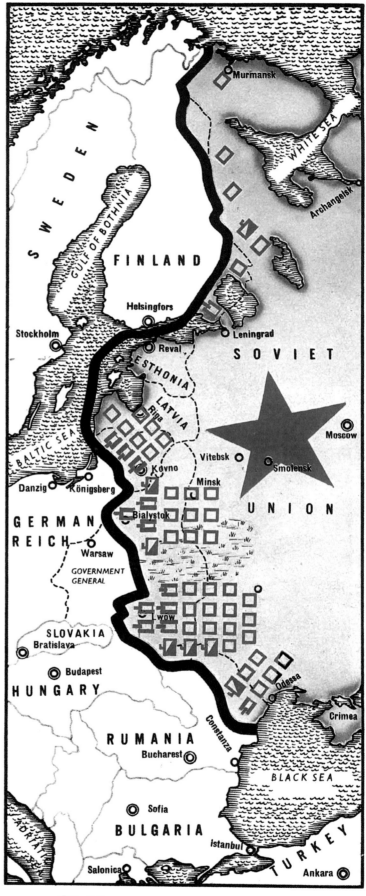

1941:

**The gigantic concentration
of Soviet troops against
the German Reich**

▢	= approx. 3 infantry divisions
▨	= approx. 3 cavalry divisions
▤	= approx. 3 tank brigades

Drawings: Seeland

An inconceivable sight. *Over the enclosure surrounding the Ogpu prison in Lemberg, the inhabitants of the city are gazing at the corpses of the thousands of defenceless Ukrainians who had been murdered there. In this city alone 2,300 men, women and children fell victims to the terror*

Horror

Lemberg was the first of the many places where, during their advance, the German troops came across the terrible traces of the Ogpu

She still cannot realize *that these fearfully mangled bodies, which she managed to identify by the fragments of clothing, were her relations*

An orphan. *Filled with despair, a girl whose parents were among the victims of the murderous Bolshevist fury, throws herself into the sheltering arms of a friendly neighbour*

A small section of the vast picture of annihilation. *The amount of material of all arms either captured or destroyed in the great encircling battle of Kiev will greatly weaken the enemy. These tremendous losses cannot be made good by deliveries from Great Britain and America. According to the first count, no less than 3,718 guns were captured or destroyed during the battle*

Ruins as far as the eye can see

After the great battle of annihilation east of Kiev

Tanks of all sizes *from the light 15 tonner to the terrific monster weighing 52 tons were employed by the Soviets in the fight against the German units where their fate overtook them. 884 tanks were destroyed or captured*

15,000 Soviet vehicles *are lying in chaotic confusion in the ring round Kiev. As a result of the increasingly heavy blows dealt at Soviet industry, this figure represents an important part of the annual production in Soviet Russia*

Inconceivable quantities of important war material *are strewn over the battlefields round Kiev. The Soviet four-barrelled M. G. also succumbed to the superiority of the German weapons*

Tanks break through the Stalin Line

and the infantry follows close behind

The tank general leaves his car for a few minutes as he drives forward to join the head of his division to give further commands to the officers of some detachments which are waiting to go into action

The road to victory. Enveloped in dust, tank after tank rolls on towards the vast expanses of the east. Demolished Soviet giant tanks lie beside the roads along which the German units are advancing

Street fighting in Schitomir. With stubborn tenacity, the Soviet troops try to hold their positions in the town. With the help of heavy artillery, street after street and block after block is captured from them

On the right: **German anti-tank guns** have brought a Soviet tank to a halt, and have set on fire lorries loaded with petrol

Photographs: PK. Emil Grimm

Soviet roads...

What is that? A German motor-cycle that had almost sunk in one of the bottomless bogs that are called roads in Soviet Russia. The indefatigable motor-cyclist is busy trying to make it recognizable again

When it refuses to go, it must be pushed: six soldiers rescue their lorry from the deadly embrace of the sand

Photographs:
PK. Beissel
SS PK. Zschäkel
PK. Naegele
PK. Wetterau

When the motor-cycle churns the sand, it is useless to step on the accelerator. Only capable hands can save the situation

The vehicle sank *half a yard into the deep mud — the driver hopes to get it going again by running the engine all out*

Advance and Rest

"I have done the impossible". The German soldiers on the Eastern Front have been able to write these proud words in their field post letters. Not only in the desperate fighting, but also in overcoming trackless country, they have achieved things that the enemy had thought impossible. They were ready to exert their last ounce of strength at every command, and after every short period of rest they were able to rise refreshed from the deathlike sleep of exhaustion and go forward to the next attack   Photographs: PK. Wanderer PK. Jäger

Seen from a Fieseler-Storch: *endless columns of prisoners on endless roads*

The daily round on the Eastern Front

In the battery position: *21 cm shells have arrived*

The flight of a shell: a shell fired from a 15 cm. field howitzer marks its passage in the sky

Photographs: PK Front Correspondent Hanns Hubmann

The moment of firing a 21 cm. mortar: the gunner is just discharging the shell with his left hand while protecting his ear with the right

The ring round Leningrad

PK. front correspondent Hanns Hubmann, who took part in the advance on Leningrad, here shows a few sections of the ring encircling the biggest Soviet port

Kronstadt under fire from German long-range batteries. *The powerful sea fortress about 18 miles from Leningrad is the last and most heavily fortified naval port of the Soviets in the Baltic Sea and is of immense strategic importance on account of its key position before Leningrad. With his long-range camera, the front correspondent took a photograph from Peterhof of one of the German attacks on the fortifications, shipyards and docks of Kronstadt and on the units of the Soviet Navy which had taken refuge in the bays of the island*

Soviet steamers in flames. *Using the narrow sea route, the Soviets tried to break through the ring round Leningrad in order to supply the city with provisions. German reconnaissance planes recognized their purpose in time and German dive bombers set the ships on fire. This photograph was taken from the village of Uritzk*

The last road from Moscow to Leningrad *is in German hands as a result of the rapid advance of the German troops. The Soviet artillery vainly tries to hold up the march of the German infantry by heavy fire*

Encircled Leningrad photographed from a distance of 2½ miles. *From the foremost German lines near the village of Uritzk, the silhouette of the encircled city with the Isaac Cathedral is clearly visible. The factory chimneys of this city of 2 million inhabitants are still smoking. But the vehicles and the tram in the foreground are already in the fighting zone*

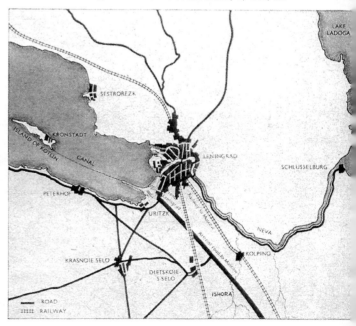

The environs of Leningrad. *While the German troops coming from the south have closed around the city, Finnish units have cut it off from the north*

Schlüsselburg, the gate to Lake Ladoga. *With the fall of Schlüsselburg, the old fortress on the Neva, the Soviets were deprived of the last possibility of supplying Leningrad by sea. The ring is closed. The German flag is already fluttering from the church, but the Soviets are still trying to set fire to the city from the opposite bank of the Neva*

Lying in an advanced position *opposite Kolpino, the strongly fortified factory city of the Soviets, two wireless operators are transmitting the reports from the foremost lines*

banks of the River Ishora, *a tributary* e Neva, *had been mined. But this did* revent the German formations from sing the river. German soldiers, using sticks tipped with iron, clear the in of mines   Photographs: PK. front spondent Hubmann, Drawing: Seeland

From his camouflaged position, *the German observer tensely watches all the movements of the enemy along the outskirts of Kolpino. The security of the ring round Leningrad depends on him too*

"We are happy". *Three brothers from Copenhagen with their company leader in the SS training camp in Upper Alsace. They have fulfilled all the conditions relating to questions of race and health and are now enjoying the manly open-air life in the camp in the woods*

"I want to fight for the new Europe"

"Signal" visits the Germanic volunteers serving in the **SS**. Among them are Flemings, Dutchmen, Danes, Norwegians, and representatives of other Germanic countries

On the dagger of an SS officer *the volunteer swears the oath. He pledges loyalty to Adolf Hitler, the leader in the fight for a new Europe. The picture shows on the left Björn J., the secretary of the Norwegian Minister of Labour, and on the right Erling H., an electrician from Copenhagen*

Much of their time in the Training Camp is devoted to sport. *Almost all the Olympic events are practised. The winner of this obstacle race said: "Our time here is like a holiday for us. We are given a good physical training. It is Prussian drill, but the German organization is agreeable"*

A practical lesson in German. *On the first day of their training the sergeant writes up the German words of command*

For the first time: the Germanic salute. *The man with his hand raised is Karl F., a student from Antwerp, one of the best amateur boxers of Belgium, 'a champion light heavyweight*

The Dutch have a definite gift for shooting. *Josefes K., formerly a business employee at The Hague, is being trained as a sniper in the use of telescopic sights*

The military training *teaches the volunteers up-to-date tactics. Complete familiarity with the ground and the art of camouflage are essential for success*

"Veronica" or the most beautiful hour of the day: *Practising a German soldiers' song*

Horses and tractors before shooting practice at
the artillery training centre. The campaign
on the Eastern Front has given the well-bred,
well-treated horse an honourable position be-

FORTRESS EUROPE

December 1941 was a turning point in the war in two ways. Defeat and retreat outside Moscow put an end to the Wehrmacht's reputation for military invincibility. By the end of the year, the war had become a war of attrition. It was a battle that Germany was doomed to lose, especially after, following the Japanese attack on Pearl Harbor, Hitler gratuitously declared war on the USA that selfsame month. The Americans could produce quantities of weaponry that the Third Reich was simply unable to match. Both the USSR and Britain were out-producing Germany as well. For Hitler, if he had taken note of the figures his technocrats were producing, the writing was on the wall. He had to win the war in 1942 or not at all. To this end, he began turning Occupied Europe into an armed fortress. But, as the RAF and the USAAF were to demonstrate, unfortunately for him it had no roof.

At War with America

On December 7, 1941, Japanese carrier-borne aircraft inflicted massive damage on the US Pacific Fleet, taken unawares at anchor at its base at Pearl Harbor. Four days later, Hitler decided to honor a verbal promise he had given to the Japanese Foreign Minister and declared war on the USA. The Fuehrer had a low opinion of American military capability; in any event, he thought the USA would concentrate on fighting Japan, rather than Germany. It was a miscalculation that, in the long term, would have disastrous consequences for the Third Reich. Roosevelt and Churchill decided together that Germany must be defeated first, not Japan.

As far back as the late 1920s, Hitler had postulated that, at some point, Germany would have to fight the USA. When the time came, he seized the opportunity. "Now it is impossible for us to lose the war;" he assured Walter Hewel, a foreign office liaison officer, "we now have an ally who has never been vanquished in three thousand years." Joseph Goebbels noted excitedly: "The Fuehrer is extremely pleased at this development...Now this is a world war in the truest sense of the word."

In the short term, Hitler thought that the Japanese attack would weaken the Americans by dividing their military efforts, giving him time for his U-boats to win the battle of the Atlantic, and so cutting off shipments of war supplies to Britain and the USSR. In his view, it was preferable to fight the USA sooner rather than later, before the American military build-up became overwhelming. His answer was to knock the Russians and British out of the war before this could occur.

The arms race

Hitler was aware of the rapidly increasing quantities of military equipment the USA was producing. By December 1941, it was already churning out armaments in quantities that Germany so far had given no signs that it could match, let alone surpass. Heinrich Koppenberg, the general manager of the Junkers aircraft factory at Dessau, was one of the first German industrial technocrats to become alarmed. Albert Speer, Hitler's personal architect whom the Fuehrer appointed Minister of Armaments in February 1942, recalled that, when he visited the Dessau plant, Koppenberg took him "into a locked room and showed me a graph comparing American bomber production for the next several years with ours. I asked him," Speer continued, "what our leaders had to say about these depressing figures. 'That's just it, they won't believe it,' he exclaimed, "whereupon he broke into uncontrollable tears."

In public, Hitler poured scorn on the USA's political leaders and on its potential economic, industrial, and military prowess. "What is America but beauty queens, millionaires, stupid records, and Hollywood?" he asked rhetorically in 1940. If he seriously believed this, he was living in a dream world of his own devising. By the end of 1942, the USA's armaments' output already exceeded the combined efforts of Germany, Italy, and Japan. By 1944, US aircraft factories were building an airplane every five minutes, while its shipyards were launching fifty merchant vessels a day, and eight aircraft carriers a month.

Put another way, in 1942 the USA produced nearly 48,000 aircraft. The following year, the figure was nearly 86,000 and, in 1944, more than 114,000. This contrasted with Germany's 11,000 new aircraft in 1941, and getting on for 15,000 in 1942. The German figures did shoot up in 1943, when more than 26,000 airplanes were produced and, in 1944, when nearly 40,000 rolled off the production lines, but even this last figure was less than a fifth of the total chalked up by the USA, Britain, and the Soviet Union the same year.

Elsewhere, the story was identical. According to the Oberkommando der Wehrmacht's own figures, the Reich managed to manufacture only between 5,000 and 6,000 tanks a year from 1942 to 1944. Britain produced 6,000 to 8,000 tanks over the same period, and the USSR around 19,000. US tank production rose from 17,000 in 1942 to more than 29,000 in 1944. The same was true of other weapons as well. In 1943, the combined Allied production of machine-guns totalled 1,110,000; the Germans managed just 165,527.

Slave labor

Though many Nazis refused to recognize such unwelcome facts, it

Hamburg: Halifax bomber, 7 men, 6 dead

Western Germany: British bomber, 3 men burned

Hamburg: Lancaster bomber, 8 men, 8 dead

Holland: Lancaster bomber, 8 Australians dead

Holland: Lancaster bomber, 8 Australians dead

Channel Coast: Lancaster bomber, 8 men, 5 dead

On the Channel: Liberator bomber (U.S.A.), all dead

Hamburg: British bomber, none saved

Dutch coast: Liberator bomber, 10 men dead

Hamburg: Wellington bomber, 6 men, 1 dead

Northern France: American bomber, all men killed

Hamburg: The remains of a "Flying Fortress"

Hamburg: American bomber, 10 men, 9 dead

Hamburg: British bomber, exploded in the air

Channel Coast: American fighter none saved

Holland: Lancaster bomber, 8 men, 6 dead

Hanover: British bomber, 7 men, 6 dead

Northern France: British bomber, 7 men, 7 dead

Channel Coast: All that remained of a British bomber

Channel: A Wellington bomber being taken to pieces

Hanover: Halifax bomber, 7 men, 6 dead

Channel Coast: Stirling bomber, wrecked in crashing

Northern France: British bomber, all killed

Holland: Lancaster bomber, 8 men, 4 dead

Hamburg: Wellington bomber, 6 men, 4 dead

Hamburg: Lancaster bomber, 8 men, 3 dead

Hamburg: what remained of a British bomber

Hanover: the wreck of a Wellington bomber

Western Germany: British bomber, 8 men, 4 dead

Holland: Liberator bomber, 10 men, 9 dead

Atlantic Coast: British bomber, 5 men, 1 dead

Channel: 3 men rescued in an inflatable boat

steadily became clear that, despite Speer's herculean efforts after he became Minister for Armaments, the Reich was losing the critical battle of production on the armaments front. Things had worked well enough during the initial phases of the war, when sheer speed, the element of surprise, and its revolutionary blitzkrieg tactics had won the Wehrmacht a string of spectacular cheap victories over its unready opponents. Once these advantages had been lost, the chances of Germany being able to deliver a knock-out blow against its enemies dwindled until ultimately it disappeared completely.

Hitler's constant changes of priority made matters worse. In July 1941, for instance, he ordered the construction of a new high seas battle fleet, at the same time as demanding a fourfold increase in the size of the

Heinkel III bombers are pictured on the production line. By this time, German aircraft production was lagging far behind that of Britain and the USA, and the Luftwaffe was losing the battle for air supremacy.

Luftwaffe, and the expansion of the number of motorized divisions in the army to thirty-six. Though German industry was incapable of meeting such unrealistic demands, it did not stop the Fuehrer from making them. Shortages of raw materials and manpower also bedevilled its attempts to out-produce Germany's three main enemies.

As far as raw materials were concerned, the Reich shamelessly plundered the territories it occupied. After the fall of France, for instance, massive amounts of raw materials were sequestrated and shipped back to Germany—the figures included 81,000 tons of copper, a year's supply of tin and nickel, and substantial reserves of gasoline and oil. The army got its hands on more than 300,000 French rifles, over 4,000 guns, nearly 4,000,000 shells, and 2,170 tanks. Many of the latter were still being employed by the Germans in the latter stages of the war.

Even more crucially than raw materials, Occupied Europe provided Nazi Germany with the workers it so desperately needed

to keep its economy afloat. Despite appearances, the Reich was far from being geared up for total war. As opposed to the USA and Britain, where thousands of women took the place of men in the factories, Germany lagged far behind. Hitler himself was opposed to the conscription of women into war industry. He believed firmly that a woman's place was in the home.

The process began in 1940. That May, 1,100,000 prisoners of war—practically all Poles—and foreign civilians were working in the country; by October, the number had risen by a further 1,200,000. Following the invasion of the Soviet Union, there was another massive increase, although only 5 per cent of the 3,350,000 Soviet troops the Germans had taken prisoner by the end of March 1942 were actually put to work. By the end of November, the total number had risen to 4,665,000. It was still not enough.

Facing an ever-increasing shortfall, Fritz Sauckel, a hard-line Nazi whom Hitler personally had put in charge of solving the Reich's labor

problem, turned to compulsion. It started in France, with the institution of the *Service du Travail Obligatoire*. By December 1943, more than 666,000 French workers had been compulsorily relocated to Germany, together with 223,000 Belgians, and 274,000 Dutch. They were joined by 650,000 Italian prisoners of war, forcibly deported as forced laborers following Italy's surrender to the Allies that September. Up to 50,000 of them died of malnutrition and disease. Nevertheless, the numbers grew and grew. By fall 1944, there were nearly 8,000,000 foreigners at work in the Reich.

Lend-lease and the draft

If Hitler dismissed US ambitions to become what President Roosevelt called "the arsenal of democracy," he was even more dismissive of US military potential in the field. Even before the USA entered the war, Roosevelt had begun preparing in case his country was forced to enter the conflict. In 1940, he authorized the doubling of the US Navy, persuaded Congress to agree to the first peacetime draft in US history, traded fifty old US destroyers to Britain in return for leases on British bases in the Caribbean, and got Congress to pass the Lend-Lease Act. This allowed the President to sell, trade, or simply supply gratis weaponry to any country he considered would use it to further the security of the USA.

The draft law was possibly the most significant of these measures as far as American daily life was concerned. Around 1,200,000 men of military age were drafted for a year's service; 800,000 reservists were recalled to the colors in October 1941. The same month, Congress voted to extend the period of the draft, though the vote was a close one. The extension was agreed by only one vote.

Hitler knew all this. He also knew that many Americans did not want to get entangled in another European war. They certainly did not share the President's view that war with Germany was inevitable. The America First Committee and the Keep America Out of the War Committee reflected this spirit of isolationism. Both had a substantial membership and even more sympathizers. Both won celebrity support. Charles A. Lindbergh, the American hero who had won fame by becoming the first man to fly solo across the Atlantic, was America First's most prominent spokesman. Other celebrated supporters included author Sinclair Lewis, the publishers of the *New York Daily News* and the *Chicago Tribune*, and the film producer Walt Disney.

Operation Torch

For the Americans—and indeed Hitler—the question was where the vast new armies the USA was raising would first be employed. The Fuehrer regarded Fortress Europe, as he christened it, to be impregnable; the blood shambles of the Dieppe Raid launched by the British in August 1942 confirmed him in this belief. Nevertheless, US military chiefs pressed for the launch of a full-scale invasion. In their view, the Germans could be beaten only in northern Europe. This meant successfully invading northern France.

For once, Roosevelt did not defer to his military advisers. Instead, he decided to go along with the British plan to land an invasion force in French North Africa. Such a move would give the USA its chance to begin asserting its predominance in the western Alliance. More pragmatically, it meant that US troops would get their first experience of combat in a region where the Axis powers were comparatively weak. On July 25, Roosevelt told General George Marshall, the US Army's Chief of Staff, to move "full steam ahead" on the planning of what was now named Operation Torch. Lieutenant-General Dwight D. Eisenhower, who had previously been named commander of US forces in Europe, was put in overall charge.

The landings took place on November 7. The 20,000-strong Eastern Assault force, consisting of American and British troops, was tasked with seizing Algiers. It would then move east into Tunisia. The Central Assault Force of 19,000 American troops stormed Oran, while the 25,000 Americans of the Western Assault Force landed on Morocco's Atlantic coast. The invading troops met patchy Vichy French resistance before the French called for a cease-fire.

Hitler, fooled by Allied intelligence, was taken totally by surprise. Fresh tanks and troops were rushed into Tunisia by air and sea. On December 1, they were ready to counter-attack the slowly-advancing Anglo-American 1st Army. On December 8, Colonel-General Jurgen von Arnim arrived hotfoot from the Eastern Front to take command of what Hitler grandiloquently christened the 5th Panzer Army.

There was no quick end to the fighting. Hitler ordered his forces to turn Tunisia into "the Verdun of North Africa." Despite some tactical successes—notably at the Kasserine Pass, where twenty US tanks were destroyed, shortage of supplies led to an inevitable Axis collapse. On May 7 and May 8, Hitler exhorted his troops to fight to the last bullet. Two days later, what remained of 5th Panzer Army and Rommel's Afrika Korps, which had retreated in southern Tunisia at the end of January, capitulated. Hitler's attempt to hold onto Tunisia had led to another military disaster.

JAPAN'S LONG ARM

Revolutionary air strategy in the Pacific

The Pacific Ocean, on which Japan is fighting out her great struggle for the new order of Eastern Asia against the United States of America and Great Britain, is the largest theatre of war ever known in the history of the world. This great expanse with its extensive archipelagos imposes its own peculiar laws upon the conduct of the war, particularly upon war in the air. Japan long ago realized the particular features of this great expanse and in every way adapted her armaments to suit them. In this connexion, Japan's particularly zealous development of the air arm of the navy is characteristic. Special attention was paid to aircraft carriers and aircraft depot ships. These weapons are able to operate at very great distances and are therefore the obvious instruments of war in large spaces.

The encirclement which failed

Japan's strategical position on the outbreak of war in Eastern Asia was at first by no means particularly favourable. The encirclement of Japan aimed at by the United States had to a certain extent been achieved by the development of a number of groups of islands under American rule, some of them even being situated inside the Japanese living space, to form modern naval and air bases. In

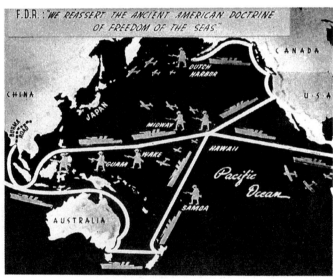

Franklin Delano Roosevelt: "We reassert the ancient American doctrine of freedom of the seas." (From the "United States News" of 6. 6. 1941). This freedom meant in reality the complete tyrannization of Japan by bayonets, air and sea power

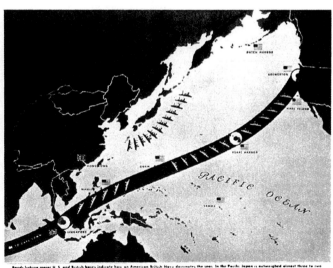

HOW THE U.S. NAVY WILL FIGHT THE AXIS

"How the U. S. Navy will fight the Axis." (From the "United States News" of 8. 8. 1941). The black line between the American and British bases was meant to show how Japan can be blockaded and overcome by the superior joint American-British Fleet

addition, Great Britain had also definitely directed her predominance in the China Seas against Japan.

From the purely military standpoint, the situation before the outbreak of war, bearing in mind the relative strengths at that time, was approximately as follows.

The American Pacific Fleet, with its bases on Hawaii, the Philippines and other advanced outposts, in conjunction with the available air forces, was able to guarantee with relative certainty the protection of the west coast of America including the Panama Canal. Danger from the air threatened at most the advanced American bases in the Pacific but scarcely the American Continent itself. The distances from the nearest Japanese base in the Pacific to the western coast of America were too great for this to be the case. It seemed impossible for aircraft carriers to penetrate very far into the American sphere of power as long as the fleet of the United States remained intact.

The situation was very similar in the south-western Pacific, that is to say, in the British sphere of interest which extends from India via the Malay States to Australia and New Zealand. Here, too, the possibility of a direct menace from Japan appeared to be only small, especially as it was considered that her air and sea power were held in check by the United States.

On the other hand, a threat to the Japanese Empire coming from Hong-kong, the Philippines, or Guam, was by no means out of the question. The flying distances from these points to Japan are very great, it is true, so that air attacks on a large scale were not very probable, but the possibility that a strong British and American naval force could blockade and hamper Japan could not be lightly dismissed.

These conditions have been decisively changed during the first few weeks of the conflict with the United States and Great Britain by the action of the Japanese forces. The capture of the American bases Guam, Wake and the Philippines as well as the rapid occupation of the British fortification of Hongkong removed the most important enemy bases in the Japanese living space and, more particularly, placed the war in the air on a different footing. The reactions caused by the newly created situation are so great that they also affect the European theatre of war.

The hunting ground of the aircraft carriers

The great distances in the Pacific, which according to European standards make war in the air impossible, have not become smaller as a result of Japan's successes. But the considerable weakening of the American Pacific Fleet in the battle of Hawaii and the annihilation of the heart of British sea power in Eastern Asia by the sinking of the battleships "Prince of Wales" and "Repulse," which occurred simultaneously, have given the Japanese Navy its liberty of movement and consequently every opportunity to carry out offensive operations. The Japanese aircraft carrier fleet is now in a position to carry air warfare to the ex-

treme coasts of the Pacific Ocean. Who could today seriously make an attempt to prevent the fast Japanese aircraft carriers from suddenly appearing, for example, on the west coast of America and there attacking the numerous military objectives? The effectiveness of the aircraft carrier resulting from the present relative strength in the Pacific must not be underestimated. The Japanese Navy has a considerable number of aircraft carriers of high speed at its disposal as well as several aircraft depot ships from which seaplanes can carry out their attacks. This fleet of aircraft carriers is supported by a considerable battle fleet which is today perfectly well able to deal in the Pacific with the united British and American naval forces. This battle fleet is therefore able to protect the passage of the aircraft carrier fleet to the most distant coasts of the Pacific Ocean.

Japan has already shown on several occasions to what use she puts her aircraft carriers. The Japanese Navy has passed beyond the old points of view that the aircraft carrier is to a certain extent the eye of the fleet, that is to say, that it carries out reconnaissance duty, or that it merely undertakes the air defence of naval units. Rather does it regard the aircraft carrier as a potent weapon of offence and uses it as such. The Japanese successes have sufficiently demonstrated what possibilities are made available to a fleet by these revolutionary tactics. Japanese aircraft carriers played a decisive part not only at Hawaii, where bombers and torpedo bombers starting from aircraft carriers smashed the American battle fleet, but also during various landing operations.

The aircraft carrier fleet makes the air arm of the Japanese Navy a very mobile, far-reaching weapon particularly suitable for use over long distances. Its mobility is all the more

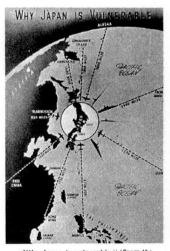

"Why Japan is vulnerable." (From the American periodical "Look" of 1. 7. 1941). A picture of the total encirclement. The military and economic strangulation of Japan was considered easy

dangerous for the enemy as the Pacific is for Japan a theatre of war offering the advantages of a struggle on the interior line in

*Everything has turned out differently: Japan
tore the meshes which strangled her. Whilst
Japan is operating on the interior line, her
enemies are conducting a difficult defence
which splits up their strength along the
tremendously wide circle of the exterior line*

nothing less than classical form. It enables offensive operations at any point on the extreme edge of the Pacific to be effectively supported by concentration in the air, whilst the enemy can move his air defence forces only to a restricted extent and never sufficiently quickly on account of the tremendous distances. Thus, for example, mutual support of the American and British air forces in order to ward off surprise attacks by Japanese aircraft carriers appear completely impossible, and even on the eastern or south-western sectors of the Anglo-American exterior line the distances are so great that the air defence is in an extremely difficult position.

Both of Japan's enemies, the United States and Great Britain, have tremendously long stretches of coastline to defend against air attacks starting from aircraft carriers. As they had scarcely reckoned with this eventuality in consequence of the over-estimation of their own power, their air defence, which was established before the war, is completely inadequate today under the altered strategical circumstances in the air.

Forced to adopt the defensive

What it means, however, for the United States to oppose an effective air defence against the air arm of the Japanese Navy along their west coast becomes clear when it is realized that the American air forces must also undertake the defence of Canada. About 30 degrees of latitude separate Alaska from California and the coastline has a length of approximately 2,500 miles. In addition, the region in the neighbourhood of the Panama Canal must also be defended.

Thousands of planes, fighters and bombers, with which nobody in America had previously reckoned, will be necessary in order to provide the west coast of America even with the most scanty defence, planes which were originally intended for Great Britain, as well as thousands of A.A.-guns, searchlights, etc. And many thousands of men who could otherwise have been used elsewhere or have been employed in the American armament industry, will have to keep watch. The same is true of the British sector in the south-western Pacific. Even if the Malay States, as already appears the case, are abandoned by the British, a huge region nevertheless remains for which an air defence must be created at all costs. The fighting in Malay and elsewhere has already sufficiently shown how small the preparations here were and how difficult it will be for Great Britain to send planes and equipment to the East. The available air units were much too weak to be able to cope with the Japanese Air Force and reinforcements were not available.

Precisely what was most unpleasant for the United States and Great Britain has occurred. The Pacific has become a theatre of air war, although not in the same sense as is the case in Europe. A few hundred Japanese planes borne on aircraft carriers make it essential to develop a gigantic air defence system calling for the employment of large numbers of planes. All these forces are for practical purposes lying fallow, for they cannot be used in an offensive operation against Japan because they are prevented from doing so by the great distances in this area.

The effect which this situation has upon the European theatres of war is obvious. What Great Britain and the United States have hoped to achieve in the next few years, namely to confront Germany at some time with a superior air force, has by this time receded far into the distance. —Iz

Records of political decisions of world importance

SIGNAL here reproduces the first photographs, other than those transmitted by wireless, from the theatres of war of the Japanese partner in the Three-Power Pact. They reached Europe by devious routes and as rare and imperishable photographic records, they supplement the official Japanese reports on the onward rush of a nation which since the second week of December of last year has caused the world to hold its breath

Pearl Harbour becomes the grave of the U.S. Pacific Fleet. *In the early morning hours of 8th December 1941 Japanese bombers and torpedo bombers plunged down from the overcast sky over Hawaii towards the American battleships anchored off Ford Island. At the same time Japanese submarines broke through the mine barrages and attacked the warships. High fountains of water spurt into the air, the first signs of a work of destruction unprecedented in naval history*

"Surprise—attack—success" was the message transmitted by the commander of the Japanese aeroplane squadron to his aircraft carrier half an hour after the opening of the attack. Justifiably as this photographic record shows: the leading battleship of the Oklahoma class (above), struck by torpedoes, is already sinking, and bombs are hailing down on the two next ships as the explosions show. The two battleships lying to the side already have a list and their oil is gushing out ... On the quayside a petrol tank is exploding. And the Japanese continue to attack ...

The announcer of the Japanese victories: Colonel Hideo Ohira. *He is in charge of the information department of the Imperial Headquarters. It was from his lips that the victories at Hawaii and Hong Kong, Singapore and Java, in Burma and off the Solomon Islands reached the world. Terseness, clarity and reliability are the features of his announcements*

ROOSEVELT—
Emperor of the World?

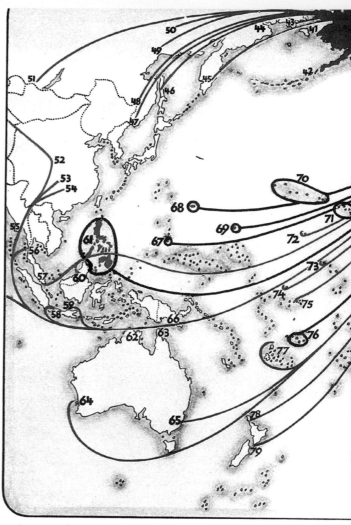

In this number "Signal" is beginning a series of articles on Roosevelt's policy. The first article that we are publishing today shows how the tentacles of dollar imperialism are reaching out over the whole world. A second article will show how Roosevelt's plans to stir up the American people's enthusiasm for war succeeded. The third article will answer the question: "Are the U. S. A. capable of ruling the world?"

Recently "Current History," perhaps the best political periodical published in the U.S.A., contained an article on "America's Destiny" by Basil C. Walker. "Current History" belongs to the publishers of the "New York Times" and has at its disposal all the home and foreign news services of this widely distributed newspaper whose close connections with leading political and economic circles in America are well known.

"Our day has come"

In his article Walker writes that it is the task of the Americans to master the present situation with bold decision and to force events into a path which leads to a world such as they wish. The only kind of peace in which they are interested is a "pax americana" similar to the one-time "pax romana" and "pax britannica." By helping Britain, he goes on, they are wearing out the arch-enemy. America's history has prepared her for the rôle she has to play. Present day developments in the world point to America as the only nation fitted for the position of leader —not to save Europe or the European system, but to make America the leader of all free people in the whole world in the American epoch that is dawning. The longer they hesitate, the harder and bloodier will be the task. A quick decision is the cleverest. Their day has come, he says. They must advance without delay.

At last, in these few sentences, the leading political monthly of the U.S.A. has made Roosevelt's real aim as clear to us as we could wish: it is not the defence of the democracies or of the western hemisphere, not even defence against the "aggressors," but purely and simply world domination, the economic and political conquest of the world. For "pax americana" means nothing other than the conquest of the world by Washington, just as "pax britannica" is nothing other than the pseudonym of that system which has subjected to the interests of London vast expanses of the earth which were not allowed to develop their own.

What Basil C. Walker reveals in his article is the programme for a campaign of aggression not only against Germany but against the whole of Europe and the great complementary territory of Africa, not only against

Japan but against the whole of Asia and the South Sea countries. The fact that the South American States are treated as mere political vassals by their big brother in the north interests Germany particularly because many of them are united to her by ancient ties of friendship. As for the rest, Europe, England excepted, has always respected the Monroe Doctrine. We have always left the states in the two Americas to settle their own affairs among themselves. We do not interfere.

All the more urgently, in consequence, do Europe and Eastern Asia demand respect for their own "Monroe Doctrine." It is up to Amernica to do as much as she will for the defence of the western hemisphere, but even a child cannot be persuaded that this hemisphere must be protected in Central Africa, in Batavia, or in the Urals. Roosevelt wants to make himself the Emperor of the World. He would like to play the rôle of a modern Louis XIV for whom the whole world offers just enough scope for the realization of his imperialistic ambitions.

Two world powers fade into nothingness

Roosevelt has already to his credit two big successes in which nobody would have believed two or even one year ago. The two greatest powers of modern times, the British Empire and the Soviet Union, have resigned their leading positions in favour of the U.S.A. and from day to day are becoming more and more dependent on Washington. Today these two powers are begging America for help and are ready to surrender in return their most valuable possessions, even their independence, if one were to believe what many Britons say. They know that without this help they cannot stand out alone against Europe which is defending herself with supreme energy. For this small Europe is fighting stubbornly, tenaciously—and victoriously against the hideous danger of Bolshevism. And at the far end of the Euro-Asiatic continent is Japan watching, silent and patient, and prepared to reply to each move with a counter-move. But both are occupied. One is busy with the war against the Soviets, the other with the war against Chungking. They are, therefore, not in a position to defend themselves as efficiently as if they

were free. And Roosevelt is taking advantage of this situation to encircle Europe and Japan, to place around their necks the rope with which he intends to strangle them. He is even prepared to make an alliance with Moscow if it will facilitate a landing in the Asiatic continent from where he can launch an attack on Japan.

America is trying to establish herself in every corner of the world which offers a starting point for attacks on Europe and Eastern Asia. She is prepared to use any means to further her aims: economic pressure, military power, political intrigues, cultural propaganda. A tour around the world will be sufficient to prove it.

Stepping-stones across the Atlantic

As the "New York Times" reports, the U.S.A. wants to induce Brazil to take over the protectorate of the Azores. Portugal's firm attitude in the face of the only too clearly manifested "interest" of the U.S.A. in the islands off the west coast of North Africa has made Washington cautious.

Perhaps—they are saying in the U.S.A.—the Portuguese will be less hostile to the occupation of the Azores if it is done by Brazil and not by the U.S.A., for Portuguese is spoken in Brazil too. Perhaps this proposal will succeed in sowing discord and mistrust between Portugal, the little mother country in Europe and Brazil, the big daughter in South America. Every attempt to upset the relations between

Europe and South America is welcome. Portugal has, however, consistently reinforced the garrisons of the Azores, of the Cape Verde Islands, and of the Madeira group. Washington does not yet dare to use force, for using force against the tiny country of Portugal would serve to reveal its clear intentions only too clearly, and therefore Brazil is pushed forward.

The occupation of these islands to which the Spanish Canaries also belong, would do more than protect South America from the "aggression" of the totalitarian states. More important is the fact that if she controlled these, America could control the sea routes between Europe and Africa south of the Sahara. Washington knows well enough that South America is threatened neither by Germany nor Italy—it wants to gain control of the stepping-stones across the Atlantic from where it would be able not only to attack South-Western Europe but also to extend its influence far into Africa. This is what the Americans have in mind. They want to build themselves a bridge-head in West Africa against Europe.

Why Wavell had to go

As the "Washington Times" reported in the middle of July, the difference between Churchill and Wavell which led to the recall of the latter from the post of Commander-in-Chief of the Eastern Mediterranean were due to the fact that Wavell, like the Americans, was of the opinion that Britain's posi-

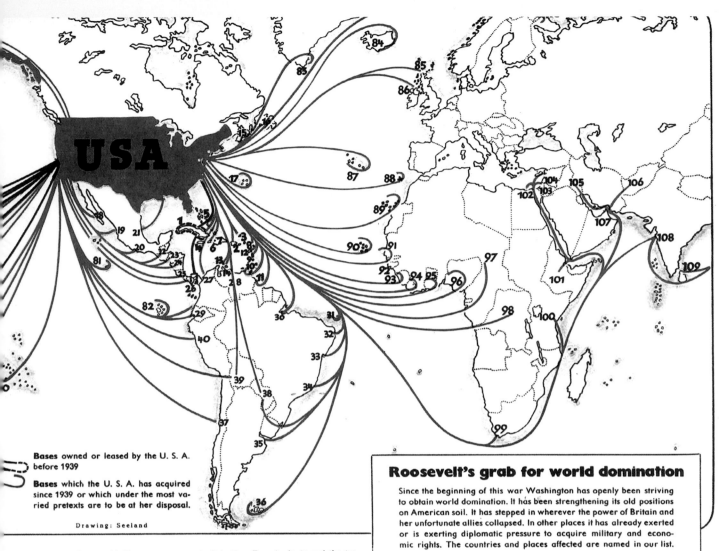

USA

Bases owned or leased by the U. S. A. before 1939

Bases which the U. S. A. has acquired since 1939 or which under the most varied pretexts are to be at her disposal.

Drawing: Seeland

Roosevelt's grab for world domination

Since the beginning of this war Washington has openly been striving to obtain world domination. It has been strengthening its old positions on American soil. It has stepped in wherever the power of Britain and her unfortunate allies collapsed. In other places it has already exerted or is exerting diplomatic pressure to acquire military and economic rights. The countries and places affected are named in our list.

West Indies
1 Guantanamo (Cuba)
2 Puerto Rico
3 Virgin Islands
4 Jamaica
5 The Bahamas
6 Haiti
7 San Domingo
8 Antigua
9 Santa Lucia
10 Trinidad
11 British Guiana
12 Martinique
13 Aruba
14 Curaçao

Canada and the Bermudas
15 Halifax
16 Placentia Harbour
17 The Bermudas

Central and Southern America
 MEXICO
18 Santa Margarita
19 Acapulco
20 Salina Cruz
21 Vera Cruz
22 GUATEMALA
23 FONSECA BAY
24 NICARAGUA
25 COSTA RICA
26 PANAMA
27 COLUMBIA
28 VENEZUELA
29 ECUADOR
 BRAZIL
30 Marajo (mouth of the Amazon)
31 Fernando de Noronha
32 Pernambuco
33 Bahia
34 Rio Grande do Sul
 ARGENTINE
35 La Plata

36 FALKLAND ISLANDS
 CHILE
37 Valparaiso
38 PARAGUAY
39 BOLIVIA
40 PERU

Alaska
41 Nome
42 Dutch Harbour

Siberia
43 Providentia
44 Anadyr
45 Petropavlovsk
46 Alexandrovsk
47 Vladivostok
48 Chabarovsk
49 Ochotsk
50 Verchme-Kolymsk
51 Irkutsk

South Eastern Asia
52 Lanchu
53 Chungtu
54 Chungking
55 Rangoon
56 Thailand
57 Singapore
58 Batavia
59 Surabaya
60 Brunei (British Borneo)
61 Manila

Australia
62 Port Darwin
63 Thursday Islands
64 Fremantle
65 Sydney
66 PORT MORESBY
 (British New Guinea)

South Seas
67 Guam
68 Marcus Island
69 Wake Island
70 Midway
71 Hawaii
72 Johnston

73 Palmyra
74 Howland
75 Enderbury (Phoenix Islands)
76 Tutuila (Samoa)
77 Fiji Islands
78 Auckland (New Zealand)
79 Wellington
80 Tahiti
81 Clipperton
82 Galapagos

The Atlantic
83 Greenland
85 Iceland
85 Northern Scotland
86 Northern Ireland
87 The Azores
88 Madeira
89 Canary Islands
90 Cape Verde Islands

Africa
91 Dakar
92 Bathurst
93 Freetown
94 Liberia
95 The Gold Coast
96 Nigeria
97 French Equatorial Africa
98 Belgian Congo
99 Cape Town
100 Kenya
101 Abessynia
102 Egypt

The Near East
103 Palestine, Transjordan
104 Syria
105 Iraq
106 Afghanistan
107 The Bahrein Islands

India
108 Bombay
109 Trincomali

Arctic Ocean
110 Murmansk

---

tion in the Eastern Mediterranean was untenable in the long run. The front should be moved back to a line running south of the Sahara across Africa. This would mean that the hard pressed British Mediterranean Fleet would be free for action in the Atlantic. The Americans and the British could then concentrate their energy on West Africa. Wavell had a good press in the U.S.A., but he was not able to put his plans into action. Instead he was transferred to India. The attack on Dakar has not been repeated up to now.

The encirclement of Europe

To accomplish this, comparatively unimportant harbours on the African coast were garrisoned with American consuls, regular air lines were opened up and the steamship companies put on more steamers. In 1940 as compared with 1939 the U.S.A.'s foreign trade with Africa increased approximately 40 %. Since 1939 America has been exporting to Africa important armaments and articles for the equipment of troops. This fact is explained if one recalls that the southernmost part of the French Empire in Africa, French Equatorial Africa, has split away from the Vichy Government and is under the control of people who have joined forces with de Gaulle. From French Equatorial Africa across Belgian Congo which is likewise hostile to Europe, to Anglo-Egyptian Sudan and across Kenya to the eastern projection of Africa an American cordon which is to be prolonged across Egypt northwards

to Palestine, Transjordania and the territories of Syria and Iraq that have been forcibly suppressed.

In the Persian Gulf the tentacles radiating eastwards from America over the whole of Europe meet those reaching out across the Pacific and the Indian Ocean to strangle East Asia. For in the petroleum fields in the Behrein Islands American capital supplies oil to the British troops and ships in the Indian Ocean and the Red Sea. From the Persian Gulf the encirclement of Europe is extended to include India. Here the intermediate links, Turkey and Iran, are missing. Although these states desire nothing more passionately than to preserve their neutrality, from day to day it becomes more and more apparent that the Anglo-Americans will display just as little respect for the sovereignty of Iran as they previously did for that of Iraq and Syria. As usual the "intrigues of German citizens in Iran against Britain" must furnish the pretext although the Iran Government officially announced that the behaviour of the 650 Germans in Iran is correct in all respects and a threat is out of the question. Under the most varied pretexts the Americans and the British are trying to induce Afghanistan to join the front against Europe.

Europe, an American economic colony?

If one bears in mind also that the Union of South Africa, with its gold

Continued on Page 33

Roosevelt — Emperor of the world?

production as the deciding factor, is almost entirely dependent on the U.S.A.'s willingness to purchase—for the agricultural products of the Union are practically unmarketable today—and that that part of Africa which lies south of the Sahara urgently needs the U.S.A. who are the only customers on whom it can reckon, one can clearly recognize the U.S.A.'s intention of making the whole of Africa dependent on her good will and finally of bringing the continent not only under her economic but also under her military and political control.

When one hears that American engineers, technicians, and trained workmen are building aerodromes, landing-grounds and living quarters on African soil (British Gambia south of Dakar), that intervention in Liberia has already been announced, that the occupation of Greenland and Iceland are already accomplished facts, and that American experts are developing air bases in Northern Ireland, one realises beyond a shadow of a doubt that America desires to subdue not only Germany and Italy but also the whole of Europe, England included. She hopes to be able to prove that Europe depends on America's good will for her food supplies and that at the same time the U.S.A. can even mete out military chastisement. Europe, including England, is to be transformed into an economic colony that owes obedience to America, and the difference between the individual European states is to disappear.

Finally, when one observes the unconditional support given by the U.S.A. to the Soviets whose designs on Europe have been established facts for some time—if they had succeeded Europe as a cultural conception would have been destroyed—the whole body of the European states reveal themselves as a community facing a common fate and with common rights to live which must be defended against the threats of a common enemy.

The tentacles reaching out for Asia

With the same consistent ruthlessness as in the case of the Atlantic the U.S.A. are reaching out to seize Asia. Here it is Japan and powers allied or friendly to her, Manchukuo. Nanking-China, French Indo-China, and Thailand, that are exposed to the ever increasing pressure exerted by America. Here, too, Roosevelt is trying to tighten his grasp. Using all the strength and means at her disposal, whether military, political, or economic, America is proceeding with the encirclement of Japan, the leading power in Eastern Asia.

Since Bolshevism, hard pressed by the fighting forces of Europe, is taking refuge in a vassal relationship to the U.S.A. as has already been done by the British Empire, it has been possible for Roosevelt to approach Japan from the north, a move which had had up to now only very imperfect success. Alaska, the western point of which is only a few miles distant from the extreme eastern point of North-East Siberia, and which combined with the long chain of Aleutian Islands provides a kind of bridge to the northeast of Asia, was already a long time ago developed into an important American air and naval base. The naval port Dutch Harbour on Unalaska, one of the large islands of the Aleutian group, was built up into a northern counterpart of Pearl Harbour on Oahu, the most important of the Hawaiian Islands. Hawaii was the heavily fortified key position of the American naval forces concentrated in the Pacific.

In the north no real progress was made because frequent storms and dense fog lessen the strategic value of the Aleutian Islands and the south coast of Alaska. Now the Americans, who do not grant help to the Soviets for nothing, want the Bolshevists to make over to them bases in North-Eastern Siberia. As they have already promised support to the Soviets in a formal agreement, one can safely assume that they have already landed or are about to land soon in Kamchatka, on the coast of the Ochotski Sea, at the mouth of the Amur, perhaps even in Vladivostok. They could send formations of the Air Force there by this route across the Asiatic continent without even touching Japanese spheres of influence. By so doing they would be within easy reach of the heart of Japan. It must be mentioned here that the northern part of the long island Sachalin that lies at the mouth of the Amur belongs to the Soviet and the south to Japan.

In the central Pacific, America's striving for supremacy has been becoming more and more apparent. The bridge from Hawaii to the Philippines, to whom the U.S.A. have promised a mock-freedom dating from 1946, and which today extends on to Thailand, Singapore, the Dutch East Indies and British India, was systematically improved. The bases on Johnston and Palmyra— south-west and south of Hawaii—were completed on the 15th of August. Farther to the south-west work is in progress on the islands of Howland and Enderbury in the Phoenix group. The American naval and air base Tutuila in the Samoa Islands is already old, having been completed some time ago; with the British Fiji Islands it completes the bridge to New Zealand and Australia. Farther to the north, in the direction of the Philippines, Midway, Wake, Marcus, and Guam are being developed.

The U.S.A. is working at high pressure on the further development of Corregidor and Cavite in Manila Bay in the Philippines. American bombers flew to Java, for the Dutch East Indies have long since degenerated into a mere tool of American politics. In Borneo aerodromes are being built which will serve to protect Singapore from the flank in the southern Chinese Ocean. Singapore itself, in a case of emergency, could perhaps be defended only with the help of American naval and air forces.

The existence of a military alliance between the U.S.A., England, British India and the Dutch East India, Chung-

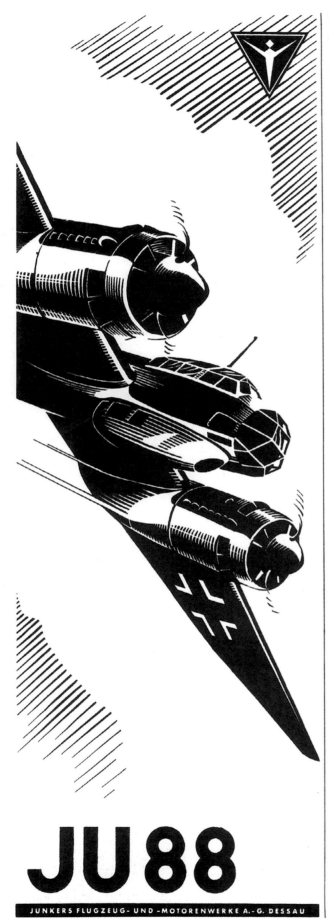

king China, Australia, and New Zealand is an open secret in the Far East. In connexion with this co-operation which is under the guidance of the U.S.A., America has set aside 40 million dollars for aerodromes in the south-west of China. The U.S.A. and England wish to prepare 600 machines for service in Kweiyang and in other places in South-Western China, and to detail 200 pilots there. In addition Hopkins, Roosevelt's Extraordinary Ambassador in Moscow, has prepared the conclusion of a military alliance between the Soviet Union and Chungking. Further, Moscow is to undertake to complete with Anglo-American help the branch of the railway running eastwards from Turksib to Central Asia as far as Lantschau in Kansu straight across Hsingkiang.

Along the Thailand, Indo-China, and China frontiers of Burma, petrol dumps, hangars, and living quarters are being erected by American engineers with the help of American money. The reinforcement of the British garrisons in Singapore, the Malay States, and in Burma point at the unmistakable fact that an Anglo-American action is being prepared against Thailand which would be offering similar violence to a small state as was offered to Iraq and as British policy has been offering to India and Egypt for many years. By making a timely agreement with the Japanese and by calling upon them to protect both of their interests the French Government has saved Indo-China from Anglo-American intervention. Thailand too, as her last actions prove, is inclining to the Japanese side.

It is a matter of course that there is something behind the granting of transport planes and the recent additional loans (10 million pounds sterling and 50 million dollars) to Chang Kai Chek, the tenacious defender of the rest of China He is the Anglo-American's continental dagger which is threatening the Japanese position in South-Eastern Asia and which under no circumstances must be withdrawn. For the Americans the important thing is to open up the gigantic possibilities of the Chinese market for exploitation by their economic imperialism. If the American plans succeed, Chang could retire after doing his duty. Just as Britain by her clever policy of the balance of power kept Europe powerless by always supporting the weaker side against a stronger adversary, so the U.S.A. today are acting in the gamble for Asia. They are supporting the weakened Soviet Union and Chang Kai Chek who has been driven back to the remotest provinces in the south-west in order to overcome Japan who has earned the leadership in the Far East by her achievements and her strength.

And why? Escape from her own problems!

Just as in Europe, the U.S.A. wish to prevent by all the means in their power that the states of the Far East should arrive at a suitable solution of their justifiable demands. If this were to happen America's attention would be directed to her own problems. In Roosevelt's own country all the questions and tasks which cannot be solved in the old-fashioned way are waiting for solution; it is easier to interfere everywhere and to make the world into the battlefield of American imperialism of the Roosevelt stamp.

Even though the countries belonging to the British Empire voluntarily content themselves with the position of vassals of Washington, it is no reason why the old homes of culture, Europe and Eastern Asia, should bow before that class of Americans whose standard of values is the dollar and for whom the films of Hollywood are cultural achievements of the highest grade.

JU 88

Drive to the Caucasus

As the Russian snows began to melt, and winter gave way to spring in early 1942, Hitler began planning another summer offensive that, this time, would win him final victory over the USSR. Instead of striking toward Moscow again, he decided to attack in the south with the aim of seizing the rich Caucasian oilfields and capturing Stalingrad, a prominent city on the River Volga. His generals warned that the Wehrmacht was not strong enough to tackle both objectives, but the Fuehrer overruled them. Hitler said that Stalingrad would not only deprive the Soviets of a major transportation hub; its fall would deal a crushing blow to Soviet morale.

The preliminaries to the offensive proper began on May 8, when Field Marshal Erich von Manstein's 11th Army struck at the Soviet forces defending the neck of the Kerch Peninsula in the eastern Crimea. By May 20, the battle there was virtually over, and Manstein was free to besiege Sebastopol, which fell to him a month later. Out of the 300,000 Soviet troops who faced the German onslaught, 200,000 were killed or captured.

Hitler was pleased with Manstein's progress, but less than satisfied with what he saw as von Bock's slowness in exploiting his defeat of the offensive the Russians had launched against him around Kharkov. He sacked Bock on July 15. The following day, he arrived at his new field headquarters near Vinnitsa in western Ukraine to take personal command of operations.

Divided objectives

Codenamed Operation Green, the attack actually began on June 28 east of Kursk. Two days later, the Germans thrust forward east of Kharkov. By July 6, they were fighting their way through Voronezh. All seemed to be going according to expectations, but then the Fuehrer amended the plan radically. Following the fall of Rostov on July 23, he divided Army Group South in two.

The new Army Group A, the southern group, was tasked with capturing Maikop and the other Caucasian oilfields around Grozny hundreds of miles to the southeast. It was then to advance to the Caspian Sea and on to Baku. Having captured Stalingrad, the new Army Group B, the northern group, was to swing down the Volga to reach the Caspian Sea at Astrakhan. Both General Franz Halder, the Army Chief of Staff, and Field Marshal Wilhelm von List, the commander of Army Group A, protested that the Wehrmacht was strong enough to secure the lower Volga or the Caucasus, but not both. Hitler brushed their objections aside. In his view, the Soviet armies were finished as an effective fighting force. His problem was with some of his own generals, whom he believed were being excessively cautious and so holding up the advance.

"Discussions with the Fuehrer today," Halder recorded at the end of August, "were once more characterized by serious accusations leveled against the military leadership at the top of the army. They are accused of intellectual arrogance, incorrigibility, and an inability to recognize the essentials." On September 9, Hitler sacked List, taking direct command of Army Group A himself. On September 22, he replaced Halder with Major-General Kurt Zeitzler, previously in charge of coastal defences in the west. Unlike his predecessor, Zeitzler was a committed Nazi. This suited Hitler down to the ground. He told the sacked Halder, "We need National Socialist ardor now, not professional ability."

To add to these problems, Hitler constantly changed his mind about which attack was to take priority. Thus, the 4th Panzer Army found itself being switched from one front to the other, and then back again. To compound matters, the Fuehrer ordered 11th Army, his only substantial strategic reserve, north to reinforce his troops still besieging Leningrad. The city had been cut off from the rest of the USSR since September 8, 1941.

Why Stalingrad?

Why Hitler became obsessed with capturing Stalingrad is unclear. There were sound strategic reasons for trying to capture the Caucasian oilfields, though, by the time the Germans got to Maikop, the retreating Russians

had successfully sabotaged the oil-wells there. Stalingrad, as Tsaritsyn had been renamed in 1925 as the drive to transform it into a model Soviet city began, was a tempting target, but not so important as to make it a vital objective. There was no real reason for attacking the city head-on other than to ensure its elimination as a potential bridgehead from which the Soviets could launch a counter-attack across the Volga.

As things turned out, Hitler would have been better advised to lay siege to Stalingrad, neutralizing it through aerial and artillery bombardment. This would have left General Friedrich von Paulus, in command of 6th Army which was tasked with attacking Stalingrad, with stronger flanks plus a mobile reserve. The Fuehrer, however, was in no mood to be gainsaid. "The entire male population must be eliminated," he ordered, "as Stalingrad with its one million uniformly Communist inhabitants is extremely dangerous." Once the city had fallen, Hitler planned for his panzers to strike north up the Volga into central Russia, attacking Moscow from both west and east. At the same time, German forces would advance from the Caucasus into Persia to join up with Rommel's Afrika Korps, which, after breaking through the British positions at El Alamein, would cross the Sinai and move forward into Jordan and Iraq. Ultimately, the intention was to invade India and link up with the Japanese.

For this ambitious strategy to work as Hitler intended, the capture of Stalingrad was essential. The

Confronted with the Russian winter, the Germans were forced to rely on horse-drawn transport as the motors in their trucks froze solid. Signal did not mention this, the lack of adequate winter clothing, or that the Russians were driving the Wehrmacht back.

city also was an objective for which Stalin had decreed his troops must defend to the last man. With his consent earlier in the summer, the Soviet armies in the south, rather than fighting every step of the way until they were surrounded and destroyed, had engaged in a series of tactical retreats. At Stalingrad, this would not be the case. Once 6th Army had been pinned down trying to fulfil Hitler's demands, the Soviets would unleash a devastating counteroffensive to destroy it. This time, said Stalin, they must succeed.

European DECISION 1940

Sept. 3rd
1939

England, Fran
ce and Polan
are war zone

Germany banished the war from the Continent

1939: War on two fronts again?

On the Sunday following Compiègne, at an early hour in the morning, the Führer arrived in Paris and visited Napoleon's tomb in Les Invalides. The man who had once and for all destroyed France's hostile power and initiated the German epoch in Europe stood plunged deep in thought in front of the red marble sarcophagus. Once more it had been necessary to conquer the Continent, because the nations yield only before the might of experience. In the eyes of the world, Adolf Hitler had now succeeded to Napoleon's position, and beyond that this process was in course of development which the Corsican had once foreseen while a prisoner in the hands of the British: the urge for unity, which in the long run no European nation could now escape, must be welded to a mighty will in order to appear immediately with the impetus of a natural phenomenon. It was a question of life and death whether in spite of all reactionary calculations the great simplification would succeed early enough for the good of Europe.

Even the most sober observer had been forced since the summer of 1940 to come to the conclusion that, with the German front along the Atlantic coast and Italy waging war in the Mediterranean, not only was France eliminated as a hostile power and England given the choice between renunciation and annihilation, but that the peoples of Europe did also in truth expect from the conqueror a complete reorganization of their own conditions and of conditions in general.

On the other side of the demarcation line, in the unoccupied part of France, the more or less honourable acknowledgement by the French, from the minister down to the lowliest reservist, that the collapse of the old world which had opposed Hitler and Mussolini was complete, corresponded to the completely natural transition which took place without any delay from the armistice with France to the total attack against England. With the Maginot Line there fell also the Chinese Wall which France had built between herself and the future of Europe.

The European Civil War

At that time a comparison involuntarily imposed itself with an upheaval on the American Continent which, however, from a military point of view took place in quite different circumstances. The secession of the Southern States which resulted in the American Civil War had not been merely a regrettable misunderstanding, but the avowed final struggle of an old civilisation which could brook no compromise with a young one. The future was with the Yankees. Their very real superiority corresponded to the inexorable path of America's destiny which was pushing forward towards a social break-through along the whole line. The Alliance of the Führer with the Duce resulted at the outbreak of war in a similar superiority in strength, for Germany and Italy who were forced to take up the struggle with the powers of European reaction, were able from the very commencement to act in the spirit and on behalf of the whole continent, the unification of which was to be the outcome of their victory. Hitler and Mussolini believed in this European solution because they were firmly convinced of the necessity of European reform by the process of the social rejuvenation of the German and Italian peoples. Herein lies the fundamental difference which distinguishes them from Napoleon who sought a solution of Europe's problems in half a dozen victorious campaigns and was not able to find it, because each time he merely conquered a further portion of Central Europe as a French glacis.

Adolf Hitler at Napoleon's tomb
Paris, June 1940

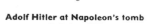

"I was forced to conquer Europe by arms.
Today Europe has to be convinced."

Napoleon in 1821 on the island of St. Helena

What Germany and Italy with their whole strength thought themselves capable of when the hour of the challenge came, what England and France feared, and yet would not recognize was regarded even before the outbreak of war as inevitable by the world beyond the boundaries of Europe in spite of all propaganda to the contrary. Even before England on September 3rd, 1939, took the step leading to armed conflict, Americans, Russians and Japanese all agreed in an impartial recognition of the fact that if war came, the Axis would revolutionize Europe. That is the chief reason why Stalin had no desire to pick the chestnuts out of the fire for the defunct Western Powers and why the Americans, in spite of their sympathies, judge the chances of European democracy in extremely sceptical fashion. It was for the same reason that the war in Europe accelerated the change in political structure aimed at in Japan and now realized by Prince Konoye: The final estrangement from England and the Three Power Pact between Japan and the Axis Powers. This time the last European civil war is being fought out before the eyes of the world and its outcome, by reason of its very finality, must appear to the powers outside Europe as the signal for an intercontinental reorganization. Whilst seeking to cover England's withdrawal from the Continent, the Americans believed they would be able to retard automatically the future course of events, whereas the Russians from the time of the pact with Germany until their occupation of Bessarabia established for themselves a new position based on facts.

No more war fronts on the Continent

The decision reached on the continent of Europe was the unprecedented result of one single year of war on European battle fields. Considering in retrospect the events of the year which began in the late summer months of 1939 and lead up to the siege of Great Britain, it becomes apparent that the German Command in collaboration with their Italian ally have systematically and step by step liberated Europe from war. The transference of the war from Poland via Norway to the Western front and later on its advance to the Western edge of the continent corresponded to the logical military conclusion that England's war had to be waged against England herself. Italy's entry into the war which was first directed against France, was accompanied by an essential feature of the war, the extension of the total anti-British front along the Southern border of Europe. An unprecedented application of military strength and a dogged consistency in the conduct of foreign policy during the war had been required in order to eliminate completely the military fronts within Europe during the course of a single year and to do away with the antiquated national ideals which have existed for centuries. It also becomes apparent, that the longest front against England stretching from the North Cape to the Bay of Biscay through the Mediterranean as far as the Indian Ocean and finally being completed by the Three Power Pact with Japan was at the same time the most economical and the shortest front possible.

Continental European Autarchy

The defeats suffered by the powers of the old Europe corresponded to the slogans of the re-

1940: Successful conduct of war banishes war from the European Continent

volutionary propaganda in Germany and Italy. The English war itself provided the economic unification of Europe with a great impetus. There has never been any creative reorganization in the lives of nations which was not the result of exceptional circumstances. The misery during the great economic crisis had finally led Germany, then an impoverished State almost despairing of its own existence, to pursue a long-sighted policy of self-help. German autarchy as seen in the two Four Year Plans was neither a programme chosen at random nor an ideal condition. The same applied to Italian autarchy after the experiences of the British sanctions war during the Abyssinian campaign. The European autarchy which we are experiencing today could never have been carried through in peacetime even by the boldest pioneer of large-scale regional economics, although the victorious powers have made of it a vast act of peace in the midst of war. Necessity and discernment were on this occasion once more the teachers of the peoples. It was not the Nazis, but the English war which inflicted this necessity and this compulsion upon Europe. The blockade at sea, in contrast to the lack of effect which it had upon Germany in a state of war, did in fact economically sever Western Europe with the exception of France from England and oversea countries even before the German victory in the West. As a counter-measure the new powers in Central Europe extended at an accelerated pace due to war conditions the system of exchanging goods in German Central Europe and in the autarchic Italian Imperium which already existed against the background of the economic agreements with Russia and the free arrangement concerning export goods from the Danubian countries. When then first Scandinavia and very soon afterwards the whole of Western Europe came within the sphere of power of England's enemies, everything had already been prepared for the assimilation of the national economies of the countries concerned

into the new Continental System. Three necessary factors did the rest. They were:

1. The immediate use of all reserves in the occupied countries for increasing the war potential against England,

2. The reconstruction work in the elimination of the material damage during the war, and finally,

3. The creation of work and the maintenance of the millions of people belonging to those nations which had unwillingly crossed over to the camp of the victors.

Max Clauss, the author of

"EUROPEAN DECISION"

will discuss the reorganization of the world without England and the obstacles placed in the path of Pan-Europe in two further articles.

Every month of the war witnessed a further step towards the development and perfection of the German-Italian economic continental system. For now, in the compact region extending from Sweden to the North of Africa, the creative impulse of all the highly developed national economies which previously had not co-operated in a manner even remotely similar to this, took effect in accordance with a mutual project.

In the German Sphere of Power

During the autumn of 1940 Germany occupied as a result of the war approximately one million square kilometres of European soil with a total of approximately 66 million inhabitants. These figures included Norway, Denmark, Holland, and Belgium whose inhabitants with the exception of the Walloons in Belgium are of pure Germanic blood and a proportion of whom is racially closely

related to the German people. From the very outset Denmark occupied a special position, for her political independence was in no way influenced by the German troops which occupied the country to guarantee her defence and in order to protect German interests. There is no German military administration in Denmark and Danish agriculture, after the complete standstill of its oversea trade during 8 months of the war, adapted itself to the requirements of its German neighbour and took its place in the Continental System. The attitude of the German government towards relations with the Norwegians, the Dutch and the Belgians after the occupation of their respective countries was demonstrated by the release of the prisoners of war of all three countries soon after the conclusion of hostilities and whilst Germany was still waging war against England from their territories. Politically speaking there were on the one side the most unconditional respect for the closely related national characteristics and the no less unconditional determination not to tolerate any platforms hostile to Germany on the Western fringe of the continent and, on the other hand, the two poles between which the reorganization during the war would be carried out under the German occupation. This included the principle of not making any alteration in the sound institutions of the countries' administration as far as the necessities of war would allow and to leave the government of the respective nations in their own hands.

The broad basis of understanding was continually provided by the complete economic and social common destiny which was the result of the force of circumstances. The Danish and the Dutch peasant both enjoy the same advantage of the closest economic incorporation into Germany. The Belgian workman derives great profit from the reciprocal penetration of the heavy industries in his own country and those of Germany, all the more so since by Germany's incorporation of

Europe restored to peace: The protection and administration afforded by the victors replaces war

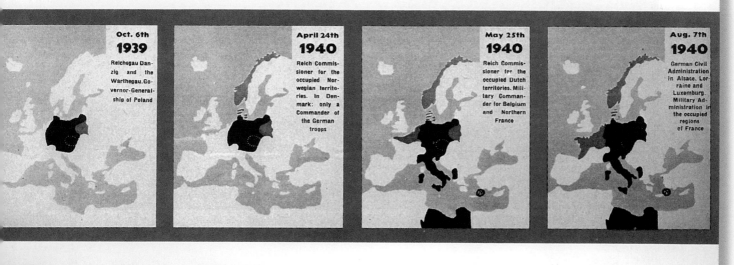

The decision in Europe

Luxemburg and Lorraine the most powerful centre of production in modern Europe has now been formed for the first time into one complete block. What had previously taken place in Silesia and Bohemia now also took place in the industrial area between the Rhine and the Meuse which suffered no damage when the German offensive broke through the Maginot Line and its extension towards the North. The war system of economy accelerated rationalisation and brought about that effective concentration of production with the technical pre-requisites of which the manufacturers had long been familiar before the customs barriers eventually fell. It would be a misrepresentation of methodical planning of the German government if the attempt were made to bring under the same category in the scheme of things the new relations with Germany which have been developed during the war in Holland, Belgium and in Scandinavia—for it is natural that Sweden also both politically and economically reorganized herself in accordance with the new continent. On the other hand it is immediately obvious that France in every way was a special case. France as a great power had wittingly sacrificed herself and accepted servitude to Britain. The German provinces of Alsace and Lorraine, in the same way as Luxemburg which is also German, were again incorporated into the German customs area. The political fact that the Gauleiters of Baden, Saarpfalz and Koblenz-Trier took over the civil administration of Strasburg, Metz and Luxemburg respectively emphasizes the definite reorganization in accordance with the homogeneity of neighbouring territories and ancient German tradition. The remainder of France was not merely divided into the occupied and unoccupied areas, but wide expanses of the occupied area continued to form part of the war zone facing England. There was, in addition, the special position of the French colonies. Although the victorious powers themselves had left the problem completely open during the Armistice, the brutal British attacks, the last of which took place against Dakar in West Africa, provided the French army, navy and air force with the opportunity of proving to the British that France, although she had been vanquished, still had enough spirit to draw her own conclusions from these acts of British treachery.

The Axis System

The axis of the reorganization of Europe in wartime was that of the victorious nations themselves: The Berlin-Rome Axis. The real origin of the new Europe will always be that moment during the autumn of 1936 when the great national revolutions of National-Socialist Germany and Fascist Italy, each of which had until then marched along its own road, were brought together by what was politically and economically a senseless invention, Britain's war of sanctions against Italy. This was the classical example for the transformation of two national wills which had been developed to the highest degree, into one community which went beyond the barriers of nationality. The mystery of the quite open European conspiracy between the Führer and the Duce was as simple as it could be ; the elimination of any and every reason for friction between the two nations, the systematic removal of every harmful competition between the two Empires on either side of the Alps. And all this with the aim of immediately beginning to double German and Italian efforts in every sphere. Economically viewed, the agreement between Germany and Italy was the point where these two countries' autarchic systems which were of separate origin, by their systematic completion of one another rebutted the reproach made by the gold bloc of that time consisting of France, England and the United States of America, that autarchy was synonymous with isolation. In reality the determination of both countries to achieve economic independence as a pledge of political independence was directed towards the permanent establishment of a greater European sphere. The wholesome necessity of extracting the greatest advantage from a most restricted use of currency, even during the years before the European war, made the political experts in economics of the Axis Powers very inventive. There was scarcely a problem of organization in the whole range of the highly industrialised economic system to that of agricultural or colonial raw materials which had not been jointly planned by Germany and Italy even before the victory of the Axis Powers had brought Europe under their influence.

As soon as the land communication across the Pyrenees had been re-established as a result of France's retiring from the war and the Italian control in the Mediterranean had been guaranteed, Spain was once more able to assume her national place in the system of the Axis which now comprised all the areas occupied by Germany north of the Alps as well as South Eastern Europe which had not become a theatre of war. The constructive policy of the Axis in the Danubian countries, the obvious success of which was the settlement of the territorial revision between Hungary, Rumania and Bulgaria, was, like the co-operation between Germany and Italy itself, based upon the principle that it was necessary to break down the internal fronts between the nations and systematically to organize the vast resources of the entire Danubian region for the benefit of Europe.

No blockades in the future

The reorganization of Europe in wartime had two precursors: Napoleon's Continental Blockade and the German Customs Union. The coercive method of the Continental Blockade was in accordance with Napoleon's purely military line of thought, whilst Prussia at a later date through the Customs Union laid the foundation stone of German industry and provided thereby the decisive impetus towards the unification of the Reich. Already in 1914 German production as well as that of North America had meanwhile surpassed that of England who now feared that the Central European Powers of those days might combine a repetition of the Napoleonic situation with the final establishment of an economic monopoly on the continent. These pre-requisites exist today and are, moreover, supported by a technical revolution in the entire economic system of supplies which in its turn has its origin in the years of misery and necessity through which Germany passed after the last war. A continent which supplements its own rich resources in natural products by products of colonies in Africa, can never again be blockaded.

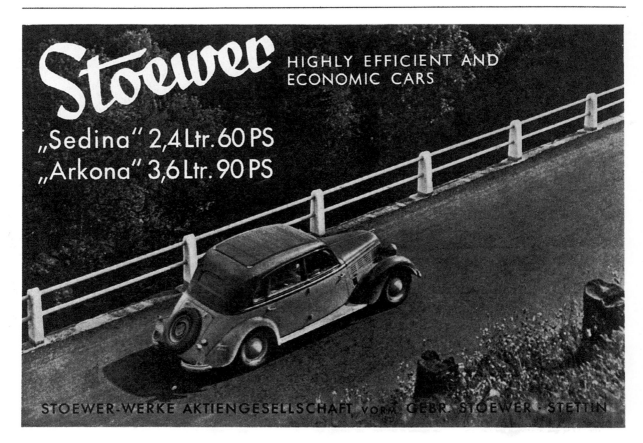

At the window of the "New Palace" in Potsdam

The Japanese Minister for Foreign Affairs, Matsuoka, gained a true impression of the German soldier at historic spots in Potsdam. The visit, the purpose of which was that the statesmen of the friendly nations should become mutually acquainted, resulted in a particulary close contact being established between the Foreign Ministers of Germany and Japan. Illustrations on pages 6 and 7

Matsuoka in Berlin

Norwegian Girls in Berlin

The „Signal" pays a visit to a group of Norwegian girls. They came voluntarily to Germany and are following various professions here

Dinner in the canteen : *Eva and Evelyn are two Oslo girls belonging to a group of merry Norwegians who have been in Berlin for some months already. Eva was a companion-help and her friend a dental mechanic's assistant. Both wanted to get to know Germany and they could not find work in Norway, they came to Berlin*

Neither Eva nor Evelyn had expected to see so much snow in Berlin! *But they had brought their skis from Noway in ease. On Sunday they go to Grunewald, the ski paradise of Berlin*

„Is that right ?" *In the beginning the work was difficult, but her companion, a girl from Sudetenland, was always ready to help (Picture left)*

Fun in the snow — just like in Norway! *The snowball fight is over: Eva has won all along the line (Right)*

"BY THE FRENCH
FOR THE FRENCH"

This is the slogan of a variety troupe from Paris which acts and sings for their fellow-countrymen who have found good positions in offices and factories in Berlin and other German towns. Aimée and Lucienne and Marcel, too, who is serving with the volunteer legion, lose themselves in rapturous enjoyment of the performances in their native style and language

He knows they like his chanson. Costume and pose compel applause from every member of the audience

A PARISIAN IN BERLIN

My first impression was that Berlin is a city with electric tramways. That is not especially interesting, you object. But it is; for in the trams you can see all kinds of things and acquire there a preliminary vocabulary. After ten stops you know the German for wood, coal, butcher's shop, restaurant, bakery, hairdresser and tobacconist's shop. Such things are most important today.

Living conditions here are more or less the same as in Paris: the essential food supplies are guaranteed by rationing. Tickets for everything, nothing without tickets. But there are no queues. There are no crowds in front of the shops. There is no grumbling. It is unnecessary for policemen to supervise women shoppers. On the contrary, very few of the "arms of the law" are to be seen. People maintain order voluntarily so that policemen are superfluous. They can still be seen, however, at the busy crossings. There they stand alert, their eyes watchful under the patent leather helmets. If you should dare to cross the street at the wrong time they beckon to you with a compelling gesture and you forfeit a mark.

It is a fact that the French are popular in Berlin. They arouse people's tolerance, curiosity, and sympathy. It cannot be denied that we have all kinds of peculiar habits. It is clear that our manners are quite different from those which prevail here. They call forth surprise and do not always meet with approval. For instance we like to evade prohibitions; that offends the disciplined German. But they forgive us much and try to make things easy for us. Tolerance.

Curiosity? Of course, but it is never indiscreet. It is the kind of curiosity that seems to say: "So you are a Frenchman? How strange to meet you here in wartime after all the ... But now that you have come we are glad ..."

And sympathy? Several thousand French citizens are working in Berlin. Not one of them has not encountered the German's need to find common ground, to make conversation about the events of the past, conversations full of compassion and hope for the future. I have exchanged cordial handshakes and a hearty "I hope we meet again soon" with many a German.

In conclusion I should like to turn aside from mere impressions. Berlin has two French embassies. the one in Pariser Platz, a dignified building in the most beautiful quarter of a city which boasts of much architectural splendour. The shutters are closed. And then the other embassy in the street, alive, full of activity, consisting of those thousands of ambassadors, consuls and chargés d'affaires who are accredited to factories, landladies, families, business men, and offices. Each one of them should be conscious of his rank and fulfil his diplomatic mission with devotion. That is imperative and important for the future.   M. B.

Battle for Stalingrad

When Field Marshal Friedrich von Paulus, and the starving remnants of what once had been the crack 6th Army, were finally forced to surrender to the Russians at Stalingrad on February 2, 1942, it was the turning point of the war on the Eastern Front. Altogether, some 235,000 German, Romanian, Italian, and Hungarian troops were captured during the battle; more than 200,000 were killed. There could be no explaining away the scale of the defeat. "Today is the blackest day for Germany in the history of our war," Lore Walb, a young student, noted despairingly.

As 6th Army, commanded by General Friedrich von Paulus, and General Hermann Hoth's 4th Panzer Army, powered southeast in June and early July 1942, Stalingrad looked ripe for the taking. Hitler, however, made a maladroit intervention that seriously compromised the seemingly inexorable German advance. He detached Hoth's armor and sent it south to the Caucasus. As a result, he let slip the opportunity to enter the city before the Soviets could rally and organize its defense.

It took the Fuehrer a fortnight to change his mind and order the 4th Panzer Army to turn northeast and head for Stalingrad again. However, shortage of supplies forced Hoth to a halt a hundred miles short of the city. Hitler had forfeited his best chance of winning a quick, relatively bloodless, and possibly decisive victory.

In the meantime, 6th Army had fought its way across the River Don. By August 23, it had reached the River Volga's right bank north of Stalingrad, and was readying itself to infiltrate its way into the suburbs. However, Paulus met stiffening Soviet opposition as Stalin and his supreme command rushed reinforcements to the stricken city. Marshal Georgi Zhukov, now promoted to Deputy Supreme Commander-in-Chief, later recalled how Stalin had decided that Stalingrad must be held at all costs. "With the fall of Stalingrad, the enemy command would be able to cut off the south of the country from the center," he wrote. "The Supreme Command was sending to Stalingrad all that it was possible to send." The 62nd and 64th Armies were already pulling back toward the city. Stalin sent the First Guards Army, the 66th Army and the 24th Army to reinforce them. He gave command of the Soviet forces inside Stalingrad to General Vasily Chuikov with orders to "defend the city or die in the attempt."

Reduced to rubble

It took Paulus until September 2 to link up with Hoth; it was not until September 13 that he was ready to start pushing into the heart of Stalingrad itself, Hoth's panzers attacking the southern suburbs. As his troops began their assault, he flew to Vinnitsa to confer with Hitler at his field headquarters. He assured the Fuehrer that the city would be in German hands completely within a few weeks.

Backed by the bombers of the Luftwaffe's 4th Air Fleet, German infantry and armor commenced a mass assault through the fast-crumbling streets. The bombed-out ruins provided the Soviet troops with ideal conditions for defense as they contested every inch of ground. Digging in behind heaps of rubble, sheltering in cellars, and posting snipers in the upper floors of half-demolished apartment blocks, they took a heavy toll of the advancing Germans. Often the fighting was hand-to-hand with little or no quarter being shown by either side.

Nevertheless, the relentless German pressure slowly forced Chuikov's troops back. By October 12, Paulus had reached the center of the city—or what little remained of it. The swastika was raised symbolically over the government building in Stalingrad's Red Square. He then attacked the northern factory district, though it took him almost a month to reach the Volga there. He then readied himself to launch a new all-out assault in a final effort to complete his conquest before the Russian winter set in again. Hitler had already reiterated his order that the city was to be taken regardless of cost.

Operation Uranus

The 6th Army had fought itself to a standstill. To finish the job, Paulus desperately needed reinforcements, but, thanks largely to Rommel's rout by the British at El Alamein, and the Anglo-American invasion of French North Africa, Hitler had

no fresh reserves available to send him. Instead, General Maximilian von Weichs, in overall command of Army Group B, decided to replace the German divisions currently securing 6th Army's left flank with the Romanian ones currently in position on the River Don. Other Romanian forces and units of the Italian Expeditionary Corps had already been tasked with safeguarding 6th Army's other flank.

As it turned out, this was a disastrous decision, but, at the time, it was one the Germans thought well worth the risk. Hitler, for one, was convinced that the Soviet army was fully extended on the Volga and totally incapable of launching any meaningful attack. The opposite, in fact, was the case. For some time, the Soviet supreme command had been preparing to launch a massive counteroffensive. By October, five new tank armies, fifteen tank corps, and over a million men were starting to assemble for the operation.

What Zhukov and General Aleksandr Vasilevski, the chief of the Soviet General Staff, planned was no less than a massive encirclement that would pin down 6th Army within the city it was striving so hard to capture, and cut it off from all hope of relief. The German decision to weaken the 6th Army's flanks was the opportunity the Soviet commanders had been looking for to spring their trap. Zhukov promptly shifted two tank corps and four field armies to face the Romanians and Italians stationed northwest of Hoth's panzers, while two more tank corps were despatched to confront the Romanians holding the line in the southeast. By November 19, the Soviets were ready to launch their attack.

Closing the ring

The Soviets struck in the northwest first. Their new forces attacked a weak spot in the Romanian defences almost 100 miles to the west of Stalingrad. Some 3,500 guns and heavy mortars opened fire in the early morning mist on the unprepared Romanians, literally blasting a way through their positions for the Soviet T-34 tanks and their supporting infantry. The Romanians were swiftly overwhelmed. After putting up a brief resistance, they began to flee in panic. The next day, precisely the same thing happened in the southeast as the Soviets launched their second thrust. The Romanians, who had only a few obsolete tanks of their own and practically no anti-tank guns, found it impossible to deal with the massed columns of T-34s that were now pouring through the ever-widening gaps in their lines. When the two tank thrusts joined up at Kalach on November 23, the 6th Army was surrounded and cut off from the rear. Hoth's panzers were marooned outside the encircled area.

With twenty divisions, six of them motorized, trapped in Stalingrad with him, Paulus had two options open. The first was to try to break out of the encirclement westwards. Zeitzler, Weichs, and Field Marshal Erich von Manstein, whom Hitler now put in command of the newly-constituted Army Group Don, urged the Fuehrer to sanction the plan. Hitler, however, favored the other option—stand, fight, and wait for eventual relief. Complaining that his generals consistently overestimated Soviet strength, he was convinced the Russians were using up their last reserves and would soon be overcome. "I will not leave the Volga," Zeitzler was informed. In any event, Goering, Hitler continued, had assured him that the Luftwaffe could airlift enough supplies into Stalingrad to keep 6th Army going until it could be relieved. The bemused Paulus was ordered to fortify his positions and

hold out until the relief force could break through to him.

Manstein was put in charge of the relief effort. On November 28, he sent a radiogram to the beleaguered Paulus: "Hold on—I'm going to hack you out of there," it read. On December 12, Operation Winter Storm was launched. Manstein had concentrated two infantry and three panzer divisions for the attack. To counter it, Zhukov struck at the Italians further to the northwest. His troops quickly overran them and then headed south in an attempt to cut off Manstein's forces from the rear.

Nevertheless, by December 19, some of Manstein's panzer formations had managed to get as far as the River Myshkova near Gromoslavka, just 35 miles away from 6th Army's positions. There, the offensive stalled. With massive Soviet reinforcements arriving on the scene, Manstein was compelled to order a withdrawal. Operation Winter Storm was over. Its failure meant that Paulus and his troops were left to fight on alone.

Trapped in Stalingrad

Paulus again asked Hitler for permission to try to break out of the encirclement—seven Soviet armies were now closing in for the kill—but the Fuehrer again rejected the request. He began to devise plans for a new relief effort to be mounted sometime in February. In the meantime, the 6th Army's continued resistance would serve to tie down Soviet forces that otherwise could be deployed elsewhere on the Eastern Front. In any event, by the third week of December, the 6th Army no longer possessed sufficient mobility to take such a gamble.

Supplies of all kinds were quickly running out. Goering's promise that the Luftwaffe would be able to airlift 200 tons of supplies a day into the pocket to keep Paulus and his men going proved to be a vain boast. The embittered Paulus and his commanders soon began complaining about their "betrayal" by the Luftwaffe. In practice, the most Goering's airmen managed was little more than 90 tons a day. Belatedly, Hitler despatched Field Marshal Erhard Milch to try to sort the airlift out, but though Milch managed to boost this to 120 tons a day, it was not enough. Only a handful of supply planes managed to land at Gumrak, the last airstrip in German hands. The rest were parachuting their cargoes aimlessly into the city in the vain hope that the 6th Army's starving troops would be able to recover them once they hit the ground. Paulus icily complained to a Luftwaffe major: "Today is the fourth day my men have had nothing to eat. Our heavy guns have had to be abandoned because we have no petrol. Our last horses have been eaten." He concluded bitterly: "We speak to you as though from another world already, for we are dead men. Nothing remains but what history will write of us."

By now, Paulus's troops could do little more than try to stay alive. Squeezed in an ever-tightening vise by the surrounding Soviet armies, most of them were sheltering in cellars, underground bunkers, or in foxholes, which they tried to insulate against the freezing cold as best they could. The growing shortage of food became harder and harder to bear. "We're mainly feeding ourselves just with horsemeat," one soldier noted on New Year's Eve. "I have even eaten raw horsemeat because I was so hungry." Another wrote to his mother that he and his comrades had been issued with a single loaf of bread, which was expected to last six men three days. Ammunition was running out as well. "The Russians," complained yet another soldier, "are

attacking without a break day and night, and we've got to save every shot because the situation doesn't allow it. How much we wish we would shoot properly again."

The last weeks

Marshal Konstantin Rokossovskii, in command of the Soviet armies to the west of Stalingrad, now began advancing across the pocket from west to east, driving the starving defenders back into the ruins of the heart of the city. Many of them collapsed from exhaustion and froze to death on the ground as they retreated. Others pulled the wounded along on sledges down icy roads littered with abandoned military equipment.

Paulus rejected Rokossovskii's offer of honorable surrender terms, so the Soviet commander drove forward inexorably until the German pocket was split into two. The surviving Germans were now penned into two small areas of the city. Back in the Reich, Goebbel's propaganda machine was at full throttle, praising the heroism of the encircled soldiers as an object lesson in the necessity of fighting on even if the situation appeared hopeless. On the tenth anniversary of Hitler's appointment as Reich Chancellor on January 30 1933, Goering rammed home the point. In a speech broadcast across the nation, he compared the soldiers of the 6th Army to the Spartan warriors who had held the pass at Thermopylae against the invading Persians. Stalingrad, he said, "will remain the greatest heroic struggle in our history." The troops crouched around the radios in their bunkers were quick to take the point. The Spartans at Thermopylae had been slaughtered to a man.

Paulus listened to Goering's broadcast as well. He had already sent his own radiogram to Hitler to commemorate the occasion. "The

6th Army sends greetings to the Fuehrer. Still flutters the swastika over Stalingrad. May our struggle stand as an example to generations yet unborn never to surrender, however desperate the odds. Then Germany will be victorious." Hitler took the message as confirming that Paulus would be loyal to the end. The same day, he signaled him the news of his promotion to the rank of Field Marshal. Paulus knew exactly what this meant. Throughout Germany's history, no German Field Marshal had ever surrendered to the enemy. Hitler expected him to kill himself rather than capitulate.

It was now that Paulus belatedly turned against his master. His dark hair and incipient beard had begun to turn white and he had developed a tic in his facial muscles because of the continual strain. The secret police building in Red Square that housed him and his headquarters was on fire when, on January 31, he surrendered to Rokossovskii. Hitler ordered General Karl Strecker, in command of the troops in the northern pocket around the Red October factory complex, to fight on to the last man. "Every day, every hour which is thereby gained is of decisive value for the rest of the front," the Fuehrer signaled him. Strecker held out for another two days before, on February 2, he, too, capitulated.

Consequences of defeat

It was impossible to explain away a defeat of these dimensions. Goebbels ordered three days of national mourning to be observed. Newspapers were printed bordered in black, their back pages filled with list after list of those who had perished "for Fuehrer and Fatherland." The *Volkischer Beobachter* succinctly summed up the official view. "They died," as it put it on February 4, "so that Germany could live."

Belief in Hitler began to falter too, as bitter jokes started to circulate about him. "What's the difference between the sun and Hitler?" went one. The answer was: "The sun rises in the east, Hitler goes down in the east." The Security Service of the SS reported: "Telling jokes that are nasty and detrimental to the state, even jokes about the Fuehrer's person, has become much more common since Stalingrad ... Even national comrades who hardly know one another are telling political jokes." The report noted, too, that "many Party members no longer wear their Party badge."

The Fuehrer was determined to find someone other than himself to blame. His worthless Romanian and Italian allies had precipitated the initial collapse by failing to stand their ground and, instead, running away. As for Paulus and his senior officers, they were beneath contempt. They had preferred to lose their honor by capitulating rather than save it by committing suicide. Paulus was "that pig" whom Hitler, if he ever got his hands on him, would have court-martialed and shot. "That's the last Field Marshal I promote in this war", the Fuehrer pledged grimly. Goering was held responsible for the disaster as well. Only one thing saved him from open disgrace. "He is my own

designated successor," the Fuehrer said, "and that is why I cannot hold him publicly responsible."

As far as the hundreds of thousands of ordinary soldiers who had sacrificed themselves in the attempt to capture Stalingrad against overwhelming odds, Hitler had little time for them and their sufferings. In early November 1942, Speer, traveling to Munich with Hitler on the latter's luxurious private train, recorded what happened when an accidental encounter took place.

"In earlier years," Speer recalled, "Hitler had made a habit of showing himself at the window of his special train whenever it stopped. Now these encounters with the outside world seemed undesirable to him; instead the blinds on the station side of the train would be lowered." Later that evening, the train halted in a siding and Hitler and his entourage sat down to dinner. Speer recorded what happened next.

"The table was elegantly set with silver cutlery, cut glass, good china, and flower arrangements. As we began our ample meal, none of us at first saw that a freight train was stopped on the adjacent track. From the cattle wagons, bedraggled, starved and in some cases wounded German soldiers, just returning from the east, stared at the diners.

With a start, Hitler noticed the somber scene two meters from his window. Without so much as a gesture of greeting in their direction, he peremptorily ordered his servant to draw the blinds. This, then, in the second half of the war, was how Hitler handled a meeting with front-line soldiers, such as he himself had once been."

Hitler increasingly reduced the times he appeared in public from 1942 onward. He rarely bothered to come to Berlin. Both Goebbels and Speer repeatedly tried, but failed, to persuade him to agree to visiting bombed-out areas of the Reich. Rather, the Fuehrer spent practically all his time browbeating his generals, pouring over situation maps, and devising new operational plans, often down to the last detail. No major decisions could be taken without him. Sure of his own status as "the greatest commander-in-chief of all time," he increasingly distrusted his military subordinates. He was also ageing rapidly. This was yet another reason for his growing reluctance to appear in public. The most important one was that now he had no good news to give.

Though the forced evacuation of the Kerch peninsula was a Soviet defeat, and a chance for Signal *to lambast Russian engineering, the tide of the war was turning against the Germans.*

The leaders of a unit supported by tanks are reconnoitring the snow-covered terrain for enemy movements. Large black patches loom up against the darkness of the wooded horizon—soon the guns will roar

How an attempt at flight ended

The drivers of the Soviet tanks had maps of Germany with them, but they were not familiar with their own country. Near Tolotshin on the Drut, these gigantic Soviet tanks, each weighing 42 tons, in attempting to break through the enveloping German forces, ran into the marshy land near the river where they finished wretchedly by sticking in the mud. Whilst the Soviet soldiers tlus fall into the natural traps of their own country, the German advance continues past all obstacles according to plan.
Photograph: PK. Huschke

Flight
and
advance

A bridge is thrown across the Velikaia. *Near Opotshka, on the other side of the Latvian frontier, the retreating Soviet soldiers attempted to hold up the German advance by blowing up the large bridge. Covered by the artillery, a unit of the SS on active service quickly throws a makeshift bridge across the river and the advance continues. The German soldier remains at the heels of the fleeing enemy and forces him to the decisive struggle*   *Photograph: PK. SS Baumann*

Farther and farther into the land of the Soviets

The great battle of Bialystok and Minsk has been brought to a victorious conclusion — the cavalry vanguards of the German armies are now pushing forward far ahead of the infantry in pursuit of the enemy.   Photograph: PK. Gronefeld

Tanks
in the
steppes

The tank advance guard halts somewhere in the wide Caucasian steppes. The close range reconnaissance plane transmits the enemy's position to them. (Picture on right). The tanks immediately move forward against the enemy who is well hidden in the tall steppe grass. As contact with the enemy may come unexpectedly at any moment, the tank grenadiers advance with them keeping well under cover out of the way of the defensive fire from the Russians. Exploding shells have set the dry steppe grass on fire at a number of places.

Tank No. 633 soon encounters a Russian anti-tank gun and puts it out of action. Whilst the tank grenadiers make prisoners of the survivors of the gun crew, the tank turns off to the left towards a new enemy

PK. Photographs:
Front Correspondent Artur Grimm

Two photographs typical of the fighting in and round Stalingrad

Between the groups of houses in the town and the bank of the Volga in the background, tanks and artillery have cleared a piece of ground. A small group of tank grenadiers is slowly and cautiously making its way forward to the Volga in order to take up a fresh position

Another group of tank grenaadiers has reached a trench in the middle of the town where it is subjected to fire. The men do not dash forward to the assault but remain under cover until the tank following them has put the enemy pill-box out of action by shellfire Front Correspondent Herbert (2)

In the "Red Barricade" fighting zone

Glimpses of the Battle of Stalingrad
by Front Correspondent Lieutenant Benno Wundshammer

The author, who for many weeks took part in the raids on Stalingrad carried out by a squadron of dive-bombers, has paid a visit to the zone of fighting which the airman otherwise only sees from a great altitude. He describes a phase of this fighting concerning which a German officer says: "Stalingrad is a fortress, but it differs in one essential from a real fortress. A real fortress has a system, the secret of which can be discovered. It can then be attacked according to a plan. Stalingrad has no system, Stalingrad is a conglomeration of fortifications, you are faced every hour by fresh problems. That is what makes the fight so difficult. . ."

"Have a look at things from down below!" the commodore of my squadron of dive-bombers had said, "and be back in two days' time!"

I am in the advanced observation post of the Air Corps and from there I can see ruined houses, a roof, a stereo-telescope and in the distance a long row of houses behind undulating country and copses.

The scene of the fighting lies where the iron water-tower stretches its finger above the smoking hill. So this is "Target area Dora" which we were attacking only yesterday.

In the town

An acrid smell of burning greets us. The carcasses of horses, their bellies swollen, fill the air with the stench of putrefaction. Prisoners and fugitives totter towards us. Then we enter the town. I have already seen many towns gutted by the fires of war, yet I have never seen greater destruction. The complicated technical installation of a modern industrial town lies a chaos of burnt and broken ruins. Whole railway stations are only a tangled confusion of rusting iron. A dead soldier is lying by the roadside. Even in death he still holds his sub-machine gun tightly in his grasp and I cannot bring myself to take it from his rigid hands.

We creep past ruined houses. The enemy has an uninterrupted view everywhere, and now and then shells come howling across from his heavy artillery. The German soldiers have established themselves in cellars and vaults buried under a heap of ruins, where they cook their food and are ready for action day and night. An infantryman gives me the following account: "Every house was a fortification. The enemy fired from the storeys of the houses and the cellars. They were usually in small parties of 15 men under the command of an officer or commissar. They would not come out of their holes at any price! We laboriously crawled up to them and threw hand grenades at them as they fired. Then they lay down and died. When the German planes blew up one row of houses after another, the Bolshevists built new fortifications out of the ruins during the night and held us up with new barricades which really filled us with amazement!"

Leaping from one piece of ruined wall to the next, we stalk forward to the Volga Terrace. In the middle of the river the enemy is still occupying well camouflaged positions behind bushes and in woods. They observe every movement on this bank. Our men are lying in pill-boxes watching the river and not worrying their heads about anything except perhaps their food.

100 yards from the enemy

An armoured wireless transmission and receiving car belonging to the Air Force Signallers, which is engaged on important tactical tasks in the infantry front line, gives us a lift. I am not in a position to say any more about the work done by these men. The mere fact must suffice. The commander of the car is a lieutenant, and as chance would have it, I recognize him as the corporal who trained me as a recruit.

"We are driving to the northern part of the town, we can get close up to the front line there!" The car rumbles off, every other noise is drowned by the clanking of the caterpillar tracks. We follow roads worn by heavy traffic. On both sides of us are artillery positions. The guns roar at regular intervals. Gradually everything becomes more desolate—we can see only shellholes, carcasses, smashed vehicles, tanks and guns. There is apparently no movement on the battlefield. Here and there a cloud of white smoke rises unexpectedly from the mountains of débris and then the lieutenant says: "Grenade-throwers!" We can hear nothing.

Our untrained airmen's eyes are not yet able to distinguish details. To the accompaniment of a great din, we drive through a town of spectral ruins. Only rarely do I see infantrymen. They are wearing steel helmets and bend low as they run. When they take cover as quick as lightning in a crater, another cloud of white smoke is always due the next moment.

The car pulls up among some half burnt out wooden houses. We leave it there. The enemy is only a few hundred yards away. Invisible! That is the greatest surprise for us. The chaos of ruins appears deserted and it is only here and there that we are able with difficulty to make out the entrances of dug-outs where the infantry have taken up their positions. A surprised "landser" stares at us until a hissing whine causes him to disappear into the earth.

→

No-man's-land in Stalingrad. *The foremost position during the fighting for Stalingrad seen and photographed through the stereo-telescope by the Air Force lieutenant and SIGNAL front correspondent Benno Wundshammer. While he was in the city the struggle for the vast gun factory "Red Barricade" was in progress. The gigantic workshops rise up behind the miserable workers' dwellings. The position of the foremost German troops is indicated by the arrow*

When an open city is converted into a fortress and not evacuated . . .

"Signal's" reporter comments on the picture on the left: "Over and over again we are appalled by the state of the civilian population of this city. A street in north Stalingrad is being subjected to heavy fire from enemy grenade-throwers when suddenly a civilian emerges from his hut. After weeks of fear and anxiety he has to flee with his goods and chattels. Women come towards us, 400 yards from the firing line. What do they want? Terrified by the erratic grenade fire, one of them has lost her children who are hiding in a cellar somewhere. The other is crying. She has had nothing to eat for three days. We give her bread. Slowly, women, old men and children trickle through our advancing line of fire and collect before the city along the roads used for our reinforcements and prepare to march westwards (picture above). This stream of misery already reaches as far as the banks of the Don, hundreds of miles in extent . . ."

The "Red Barricade" fighting zone

We cross a communication trench. A glance across the parapet reveals the Volga as it flows behind fences and factories. Skyscrapers burning with a vermilion glare are silhouetted against the blue sky. An M. G. is slowly crackling somewhere, bullets whistle through the gardens. The grenade-throwers roar dully. Then come short, clear, sharp detonations. Snipers!

We take cover in a cellar. In the dim light I can make out a box of hand grenades, sub-machine guns and a Very pistol with cartridges. Such an arsenal of weapons ready to hand is a great comfort. A ladder leads up to the loft of the wooden house, which has no back wall. An N. C. O. reports when

we reach the loft. A stereo-telescope operated by a lance-corporal has been brought into position in the front of the sloping roof. I look through the glass at the streets where the enemy is ensconced only 100 yards away from us. I see only wooden huts and behind them a large factory, the gun factory "The Red Barricade", from which that whole part of the town derives its name. The lance-corporal says: "The houses are occupied by the Russians." I can see nothing. Nobody. Just over there I catch a glimpse of a slight movement. "Yes, that's one of them," says the lance-corporal. "And in front there, exactly above the yellow blob of clay, is our most advanced post."

For a matter of seconds there is a

dull gleam from a German steel helmet. The battlefield is deserted just as though there were nobody here at all. Only the detonating grenade-throwers and the staccato crackle of invisible M.G.s betray the struggle that is in progress. Well concealed, full of endurance and cunning, the antagonists observe one another.

I stare at the factory. White smoke is pouring out of the workshops. The lance-corporal explains: "We discovered a Stalin organ and several grenade-throwers there." However much I look, I can see nothing but a small cloud of dust here and there among the destroyed furnaces. The lance-corporal consoles me by saying: "That is quite enough. We don't need any more than that." A horrible roar causes us to throw ourselves down in a confused heap. There is a sudden ear-splitting explosion. "That was quite close," the lance-corporal says as he gets to his feet again. Twenty yards to our left a wooden hut goes up in flames—the lance-corporal is once more seated behind is stereo-telescope and the N.C.O. is at the telephone.

We creep, jump and crawl back. Again there is a roar followed by loud explosions above us and white clouds

of smoke. A.A. guns with fuses set high are joining in the ground battle! Shell splinters crunch into rotten wood. Two infantrymen pass by carrying a third whose head is hanging down motionless. His fine fair hair moves in the wind. We go on. Behind the next brick wall I see a soldier writing a letter on a box. He takes no notice of the artillery and the impacts of shells, he has something more important to do.

When I ask him how things are, he answers: "Quite O.K., thank you! Rations are good and plentiful and, besides, things are pretty quiet today. But it warms up in the afternoon. The dive-bombers attack ahead of us then. Damn plucky lads, they are!"

I have not the courage to tell the man that is exactly what I think of him. He would not believe me.

A section of the highway used by the fugitives seen from the air. A knot of fugitives has realized that empty German lorries on their way to the rear can take the civilians out of the danger zone. Opposite a demolished Soviet tank, the last lorry in the column is being loaded with the possessions of the fugitives, while the others wait for the next chance of a lift

63 degrees Fahrenheit of frost

A storm boat races across the Dniester . . . ... the first of many. Under the hail of fire the men at the steering wheels guide their outboard motor-boats through the muddy waters of the broad river. Every muscle is tense, every eye is fixed on the goal: the blind spot on the steep slope on the enemy bank of the river. There, the torpor of the brave infantrymen will give way to stubborn warlike ardour — for beyond the river is the Stalin Line in the Ukraine

Photographs: PK Hackl

An unusual achievement: Lieutenant Jäckel, group captain in c

The last Soviet "artery" in Stalingrad. *For months the struggle for Stalingrad went on and step by step, at the cost of much bloodshed, the city was wrung from the grasp of the Bolshevists. With the stubbornness of despair the Soviets hold on to a tiny strip along the western bank of the Volga. Deep rifts, the Balkas, run down to the river and simplify the problem of reinforcements and supplies for the enemy. With bombs of the heaviest calibre our dive-bombers hammer ceaselessly at these natural "communication trenches" annihilating considerable numbers of troops even before they can be sent into action. The picture shows one of these ravines after a bombing raid. On the island in the river Soviet A. A. batteries trying to hinder the attack by the Air Force were bombed at the same time. On a more distant arm of the river shown in the top right-hand picture the reader can distinguish a ferry used by the enemy every night*

Deadly blows at the Balkas. *The German airmen show great skill in hitting the ravines that are packed with troops. According to reliable statements by prisoners, the daily losses of the enemy vary between the strength of a battalion and a regiment*

Lieutenant Jäckel's orders are to attack the Volga ravines in Stalingrad. He identifies the objective on a reconnaissance photograph

"Far below we see the olive-green shimmer of the river and the gleam of the sandbanks as Lieutenant Jäckel's machine dives to the attack"

"Above the Volga ravine the clouds from the explosions disperse beside the burning oil tanks as we begin our return flight. Once more we had hit the mark!"

RAVINES ALONG THE VOLGA

A report on the fight for Stalingrad by Front Correspondent Lieutenant Benno Wundshammer

*"Above the city our Vees spread out to lessen
the danger from the A. A. Flying in cur-
ves we move forward towards our objective"*

"As we dive," writes our reporter, *"I see a vast
factory among the ruins of which the Bolshevists
are still hiding. It is the "Red October" works.*

n landing, Lieutenant Jäckel is congratulated by his
mrades and presented with a few bottles of something
od. In half an hour he is due to make his 601st take-off

The best picture brought back by our reporter.
Commenting on this photograph, Lieutenant
Wundshammer told us: *"After our return I developed the films in the squadron dark-room and
this is the best picture of the attack. I took it immediately after our machine, flying as Number Two
behind Lieutenant Jäckel, pulled out of the dive.
We are moving off flying close below the heavy
banks of smoke from the burning oil tanks and in
the ravine a mushroom of smoke is just rising*
*above the exploding bombs. As we dived down
alongside the rising pillar of smoke Soviet fighters
attacked us, coming unexpectedly out of the swathes
of smoke. We kept up a hail of fire to occupy
the enemy while our pilot dropped all our
bombs direct on the objective. It was not long
before German fighters were with us and after
a short battle in the air brought down a JAK 1
fighter. The pilot baled out and landed behind the
German lines among the debris of ruined houses*

MAJOR DR WILHELM EHMER:

EUROPE'S SHIELD

CONCERNING THE SPIRITUAL FOUNDATIONS OF THE GERMAN ARMY TRADITIONS

For the second winter Stalin's armies have been attacking Europe's Eastern Front in a battle of truly Continental dimensions and Continental importance. The soldiers of the German 6th Army together with a Croat regiment and two Rumanian divisions defended Stalingrad to the last man, thus binding several Soviet armies and enabling a new and strategically more favourable front to be established. The sacrifice they made can only be explained by a soldierly spirit, the foundation of which is here interpreted by a contemporary soldier and philosopher

The battles of material during the last two years of the first World War had played a large part in establishing the view that the individual soldier was once and for all doomed to disappear from the battlefield as a unit having a will of his own. Mechanical war, the war machine crushing everything in its path, was supposed to have taken his place. This opinion was held by many military writers, particularly by French, British and American theorists, but it also made itself felt in the measures adopted by General Staffs. We will here quote two examples. When the German Army was disarmed in 1918, particular care was taken to ensure that it possessed no heavy weapons, no heavy guns, no tanks and also no planes, for these had been the principal weapons employed in the battles of material. It was consequently believed that this prohibition more than anything else would render Germany defenceless. The second example is the Maginot Line. If mechanical war was going to decide the victory in the future, it was only necessary to establish a tremendous wall of heavy weapons to be invincible for all time.

It would be interesting to investigate whether the Germans, too, would have adopted this "material view" if they had not been forced by Versailles to do without the most important weapons. We doubt whether the German theorists and practical experts would in such a case have recognized the superiority of war material over the soldier. The spiritual foundations of the German military tradition had always been too firmly established in the nation itself for that. Had not, too, the individual German soldier, by defying the material superiority of his enemies for so long, proved that determined men scornful of death are superior to blind material?

Endowed with soldierly virtues by destiny

The Treaty of Versailles forced Germany where her Army was concerned to rely upon that strength which no dictate could forbid—the spirit. Where there was a lack of external means, the internal ones were mobilized and where the employment of material was restricted, the abundantly flowing spring of ideas was exploited.

The historical comparison: Leonidas, the Spartan General

Fighting to the last man, he defended the gate to Greece, the Pass of Thermopylae, against the Persian invasion in the year 480 B.C. Nurtured by the spirit of such sacrifice, the Attic naval alliance, the first great political alliance of the Greeks, came into being three years later. The Persian danger was now finally overcome. Athens began to flourish. The hour of the birth of European culture had come. The sacrifice had borne fruit

TRAVELLER, SHOULD YOUR ROAD, LEAD YOU TO SPARTA, TELL THEM THAT YOU SAW US LYING HERE AS THE LAWS WILLED IT

Inscription on the national monument erected by the Greeks in memory of Leonidas and his soldiers

The "victors" of the World War clad themselves in a heavy coat of armour and dug themselves in behind lines of fortifications built with the greatest cunning and bristling with weapons, whilst the tiny German Army consisting of but 100,000 men became the guardian of the great spiritual German soldierly tradition and at the same time developed this tradition by drawing the necessary conclusions from the experiences of the World War. The difficulties of the situation did not cause it to throw in its hand or to despair, on the contrary, they aroused all the soldierly virtues, strength of character, determination, inventiveness and courage, all of which are foundation stones on which the German soldierly tradition has been built from its very beginning.

Peoples, which have to fight for and secure their existence on a poor soil under hard conditions regard soldierly virtues as the expression of an attitude forced upon them by necessity. The two German races, which were the first to develop a genuine soldierly spirit, had to carry out tasks of a warlike character. The Prussians were obliged to wrest from their country, which had been so ungenerously treated by nature, the foundation for a modest existence as a nation and, moreover, also had to defend themselves against strong and more favourably placed neighbours. The Austrians, being the inhabitants of the frontier marches, were forced to become soldiers in order to defend themselves against the southeast. In both cases, therefore, it was not the whim of a despot which established an army and imbued the people with soldierly conceptions, but their historical fate, nature itself, which stood as godparent at the cradle of both the Prussian Army and the old Austrian Army. After again covering their colours with immortal glory during the first World War both have been organically incorporated by different processes in the young National Socialist German Armed Forces.

The Prussian Field Marshal Hellmuth von Moltke, the first Chief of the Great General Staff, once characterized soldierly virtues as follows: "Courage and self-denial, devotion to duty and willingness to make sacrifices, even of life itself." If we

... Generals Pfeffer, Hartmann and Stempel together with Colonel Crome and a handful of soldiers standing out in the open on the railway embankment ...

THE MONUMENT
OF STALINGRAD

This and the following descriptions, some of which have been illustrated by Front Correspondent Hans Liska, are based on radio messages from the German 6th Army, the accounts given by the last wounded to escape from Stalingrad and the last field-post letters brought out of the lost city by the last plane. Among them are the reports of eye witnesses such as the driver of a troop transport lorry who scorched along at breakneck speed through advancing Soviet tanks spraying 300 Soviet infantrymen with M. G. fire only because he wanted to rejoin his unit in Stalingrad. Three cooks were busy for the last time in their field kitchen when surprised by Soviet tanks. To defend themselves they snatched a few grenades lying nearby and leapt at the tanks demolishing a couple of the giants. Then they went on with their cooking. A German plane, compelled to make a forced landing among the ruins of Stalingrad, alighted in Soviet territory. Was it madness when the crew was rescued by those grenadiers who themselves were trapped in the city? What did it mean when officers and men harnessed themselves to their gun to pull it 12 miles through the snow to Stalingrad because they had neither horses nor petrol, a gun for which they had scarcely any ammunition? What kind of men were they who knew for weeks how everything would end and who nevertheless wrote home: "You know what the situation is like here, Father, and you know the solution. You can depend on it finishing honourably ..."

pply these ideas to civilian life as it as developed under the modern liberal system, we immediately see that we eally have to do with definitely soldierly qualities. Instead of courage, liberalism prefers skill in business in rder to make a way in life, it prefers omfort to self-denial, duty is often elt to be only an unpleasant compulsion and when sacrifices have to be made, it is material goods which are urrendered with the hope of avoiding he possibility of being exposed to personal dangers.

The German soldier places his faith n courage, self-denial, devotion to duty and the willingness to make sacrifices not for any material advantage but simply for the sublime conception of the fatherland and for the honour and greatness of his people. In his will, Frederick the Great wrote that it is man's destiny to work from his birth until his death for the weal of the community to which he belongs. We might add in the spirit of that great king: Not only to work but also, should it be necessary, to fight and to die. In the three wars during which he won the vital foundations of the national power for his people, which numbered only three millions and was faced by a coalition numbering 50 millions, Frederick in any case acted according to that precept. Frederick the Great was, moreover, anything but a fighter by nature, he was a highly cultivated and extremely sensitive man devoted to philosophy and to the arts. He combined with rigid discipline, unconditional obedience and an unshakable sense of duty, a self-sacrificing spirit scornful of death, determination even in apparently desperate situations and that mental liveliness which a generation later found expression in the achievements and creations of men like Clausewitz and Yorck, Gneisenau, Scharnhorst and Heinrich von Kleist.

At the same time a decisive step forward was taken. The defeat suffered in 1806 at the hands of Napoleon's Revolutionary Army had shown that the old Prussian military spirit had become rigid and was incapable of adapting itself to the new era. It required rejuvenation. Scharnhorst and Gneisenau saw plainly that military leadership could no longer remain a privilege of the nobility, but that it was necessary for fresh blood to bring a new stimulus into the army. They consequently created a genuine national army in the face of great opposition from various quarters. Even today it is still worth while reading what they wrote in their memorandum to Frederick William III concerning the necessity of throwing open the career of officer not only to the middle classes but to every German who had proved his worth in the face of the enemy.

Those thoughts, indeed the whole of that epoch, can be compared with the events of our own days. Prussia-Germany required six years, from 1806 to 1812, in order to recover her strength after her great fall and it was in a similarly short space of time that the new German Armed Forces were created from nothing. Just as in those days, the rich abundance of the nation's strength makes it possible for every capable soldier to climb to the highest positions in the services without this resulting in any depreciation in quality. In both cases the foundation consisted of the same soldierly virtues adapted to the requirements of the age, supplemented today by a new element, field-grey socialism as experienced for the first time in the sufferings undergone in the trenches and under the drum fire of the first World War.

Soldiers of a new state . . .

For the German soldier the most profound human experience of the first World War was the comradeship, the human bonds uniting him to his fellows in his misery and during the fighting, the feeling of an indissoluble community of destiny in the face of a hostile world superior in material resources. It was from this spiritual and mental factor that the Socialist idea on a national basis, National Socialism, was born in the postwar period. It was not the invention of a theorist but the practical application of experience gained in four years of war, the application of a new conception of life moulded during those years in the sphere of politics. Adolf Hitler, himself a soldier who proved his worth during the first World War, gave that experience and that conception of life both shape and expression. After the collapse of the old structure of society of the monarchic period, he carried out what was in accordance with the essential development and the meaning of German history. That is why although he originally had no resources of power at his disposal, he was able during the course of time to overcome all obstacles supported solely by the increasing faith of the people in the rightness of his intentions and his doctrine.

The soldierly elements in this development must be kept in mind in order to pass a correct judgement on the phenomena of our day. Everything ever said or written by Germany's enemies regarding a conflict between the Party and the Army in Germany is either objectively wrong or malicious calumny. The Party is the political branch and the Army is the military branch springing from one and the same trunk. The National Socialist Party has adopted many features of the soldierly tradition, for example, the principle of leadership, the rigid organization and discipline. The Army as reorganized since 1935 is imbued and inspired with the political-revolutionary spirit of the National Socialist creed.

Both were to a very considerable extent the result of pressure from outside. They owe their existence to the fact that the sated victorious powers of Versailles wished to keep the German people—the people with the biggest population in Europa and culturally one of the most important—in a state of impotence for all time to come after first disarming it and financially plundering it. To do so they used various means including such States as Poland and the artificial creation known as Czechoslovakia. Such a state of affairs was intolerable for the German people with the consequence that the re-establishment of its Armed Forces was carried out in the spirit of the new political order and at a speed verging on the miraculous.

The final struggle of the southern group in Stalingrad: the last "hedgehog" in front of the OGPU buildings

THE LAST DAYS...

The sacrifice for Europe of the German 6th Army and a Flak division, 2 Rumanian divisions and a Croat regiment

This hedgehog in the square in front of the OGPU buildings and a second hedgehog in the tractor factory a few miles away were the last strongholds defended by the Germans and all that remained of the "Stalingrad pocket" at the beginning of February 1943. People no doubt are inclined to think of other pockets during this war and draw comparisons. And it is right that they should do so. Kiev was surrounded by the Germans on 20th September 1941 and, 6 days later, 665,000 prisoners were counted. There was the famous pocket of Briansk and Wiasma closed by the Germans on 8th October 1941 and evacuated 10 days later by 663,000 prisoners. It was glorious early autumn weather at that time and the Germans were dealing with the remnants of armies. The Stalingrad pocket was held by one German army, 2 Rumanian divisions and a Croat regiment for almost 80 days. From the commander-in-chief

PK. Drawing: Front Correspondent H. Liska

down to the last private, everyone in Smlingrad knew that they, the pier supporting the entire front, had to hold out to the bitter end. In the middle of November 1942 the pier was cut off in the rear by the flood. The dead flat terrain swept by snowstorms and frozen hard as stone with the thermometer registering 35° centigrade below zero, offered no tactical barrier. But transporters could still land bringing rations and ammunition and evacuating the wounded. Five to six Soviet armies kept storming without a break, artillery and bombs hammered the besieged ceaselessly, the ring was closing in. At Christmas it was no bigger than the city of Stalingrad proper. The possibilities of landing and provisioning from the air became smaller, the daily rations were reduced from day to day, every shot fired and every drop of petrol was irreplaceable: systematically the enemy razed every remaining wall to the ground. In the cellars and subterranean passages the soldiers and the wounded had their quarters. It was the beginning of January. The men suffered

privation and hunger. At the same time, however, one single assault made by these soldiers against the northeastern front cost the Soviets 800 dead before the main fighting line of a tank division. Up to 20th January 400 enemy tanks had been destroyed. The losses in men and material by far surpassed the figures of the encircled forces and the time lost was irreplaceable. The days went by and the men in Stalingrad fought on. When the two last hedgehogs were driven together in the heart of the city the southern group hoisted the Swastika from the OGPU buildings, the symbol of the square. Without reinforcements, ammunition or rations they fought on with bayonets until February. Then they destroyed everything that could be of use to the enemy. The OGPU buildings collapsed in a gigantic explosion, the flag disappeared in a cloud of smoke, the tomb closed over the last defenders. When everything was quiet again, the noise of battle could still be heard from the tractor factory. The end had not yet come.

EUROPE'S SHIELD

In this case, reference to the German powers of organization explains but little, the decisive fact here was the spririt employing those means of organization. The German Army had not played any part in the internal political chaos between 1918 and 1933. It had watched over the military heritage and added to it the experiences of the first World War. It now became the heart of the new Army which received a further impulse from the revolutionary impetus of a political rejuvenation. This amalgamation between the best military traditions and the new ideas and the belief in new conditions of existence then made possible the amazing victories won by the German Armed Forces since 1st September 1939. They must not be interpreted only in the light of technical progress in war or material organization, for Germany's antagonists also had them abundantly at their disposal. Had they not their Maginot Line, did not armies at first far superior in numbers encircle the Reich prepared for war at a moment's notice and did they not possess the resources of the whole world? The Polish Army was swept away in only 18 days, the Maginot Line was overrun and France vanquished in something less than seven weeks, the British suffered one defeat after another from Narvik to Dunkirk and from there to Crete, the Bolshevist armies, far superior in numbers and material, were thrown far back into their own country. All this must be ascribed to the mental and spiritual strength of the rejuvenated German Armed Forces which the ohters had nothing equivalent to oppose with. The fact that Germany this time also secured strong reserves of material for herself and from the very outset adopted better precautionary measures regarding raw materials and food supplies than in 1914, was a natural consequence of the experiences during the first World War. The decisive factor was, however, and still is the ideas and ideals with which the German Armed Forces are imbued and which provide them with the strength to gain the victory.

. . . and political soldiers

Ever since the democracies so despicably threw away the magnificent chance they had in Versailles of carrying out a really just reorganization of our Continent, Germany has undertaken to provide tortured Europe with new possibilities of existence. It is in this sense that the German Army feels that it is, indeed, the executor of a political will. The view, which used often to be asserted, that the soldier must be "unpolitical has given way to the conviction that he must be political through and through, that is to say, that he must be completely imbued with the importance and the value of the ideas now championed by National Socialism. It was not the lust for conquest which caused Germany to take up arms, this war has been forced on her by the destructive aims of her enemies. The German soldier is convinced of this to the very depths of his innermost being and that is why the German Armed Forces form an invincible bloc having as its spiritual foundations the sublime ethics of a soldierly tradition. It is, moreover, inspired by the belief in the high mission of protecting the Reich and thereby also the whole of Europe against the attacks of the capitalist Powers in the West and above all against the horrors of Bolshevism.

Every German soldier knows that this is in the true sense of the word a life and death struggle. Not one of them has any illusions on that point so that the determination to hang on and to deal the enemy heavy blows wherever possible is only increased.

The distorted description which enemy propaganda customarily gives of the Reich's Armed Forces cannot stand up to a dispassionate investigation by a really neutral observer.

Germany has today in the real sense of the word a national army in which every capable soldier carries a field marshal's baton in his pack. He has not sacrificed any of the important values of his great soldierly tradition, on the contrary, he has gained many new ones. Courage, self-denial, modesty, discipline and the willingness to make every sacrifice are still the highest virtues. The principle of being more than you seem to be is still in force. The German still fights chivalrously as he always has done and does not employ the cruel methods of a brutal mercenary with which he has become acquainted during this war from his antagonists such as the shelling of military hospitals and attacks on planes engaged in rescuing men in distress at sea, air raids on open towns carried out by the British in order to terrorize the population and the terrible maltreatment of prisoners by the Bolshevists. The populations of all the territories occupied by the German Army are unanimous in their praise of the exemplary conduct and discipline of the German soldiers. One is continually surprised in such countries at the friendly relations between the men and officers in the German Army. For every German officer it is a natural duty to take a human interest in his subordinates. Here there are no clear-cut class distinctions, no social abyss exists, they all feel themselves equally pledged to a common duty. Military rank and discipline do not suffer in consequence for a single instant, they remain just as rigid as ever before.

In the service of Europe

It is consequently sublime spiritual values tested and chastened throughout the course of centuries, consolidated in many wars, handed on from generation to generation and continually inspired with new life which have enabled the German soldiers to achieve what they are now performing in the defence of a whole continent. They are the best manly virtues which every nation ought to appreciate that has not fallen a victim to the empty hurry and scurry of a noisy, materially-minded civilization as the Americans have done. Undoubtedly there are many other valuable conceptions of life besides the soldierly one, but in the struggle for existence the latter is the solid foundation without which a people must in the long run collapse when exposed to heavy crises. For the soldier who is forced to kill and destroy is also hazarding his most valuable possession, his life. By so doing he leaves behind him the sphere of dull utility and rises into a region where the conduct and value of a man are reckoned according to unchanging standards.

The most sublime example of this is the sacrifice of the troops fighting at Stalingrad which enabled the allied armies on the Eastern Front to build new dams to hold up the raging Bolshevist torrent and continue to preserve Europe from the annihilating rule of the Soviets. Cut off from all possibility of receiving reinforcements, surrounded

The Alcazar of the steppes . . . *The remnants of the 11th Army Corps under General Strecker of the Infantry have established themselves in the tractor works. The fitting shop forms the centre of the defence. The enemy have slowly worked their way forward to within 20 yards systematically destroying the walls and iron girders. Then they throw hand grenades and mines among the ruins. The defenders have taken up positions in subterranean passages and erecting pits. Driven forward by their tanks, the Soviets repeatedly force their way into the fitting shop where they are annihilated with bayonets and spades in hand-to-hand fighting. Wounded men fight on. Men suffering from severe frostbite pass the ammunition up to the others. There is not much of it left ... They still have a wireless set. On 30th January, the tenth anniversary of the Greater German Reich, they listened with its help to the Führer's proclamation amidst the detonations of bursting shells, the noise of crumbling walls and the groaning of the wounded. The last defenders of Stalingrad reported this, their last ceremony, by wireless. "...and perhaps for the last time we raised our arms to give the German greeting." Those were the concluding words of their message*

Is Europe a fiction?

Does a common European destiny really exist or do the European peoples employ the word Europe only when it appears suitable to them in order to disguise their motives? SIGNAL publishes on page 11 an article dealing with this subject by Giselher Wirsing. During these decisive weeks it particularly concerns us all:

We, the Europeans!

Attempts to demoralize . . . *Even at an early stage, the Soviets sought to demoralize the encircled German Army and its allies. They installed loudspeakers in the front lines and advised the soldiers to surrender as the struggle was hopeless. Pamphlets like the one here reproduced rained down on Stalingrad from Soviet planes guaranteeing the soldiers, both officers and men, their lives and good treatment if they laid down their arms. It was also asserted that 70,000 men had already surrendered. The "mass photograph" of German prisoners intended to confirm this statement is obviously a bad forgery and places the Soviet promises in their proper light. The same groups are repeated several times on this photograph (compare the white circles joined up to one another!). It is a composite photograph. Every appeal to the Germans to surrender including two official ones were answered by force of arms until the last bullet had been fired, the last document and the last rifle destroyed*

70 000 deutsche und rumänische Soldaten und Offiziere haben sich gefangengegeben!

70 000 Eurer Kameraden sind lebendige Zeugen dafür, daß die Rote Armee den Befehl Nr. 55 des Volkskommissars für Verteidigung der Sowjetunion, **Stalin**, strikte durchführt. Dieser Befehl garantiert den deutschen Offizieren und Soldaten, die die Waffen gestreckt haben, das Leben und gute Behandlung.

70.000

„Ein Soldat, der sich in einer aussichtslosen Lage gefangengibt, handelt nicht ehrlos, sondern vernünftig. Die Kriegsgeschichte kennt viele Beispiele, wo die tapfersten Soldaten und Offiziere die Waffen streckten, wenn weiterer Widerstand aussichtslos war."

(Aus dem Aufruf des Kommandos der Roten Armee an die im Raum von Stalingrad kämpfenden deutschen Soldaten und Offiziere)

One of the men belonging to a unit holding a "dug-out village" on the Eastern Front. The position forms a part of the front in the same way as the vertebrae form the spine. Men are required here who are tough because they know what is at stake. This man's gaze travels past the approaching Soviet tank to the prospect of a future which justifies every sacrifice

A glance at this man's face tells everybody capable of reading faces that he had never dreamt he would once be numbered among the toughest men at one of the centres of fierce fighting in the greatest struggle in history. This man's courage can be seen in the earnest strength of his eyes which are full of knowledge and confidence

Cover! The enemy is just laying down a barrage

This concerns you, too!

. . . Dear friend, just take a look at these pictures! They show you something which is by no means out of the ordinary among us in the front line. A dug-out is being fought for somewhere on the Eastern Front and after the fluctuating fortunes of the engagement, the Germans are still in possession of it. Such actions have been taking place for years now and they form the daily life of our men at the front. Can you imagine what that means? For you life still runs on quietly along its normal channels — we know, of course, that many large towns are exposed to extremely heavy air-raids and yet you must admit that most of you, in spite of everything, live a different life from that. And, moreover, we are pleased you do. You must realize, however, that these nameless soldiers, who all have perfectly normal names and are not mentioned personally in any military communiqué, are out in the front line for you! Have you ever thought what it means day after day; year after year, to keep on dashing out from cover or the security of a dug-out into the murderous hail of shells from the enemy's guns and into the death-bringing no man's land where whistling bursts of M. G. fire are the only music with which these men are still acquainted? Do not run away with the idea that these soldiers have only one desire— to be soldiers! I know how much yearning for beauty and happiness is hidden behind the mask of soldierly bearing and I know how much unlavished tenderness is stored up in these hands which for long have been clasping their weapons with inexhaustible courage. It is easy, it is even intoxicating to perform a bold deed or an exacting duty if but once To do so, however, year after year with faith in your heart is a far greater thing! PK. Photographs: War Correspondents Ohlemacher and Scūrer

We understand the passionate tension in this soldier's face as he loads when we think that he has to carry out the movements with the greatest precision as quickly as possible. The concentrated energy with which the necessary actions are carried out is the energy of the soldier who realizes what the outcome of the struggle will mean

The gaze of the man, who looks fixedly but fearlessly at the low-flying Soviet planes roaring towards him proves that he is accustomed to danger and has learnt to suppress all feeling of fear. Only moral strength such as is founded upon the knowledge of a high ideal renders men capable of self-sacrifice

Grenadiers ready for hand-to-hand fighting: Bolshevists are approaching in the fog

Leaping on to an enemy tank which has broken through. Every scrap of cover is utilized

A section of the 35 kilometres long "Stalingrad Inferno"

The extensive factories of Stalingrad stretch along the bank of the Volga to a distance of 35 kilometres, for they all seek the proximity of the river. The Russians had converted this town of more than a million inhabitants into a fortress and defended it factory by factory, street by street, house by house. The German Army has systematically attacked and captured one pill-box after another. Our photograph shows a dive-bomber attack on a Stalingrad factory. The plane is just pulling out of the dive, the falling bomb can be seen obliquely under it. "Signal's" special account of the fight for Stalingrad begins on page 11 of this number

PK. Photograph: Front Correspondent Benno Wundshammer

Kursk and After

Following the 6th Army's surrender at Stalingrad in February 1943, Hitler resolved to halt the Soviet advance. Operation Citadel began on July 5. It did not go according to plan, the Soviets counterattacking successfully just ten days after the German attack started. The Fuehrer, however, had already decided to abandon the operation. On July 10, Allied forces invaded Sicily; on August 1, the Germans started to evacuate the island. The Allied success there precipitated Mussolini's overthrow. Hitler's sole major European ally finally had been knocked out of the war. The Fuehrer had to find the reinforcements to defend an entire new front.

Though Hitler would not admit it, it was clear after the fall of Stalingrad that the Third Reich was on the defensive in the east. What the Fuehrer and his generals were now debating was whether to launch a new offensive to straighten out the German front line, and weaken the Soviet army sufficiently to prevent it from launching a summer offensive of its own. The question was where would it be safest to make the move? After much debate, Hitler took the decision himself. The blow was to fall at Kursk, where the Soviet forces holding a vast salient there could be crushed in a classic encirclement. It was a gamble of such magnitude that he would later say the very thought of it made his stomach turn over.

By July, both sides were ready for what proved to be the greatest land battle ever fought. The Germans had concentrated nearly fifty army and Waffen SS divisions for the attack, more than 2,000 tanks, some 1,000 assault guns, and 1,800 aircraft. Troops from Field Marshal Hans von Kluge's Army Group Centre, spearheaded by the 9th Army, commanded by General Walther Model, and consisting of four panzer and one infantry corps, were to strike southward across the neck of the salient. Manstein's Army Group South would push northwards with General Hermann Hoth's 4th Panzer Army as the driving wedge of a Blitzkrieg-style attack.

Attack and response

On July 5, the Germans struck simultaneously as planned on both sides of the salient. The Russians were ready for them. Thanks largely to the "Lucy" spy network, Soviet intelligence had known of Hitler's intentions since April. The forces defending the salient outnumbered the Germans substantially—and that was before reinforcements began to arrive. They were positioned in eight defence lines, in places up to 25 miles (40 km) deep, and were supported by getting on for 5,000 tanks, 20,000 artillery pieces, 6,000 anti-tank guns, 1,000 Katyusha rocket launchers, and over 3,500 aircraft. "The Soviets had prepared a position whose extension in depth was inconceivable to us," a panzer commander commented after the battle. "Every time we broke through one position in bitter fighting, we found ourselves confronted by a new one." The Soviet plan was to wear the attacking Germans down before launching a decisive counteroffensive.

Manstein's thrust got off to a slow start. After two days of bitter fighting, the Germans had managed to penetrate only 7 miles (11 km) into three isolated parts of the Soviet defense system. Then, Hoth's 4th Panzer Army suddenly surged forward. For a time, a breakthrough looked as though it might be imminent, as the 2nd SS Panzer Corps secured a bridgehead over the River Psel and prepared to capture the town of Prochorovka. But, on July 9, the advance stalled. Manstein pressed Hitler to be allowed to renew the attack, but the Fuehrer refused him permission to do so. Meanwhile, Model's progress in the north had run into trouble almost from the start. Mindful of the huge Soviet reserves, the strength of the defenses confronting him, and the danger of counter-attack from the rear, the German general was unnaturally hesitant. It took him five days to advance only 6 miles (10 km). Then his attack, too, ground to a halt.

While Operation Citadel floundered, Hitler received unwelcome news from elsewhere. On July 10, British and American forces landed in Sicily. A few days later, faced with the necessity of rushing reinforcements into Italy in a last-ditch effort to keep the country fighting, the Fuehrer called off the

Eia, eia, alalà! Italian mountain troops proclaim their loyalty to National Fascist Italy with the old Fascist greeting   PK. Photograph: War Correspondent Schlickum

IN ITALY

↑ **The end of an Anglo-American tank wedge.** Hundreds of tanks and heavy weapons were either destroyed or captured
PK. Photograph: War Correspondent Lüthge (2)

The march to the rear. Many thousands of British and American troops were forced to surrender during the fighting for Italy ↓

entire Kursk attack. The Russians launched their counteroffensive immediately, forcing the Germans back to their starting lines. By August 1, they were making substantial gains on either side of the salient, forcing the Germans farther and farther back. They recaptured Kharkov on August 28, by which time the Germans were in full retreat. "It was," wrote OKW operations staff officer General Walter Warlimont some years later, "more than a battle lost. It handed the Russians the initiative and we never recovered it again right up to the end of the war."

Rescuing Mussolini

That catalyst that prompted Hitler to call a halt to Operation Citadel was probably the news that, on July 25, the Fascist Grand Council, meeting in a marathon ten-hour crisis session in Rome, had voted to strip Mussolini of his dictatorial powers. Victor Emmanuel III dismissed the Duce and had him arrested the next day. Hitler was incensed when he heard of Mussolini's precipitate fall. "We must be clear," he shouted at his staff during the evening briefing session. "It's pure treachery!"

Under Field Marshal Albert Kesselring's skilful command, fighting was still going on in Sicily. There, roughly 60,000 German troops managed to keep 13 Allied divisions at bay for 38 days. However, Hitler's first move was to order him to prepare for the island's evacuation and then to ready himself to deal with the inevitable Allied invasion of the Italian mainland. The Fuehrer made his intentions very clear. "He intends to arrest the King, take Badoglio (Mussolini's successor as Italian leader) and his entire rabble into custody, free the Duce, and give him and Fascism the opportunity to get back into the saddle and form a strong regime," Goebbels noted excitedly after a private meeting with him.

It was clear that Hitler had little or no faith in the Italians carrying on with the war once the Allied landings had taken place. "The resistance offered by the Italian troops is largely symbolic," he judged. "The Italians do not want to fight and are glad when they can give up their weapons, even better when they can sell them." The Fuehrer largely exempted Mussolini from such strictures, even though, at his last meeting with him at Feltre in northern Italy on July 18, he had harangued the Duce non-stop for two hours on the necessity for the Italians to contribute more to the fighting. He told Captain Otto Skorzeny, the daring SS commando leader he was putting in charge of a rescue mission: "I cannot and will not leave Italy's greatest son in the lurch!"

Locating where Mussolini was being held captive was the first of Skorzeny's problems. The fallen dictator was taken first to the island of Ponza, then to another island, and finally to a hotel in Gran Sasso, an isolated ski resort in the Apennine mountains in central Italy. An intercepted Italian radio message alerted Skorzeny to this last move. On September 12, he and his glider-born paratroops and SS commandos—plus a newsreel cameraman—parachuted down to the hotel, leaving their gliders to crash-land on the mountains. It took them just five minutes to overcome Mussolini's guards; they did not have to fire a single shot in the process. On the contrary, the colonel commanding the carabiniere invited Skorzeny to share a flask of wine with him.

Skorzeny saluted Mussolini with the words "Duce, the Fuehrer has sent me to set you free." Mussolini replied "I knew my friend Adolf Hitler would not forsake me." Meanwhile, Skorzeny's men were improvising an airstrip in front of the hotel to enable a tiny Fiesler-Storch reconnaissance plane to land and fly the Duce to safety. Mussolini, an experienced

pilot himself, was visibly nervous, especially since Skorzeny insisted on adding to the airplane's weight-load by squeezing in as well. He later explained that, if the plane had crashed and Mussolini been killed or injured, Hitler would have had his head.

Luckily for Skorzeny, the take-off was successful. Mussolini was flown to an airfield outside Rome, then to Vienna, and finally to Hitler's East Prussian military headquarters, where he was warmly greeted by a jubilant Fuehrer. However, Hitler's enthusiasm did not last for long. Mussolini was obviously a broken man, even though he was persuaded to set up a puppet Fascist regime in northern Italy, based on the town of Salo. He enjoyed no real power, surviving more or less as a figurehead at the beck and call of his Nazi "liberators."

Resisting the Allies Mussolini was not able to contribute much, if anything, to the Nazi war effort after his return to what passed for power. However, Skorzeny's daring exploit certainly served to raise morale at home within the Reich. People were reported as saying that it showed Germany was still capable of taking quick, decisive action to get out of tricky situations by improvising in grand style. However, their opinion of the Italians as a whole was less than favorable. Many shared Hitler's view that the Italians were utterly decadent. The SS Security Service reported that there were "marked feelings of hatred in all parts of the Reich and in all strata of the population against one people—namely the Italians."

The report continued. "Basically, people don't hold the enmity of our real opponents against them. It is felt to be a matter of fate. But people can never forgive the Italians for the fact that after they have gone to great lengths to assure us through their chosen representatives of their

Paratroops fall from the skies to attack Allied invading forces in Sicily. Signal *praised Axis resistance on the island; it did not mention that many Italians fled or surrendered at the first sight of their American and British opponents.*

friendship, they have now betrayed us so despicably a second time. The hatred against the Italian people springs from the most profound feelings."

Even before the long-awaited Allied landings took place—Montgomery's 8th Army crossed the Straits of Messina to land in Calabria in Italy's far south on September 3, with a second one following farther up the coast at Salerno six days later—Hitler had already decided that Italy must be defended, whether the Italians liked it or not. One thing was clear to him— Badoglio's repeated assurances that Italy would fight on alongside its Axis partner were not to be trusted. At 6.30 on the evening of September 8, the BBC announced the conclusion of an armistice between Italy and the Allies; Badoglio confirmed the news in a broadcast to the Italian people an hour-and-a-quarter later. The next day, he, the king, and General Ambrosio, the Chief of the General Staff, fled south from Rome to join the Allies. Many senior members of the Italian High Command joined in this stampede for safety.

Some high-ranking German commanders—notably Rommel and General Alfred Jodl, head of the Operations Staff at Wehrmacht High Command—advocated withdrawing north to make a stand at the Apennines. Kesselring, on the other hand, argued that southern Italy should not be given up without a fight. Hitler agreed with Kesselring. Even if he could not drive the British and Americans back into the sea, he could at least unleash a brutal, hard-fought battle that would inflict the maximum amount of casualties on the Allied

Shock-troops descend from the air: *A beautiful jump. The parachutes glide down like a huge bunch of balloons*

armies as they struggled to fight their way up the long Italian peninsula. Allied planners had predicted that Rome would be captured by October; it was June 1944, the day before D-Day, before the Allies managed to march into the Italian capital.

The Italian campaign was the longest and bloodiest one to be fought by the Allies in the West during the entire Second World War. In

November, reviewing the military situation with Goebbels, the Fuehrer commented: "The enemy has not won a significant military victory except on the Eastern Front. In Italy, the English and Americans are bogged down and suffering the heaviest losses there." As the battles at Anzio and for Monte Cassino were to demonstrate the following year, for once—and for a time—Hitler was right.

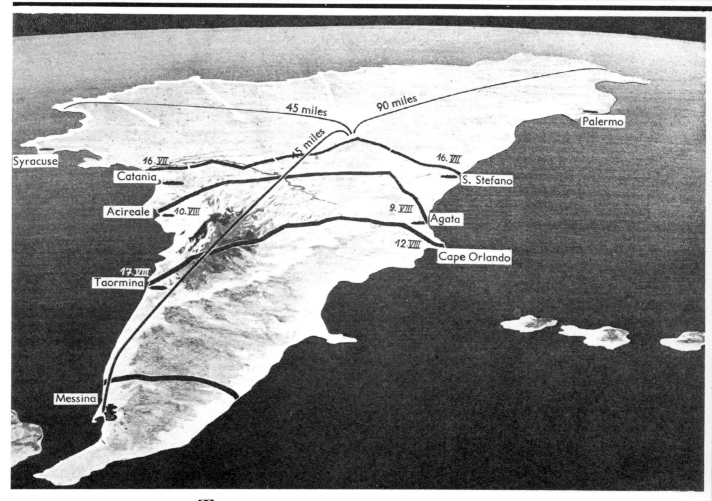

Sicily--a number of comparisons

Two British and American armies were launched against four German divisions on Sicily. Eisenhower's orders were to cut off the Germans in the shortest possible time from Messina, that is, to cut off the retreat to the Continent and to annihilate them. Sicily was to be a German "Dunkirk". But was it?

During the critical phase, the Anglo-American struggle for Sicily, which lasted 39 days, was restricted to one third of the island (1). The above sketch-map shows the successive stages of the fight for this area. In spite of repeated crises, Crete (2) was taken by storm in the thirteen days between 20th May and 1st June 1941. The German occupation of Norway (3), an area more than twelve times the size of Sicily, was completed between 9th April and 1st June 1940 with the exception of the action round Narvik which was in German hands again on 10th June. Both these landings are a proof of the efficiency of German troops and arms and of the superiority of German leadership. Dunkirk 1940 was the grand finale to a battle of annihilation. After the Grebbe Line had been penetrated, Holland capitulated on 14th May. On 24th May the annihilation of all the enemy forces still in Artois and Flanders began (4). On 28th May the ring drawn round the remnants of four enemy armies from Ostend to Lille, Armentières and Gravelines was closed.

The Belgian Army capitulated while the fragments of the British Expeditionary Army tried to escape at Dunkirk after an unparallelled defeat in three battles of encirclement (5). On 4th June Dunkirk capitulated with 88,000 prisoners. 26 days after the beginning of the campaign in France, the British had been swept from the Continent and had experienced the Dunkirk catastrophe of which Churchill said that it was "a colossal military disaster". But after more than five weeks of heroic resistance, the German troops down to the last private were able to make an orderly retreat back on to the European mainland. Read our report on the five phases of the Battle of Sicily.

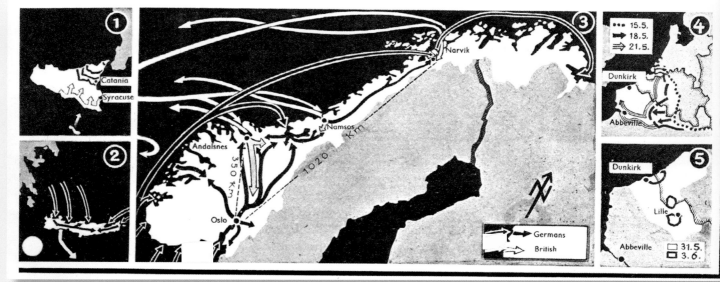

39 days···

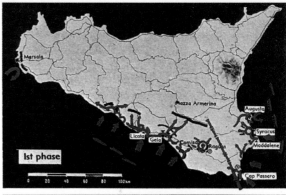

1st phase of the fighting 10th to 13th July 1943

During the night of 10th July several groups of enemy ships approached the eastern and southeastern coast of Sicily between Marsala, Cape Passero and Augusta along a broad front. Under cover of the fire from their heavy naval artillery, United States troops simultaneously began to land at various spots along the south coast in the vicinity of Licata and Gela. British divisions disembarked at Syracuse and Cape Passero. Parachutists and airborne troops were also sent into action in the Ragusa-Comiso area.

The struggle of the Anglo-American armies of invasion against Germany's and Italy's advanced guard had begun.

Whilst German and Italian coastal defence troops offered resistance to the invading enemy and immediately engaged him in embittered fighting, the British and Americans continued to land fresh troops at further places along the extensive coastline. The parachutists and air-borne troops landed behind the Axis lines were encircled, annihilated or dispersed by emergency units of the Air Force and Army as soon as they touched the ground. As early as the 10th July, the main body of the "Hermann Göring" Tank Division, which launched an attack in the direction of Gela eastwards of the Gela-Piazza-Amerina road, succeeded in collaboration with a number of Italian units in driving back the Americans who had landed at Gela into a narrow coastal strip and forcing them to take to their ships again with the majority of their strength. In the southeast of the island a unit of the 15th Tank Grenadier Division supported by units of the "Hermann Göring" Tank Division and an Italian division launched an attack against Syracuse. The enemy parachutists who had landed northwest of Syracuse were put out of action. During the course of the night and the days which followed, the enemy again landed strong contingents of troops including tank units at various places along the coast. Enemy attempts to land at Marsala and Augusta were repulsed with heavy losses.

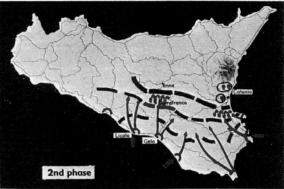

Under the pressure exerted by the British and American troops, who were continually drawing reinforcements from the bridgeheads, and in order to escape the rain of shells from the heavy naval units off the coast the German and Italian troops withdrew during the succeeding days to prepared positions lying further northwards, all the time fighting delaying rearguard actions. In spite of the stubborn resistance of the British the town and harbour of Augusta and the peninsula of Maddalena were recaptured by units of the 15th Tank Grenadier Division. During fighting for the possession of roads leading northwards through narrow mountain valleys, the German and Italian troops inflicted exceedingly heavy losses on the enemy in elastic warfare. Skilful withdrawals alternating with lightning attacks continually resulted in the cutting off from the main forces and annihilation of enemy advance guards. Once more the armour-piercing weapons of the German troops proved their superiority laying low even the heavy American "Dreadnought" tanks.

In almost uninterrupted day and night fighting, strong bomber, Stuka, fighter and destroyer units of the German Air Force attacked concentrations of enemy troops, columns on the march and disembarkations with annihilating effect. From the beginning of the landing operations until 13th July, the German Air Force sank no less than 20 troop transport ships, cargo boats and merchant vessels totalling 107,500 tons as well as numerous landing boats. 97 ships, 5 cruisers, 2 destroyers and a large number of landing boats were damaged by direct hits from bombs. Anti-aircraft guns and aerial combat accounted for 83 enemy planes.

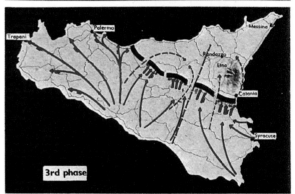

2nd phase of the fighting 14th to 17th July 1943

During the fighting which now followed, the enemy attempted by concentrating his strength not only to force a breach in the Catania Plain but also to capture the area round Enna, the centre of Sicily, by penetrating the right wing of the German defensive front. With this object in view, General Montgomery, who was in command of the British 8th Army in Southeast Sicily, reinforced the British troops held up by the strong German defence in their attack south of Catania by bringing up contingents of freshly landed troops. By the mass employment of parachutists and air-borne units northwest and south of Catania, he attempted to break the resistance of the German troops with an attack in their rear. Battleships, aircraft carriers, cruisers and destroyers were concentrated along the coastline from Augusta to Catania with the object of holding down the German troops with almost incessant shelling from their heavy guns.

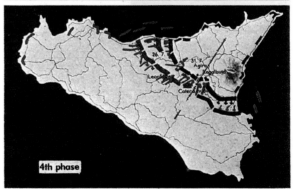

The defenders nevertheless proved in the days to follow that they were able to cope with this superiority in men and materials. The air-borne troops landed northwest and south of Catania were encircled and annihilated before being able to launch their attack. The heavy onslaughts of the British, which now began with strong tank and air support, collapsed in the face of the defenders' resistance with heavy losses after severe and embittered fighting without having reached the Plain of Catania. In only a few days of fighting, the "Hermann Göring" Tank Division alone accounted for 130 enemy tanks and 15 planes at Catania.

The offensive launched to the west by United States troops shared the same fate. General Patton, too, brought

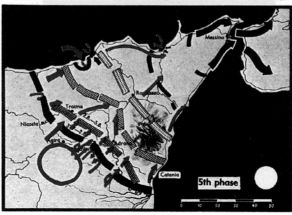

One shell after another *explodes along the enemy's front. It is only at the cost of heavy losses that he can advance at all against the desperate German defence*

up reserves from the bridgeheads at Licata and Gela in order to make up for the losses of men and material in the previous fighting. He launched an attack in the Barrafranca area with the object of capturing the town of Enna so as to be able to control and use the roads and railways converging there which were of fundamental importance for the prosecution of the fighting. Although the Americans here sought to carry forward the infantry attack by giving it strong tank and air support and covering it with massed heavy artillery fire, all their efforts did not achieve the anticipated success. They suffered very heavy losses and all their

attacks crumbled in the annihilating fire of the defenders often before the main battle line had been reached.

The chief task of the German Air Force, which gave effective support to the troops fighting on the ground, in this phase of the fighting, too, lay principally in attacks on enemy shipping in the waters surrounding the island. During the period from 14th to 17th July, the German Air Force sank 1 destroyer, 28 troop transport ships, oil tankers, munition ships, supply ships and troop landing ships totalling 94,000 tons. 5 cruisers, 5 destroyers and 53 ships of various kinds were damaged whilst 43 enemy planes were brought down.

3rd phase of the fighting 18th to 23rd July 1943

The Americans scored a cheap triumph during the third phase of the fighting in Sicily. They occupied the west and northwest of the island, which had been evacuated by the German troops, and took possession of the town of Trapani and Palermo without opposition.

The situation in the east and northeast of the island, however, was very different. Huge forces of mobile and mechanized troops were massed once more with the object of forming two spearheads. The aim of the Americans was to outflank the German 15th Tank Grenadier Division and a number of units from Italian divisions at two places and thus get possession of the roads leading northwards and northeastwards through the mountains via Randazzo to Messina.

The second spearhead was to be the affair of the British. In spite of the defeats inflicted on it during the second phase of the fighting, the British 8th Army was to make another attempt to capture the Plain of Catania along a broad front in order to cut off the German and Italian troops' line of retreat to Messina on the other side of Mount Aetna along the coastal road leading northwards.

But in this phase of the fighting, too,

the enemy was not able to reach his strategic objectives and suffered disproportionately high losses of men and material.

Wherever the enemy attacked, whether in the middle or in the eastern sector of the Sicilian front, the onslaught of his tank units was shattered by the destructive power of the defenders armour-piercing weapons. Did the enemy infantry succeed in places in advancing beyond the outposts and reaching the main fighting line, German and Italian grenadiers nevertheless remained the unquestionable masters of the situation in the hand-to-hand fighting. The nature of the tactics employed in Sicily, the elastic prosecution of the fighting and the many advantages provided by the rugged nature of the country with its narrow mountain passes, made it possible to inflict extremely heavy losses on the attacking enemy with a minimum number of defenders. During the course of the operations from 18th to 23rd July, the enemy was consequently obliged to allow increasingly long periods to elapse between his attacks in order thus not only to regroup his decimated units but also to bring up fresh reserves. The number of divisions estim-

ated as being required for the invasion of Sicily was soon exceeded. General Alexander, who directed the operations in Sicily, found it necessary in view of the successful and heroic resistance put up by the defenders to ask the Allied Headquarters for fresh divisions and to transfer them across the sea continually watched over and rendered dangerous by the German Air Force. It was on the sea that the biggest weakness of the British and Americans lay. The enemy's difficulties there increased day by day in consequence of the successful operations of the German naval units and Air Force.

The German Air Force, for example, sank 2 troop transport ships of 14,500 tons and a tanker of 10,000 tons in Sicilian waters whilst 1 cruiser and 1 destroyer as well as 21 ships, most of them of medium tonnage, and innumerable special landing boats were damaged.

A particularly courageous action was carried out by 6 German motor torpedo boats which during the night of 19th to 20th July forced their way in clear weather into the harbour of Syracuse and sank 2 destroyers anchored there

and a 3,000 ton steamer as well as damaging a big troop transport ship of 8,000 tons.

4th phase of the fighting
24th to 31st July 1943

Not until 30th July did the British feel strong enough to launch a fresh attack. By outflanking the right wing of the "Hermann Göring" Tank Division lying to the south and southwest of Catania, the enemy attempted to break through in the direction of Regalbuto with the help of strong tank and artillery support. A second group attacked simultaneously in the direction of Catenanuova. Whilst the attack on Regalbuto crumpled in the defensive fire of all weapons before the British were able to reach the town, Catenanuova was lost during the course of embittered fighting. During the night from 31st July to 1st August, the main fighting line was withdrawn to the heights northeast of Catenanuova and Regalbuto, which latter place was abandoned to the enemy.

The enemy strove by every means in his power and by the ruthless employment of his divisions to achieve the aims which he had failed to realize during the previous week's fighting. He consequently regrouped his forces and transferred the centre of his operations to the American sector in the hope that by attacking there with particularly strong spearheads, he would be able to overcome the defenders' resistance and break through eastwards along the coastal road. A second attack by strong motorized and mechanized units was to overrun the troops at Leonforte and Agira, push forward towards the north and join up with the northern group.

Whilst the Americans only skirmished along the northern front with weak forces, they launched a big attack along the coastal road on 25th July. The tank grenadier division fighting there repulsed the attack and threw the enemy back in an immediate counter-attack. When the enemy attacked again the next day, he met with no opposition.

The mobile German prosecution of the fighting proved its value during the course of the operations which now followed. The most stubborn defence and withdrawals at the appropriate time alternated with lightning attacks.

A photographic record. *Methodically, as though on manoeuvres, the last troops fighting in Sicily arrive on the mainland with ferries across the Straits of Messina*

Whilst the enemy offensive along the coast was never able to get going properly in consequence of the delaying rearguard actions fought by the German troops, the second spearhead, that of the Americans in the middle sector, encountered the inflexible determination and stubborn resistance of the German tank grenadiers. Even the assault carried out against the German rearguards at Leonforte compelled the enemy to throw in all his forces. In order to be able to storm Agira, the enemy was obliged once more to regroup his units after the heavy losses they had suffered and to bring up reserves. He then launched the big attack on Agira. After a severe struggle with changing fortunes for both sides, which forced both defenders and attackers to throw in their last reserves, the enemy's attempt to break through to Agira collapsed and the realization of his outflanking movement was frustrated.

Strong bomber and fighter units of the German Air Force were employed over Sicily and participated effectively in the fighting on land. In this phase, too, however, its chief task lay in attacking ships in Sicilian waters and the supply ports in Africa. A 7,000 ton tanker and 3 large merchant ships totalling 20,000 tons were sunk, whilst 36 transport and merchant ships, 1 cruiser and 2 smaller naval units were seriously damaged. 64 enemy planes were shot down by the anti-aircraft defence and in aerial combat.

Small fast boats belonging to the German Navy torpedoed a cruiser and sank an enemy submarine. 7 enemy planes were brought down by A. A. fire from German ships.

5th phase of the fighting 1st to 17th August 1943

Whilst the enemy during the first days of August advanced with only weak forces against the "Hermann Göring" Tank Division in the southern sector and the 29th Tank Grenadier Division in the northern sector, the main enemy attack was now transferred to the middle sector. It was not difficult to guess his intentions. He was trying to gain possession of the roads leading via Troina on the one side and Adrano on the other to Randazzo and Messina. In order to achieve this object, the enemy concentrated his main force in the middle sector in the Nicosia-Agira-Regalbuto area in preparation for a big attack. The German troops together with a number of Italian units now faced their most difficult task during these operations. If they succeeded in repulsing the enemy's attack with its vast superiority of men and material and in gaining time by means of elastic methods of fighting so that the main body could retire, then they would have succeeded in their aim. Conscious of this historic task, the German tank grenadiers resolutely faced the big attack, held it up and continually compelled the enemy to regroup his forces.

The main body of the German and Italian troops meanwhile retired towards the northeast. The enemy pushing forward in pursuit became entangled in wide expanses of dense minefields and thus lost much precious time. Counter-attacks were launched against attempts made by the enemy to hold up the retreat of the German and Italian units by landing troops in their rear. The enemy forces which had landed were encircled, destroyed or thrown back into the sea.

The transference of the troops to the Italian mainland had been going on for days past unhindered by the enemy. The unexcelled courage of the German rearguards, which prevented a more than twentyfold superior enemy from seizing the disembarkation harbours, made it possible to convey all the units fighting in Sicily together with their heavy weapons, tanks, guns, lorries and other equipment across the Straits of Messina to the mainland.

The struggle in Sicily had thus come to an end. During fighting which lasted for 5 weeks, the Army carried out the task allotted to it of acting as an advanced guard and gaining time for the concentration of the main body of their own troops. Only when the history of the war is written will it be possible to pay full tribute to the small but unprecedentedly courageous group of men who in a heroic struggle succeeded in putting out of action more than a third of the fighting strength of a superior enemy.

During the same period, the German Air Force sank and damaged much of the enemy's all-important shipping. 61 transport and merchant ships, most of them carrying men and war material, totalling 290,000 tons were sunk as well as 1 cruiser, 7 destroyers, 3 corvettes and numerous smaller naval vessels. A further 59 cargo and transport ships totalling 278,750 tons were so severely damaged that their loss may be regarded as certain. The other ships set on fire and struck by bombs of all calibres are too numerous to be mentioned.

The achievements of the German Navy, which carried out the tremendous task of withdrawing all the German and Italian troops with their weapons and equipment, nearly 10,000 lorries, 17,000 tons of ammunition, fuel and other supplies as well as more than 4,000 wounded during the first weeks of August were unique in history.

This masterpiece of military organization in the face of a more than fourfold superior enemy force could only be accomplished by troops who had prevented every breach of their lines and every outflanking movement on land, by the heroic deeds of a navy, which carried out the traffic to and from the island almost exclusively with small vessels and protected it on the flanks with light units, and by an air force which participated in the ground fighting with strong bomber and fighter squadrons, engaged the enemy in aerial combat and struck heavy blows at him by sinking and damaging valuable shipping.

Officers and men have thus performed an achievement which will go down in the history of warfare in the same way as a victorious offensive battle.

Vol. 19. First October Number 1943 / SIGNAL / A bi-weekly publication / Editor : Wilhelm Reetz, Deputy Editor: Hugo Mösslang / Signal is published and printed by Deutscher Verlag, Berlin SW 68. Kochstrasse 22-26. Copyright under international Copyright Convention / All rights reserved

The prisoner of Gran Sasso: Benito Mussolini. What are they to do with his gaolers whom they had quickly overpowered? "Set them free!" replies the liberated Duce as he makes for the Fieseler Storch

"Good luck!" At an altitude of 6,000 feet his liberators cheer the Duce. The Storch takes off. Down below in all parts of Italy thousands of Blackshirts are waiting for him, the smith of Rome, the saviour of Italy

Bombing the Reich

When RAF bombers struck at Berlin on the night of August 26, 1940, the Berliners—according to US war correspondent William Shirer—were "stunned." Goering had assured them that no enemy airplane would ever reach the Reich's capital. Hitler vowed revenge and the Luftwaffe tried its best to carry out the Fuehrer's command but it was not equipped with the heavy bombers to do the job. It was the RAF that perfected the skills of area bombing. Air Chief Marshal Sir Arthur Harris, who led Bomber Command from 1942 to the end of the war, vowed that the attacks would go on "until the heart of Nazi Germany ceases to beat."

When Hitler turned east to launch Operation Barbarossa, the attack on Soviet Russia, in June 1941, the Blitz against Britain the Luftwaffe had unleashed the previous fall came to a virtual stop. With around three-quarters of the German air force now deployed on the Eastern Front, Goering's remaining bombers in the west were incapable of waging a protracted campaign of any severity. For its part, RAF Bomber Command was slowly intensifying its bombing raids against the Reich, but, until spring 1942, the results were often ineffective. The raids were also costly.

A government investigation revealed that only a third of Bomber Command's aircraft were actually managing to get within 5 miles (8 km) of hitting their primary targets, and that flying by moonlight was vital to achieve even this level of accuracy. Most aircraft were dropping their bomb-loads blind by estimated time of arrival. Aircraft losses ballooned as well. In the first eighteen nights of August 1941, 107 aircraft were lost. In September, out of 2,501 sorties dispatched, forty aircraft crashed and sixty-eight went missing. On the night of 7 November, thiry-seven aircraft out of the 400 dispatched were lost. Put another way, 12.5 per cent of those sent to bomb Berlin, 13 per cent of those attacking Mannheim and 21 per cent of those sent to bomb the Ruhr failed to return. Only those bombing targets in Occupied France managed to make it home relatively unscathed.

The Kammhuber Line

The increase was not surprising. British air raids on the Ruhr in 1940 had prompted Goering to put General Josef Kammhuber in charge of the Reich's defenses against night attack. At first these relied principally on flak and searchlights; it was only slowly and reluctantly that Goering was persuaded to allocate more night-fighters to the defense. The problem was that both he and Hitler believed that the Luftwaffe's job was to attack, not to defend. "This whole phoney business won't be necessary any more once I get my squadrons back to the west," he assured Kammhuber when discussing the air defense of Germany in fall 1941. Meanwhile, the night-fighter force was starved of aircraft and aircrew. There were never quite enough of them to tip the scales decisively in the Luftwaffe's favor.

Nevertheless, Kammhuber managed to build up a defensive system that came within an ace of winning victory in the air war. He started by progressively setting up a belt of searchlights and sound-locators across northern Germany and Holland and Belgium between 50 and 100 miles (80 and 160 km) inland from the coast. What night-fighters he had available patrolled sectors of this line, seeking to attack the bombers as they were detected. Then, in spring 1942, came the much more sophisticated and potentially deadly Himmelbett system, based on a chain of overlapping radar-guided fighter "boxes" that had been established running the length of the coast from northern Germany to Belgium and around the Reich's most important cities.

Each "box" had its own long-range Freya radar to provide early warning of the approach of the bombers and their course, though not their height. As the night-fighters scrambled to intercept them, the short-range Wurzburg took over. Each "box" had two—one to track a bomber more precisely and the other to track an intercepting fighter. Ground controllers plotted the relative positions of the two aircraft with red and green dots projected onto a Seeburg evaluation screen. Initially, the controllers tried to trap the bomber in the cone created by a supporting searchlight battery. Later, when the night-fighters had been equipped with their own Lichtenstein airborne radar, they aimed to guide the fighter to the point at which its own radar could take over.

It was an ingenious system, but it had two drawbacks. First, it involved the use of two radar screens as opposed to the British one. Second, each "box" could control only a single interception at a time. Realizing this, the RAF developed what was referred to as "streaming"—directing the entire bombing force through a single box and so saturating the defenses. As their attacks became more and more massive, the Kammhuber Line was swamped by the sheer scale of the offensive.

Area bombing

While Kammhuber was fighting his own corner, Bomber Command was reconsidering its own tactics. It made the momentous decision to abandon its efforts to hit precision industrial targets and addressed itself instead to carpet bombing the urban areas of the Reich.

New tactics went hand in hand with the introduction of new aircraft. Four-engine heavy bombers—the Short Stirling, Handley Page Halifax, and Avro Lancaster—were starting to replace the twin-engine Whitley, Wellington, and Hampden medium bombers on which Bomber Command had hitherto relied. There were new navigational aids as well. Gee, a radio-pulse navigation system, came first. H2S and Oboe, two radar guidance systems, followed. There was also a new commander-in-chief—Air Chief Marshal Sir Arthur Harris, known to his aircrews as "Butcher" or "Butch." It was his job to attack what the Air Ministry defined as "Primary

Bomb damage in the Belgian city of Antwerp was seized on by Signal *to prove that the Allies were "air pirates" indulging in "terror bombing" of innocent civilians, rather than limiting their attacks to strictly military targets.*

Industrial Areas"—Essen, Duisberg, Dusseldorf, and Cologne—as well as its "Alternative Industrial Areas." Lubeck, Rostock, Bremen, Kiel, Hannover, Frankfurt, Mannheim, Stuttgart, and Schweinfurt all featured on this second list. Harris was also to continue harassing air-raids on Berlin "to maintain the fear of attack over the city." It was no small task, but one that the supremely-confident Harris was sure he and his aircrews could fulfil.

Lubeck was the first German city Harris selected to try out his new tactics. Put at its simplest, he chose it because it was an area that his aircraft could find, strike at, and utterly destroy. It was on the Baltic coast and so easy to locate. It was only lightly defended. Above all, it was a closely-packed medieval town that would be relatively easy to set on fire and burn. The raid, which took place on March 28, 1942, was an overwhelming success. Some 1,425 houses were totally destroyed and 1,976 badly damaged. Rostock, another coastal city, was the next target. This time, the attack was carried out over four consecutive nights. As with Lubeck, the center of the city was left ablaze.

The 1,000-bomber raid

Harris had not finished demonstrating what Bomber Command could now do. On May 30, 1942, he launched the first-ever 1,000-bomber raid against the Rhineland city of Cologne. It was the greatest concentration of air power the world had yet seen, even though, to reach the magic figure, which was double the normal strength of Bomber Command's front-line squadrons, Harris was compelled to call in every available aircraft from his Operational Training Units, the OTU pupils and their instructors, to make up the number.

The aircraft attacked in three waves—Wellingtons striking first, followed by Stirlings, with Manchesters and Lancasters bring up the rear. As they flew toward their target, the aircrews of the later waves saw a vast red glow in the sky ahead of them, which was clearly visible 125 miles away. It was the city of Cologne ablaze from end to end. On the ground, chaos reigned. Many of the flak batteries had been forced to cease fire because transport could no longer get across the city to get fresh ammunition to the guns. Searchlights meandered wildly across the sky. Below the

A damaged school in Antwerp reinforced Signal's *point that everywhere in the occupied territories was considered fair game by the Allied strategic bombers. No one was safe from savage air attack.*

attacking aircraft, 3,300 houses had been totally destroyed, more than 2,000 badly damaged, and over 7,000 partly damaged. An amazing 12,000 fires were raging among the breached water mains, severed power cables, exploding gas mains, and wrecked telephone systems. An estimated thirty-six factories had been totally destroyed, seventy badly damaged, and more than 200 damaged in part. The Rhine docks, the railways, and the tramway system had been put out of action. Some 45,000 people had lost their homes.

It was disaster on an epic scale, even though Goering would not admit it. Albert Speer, accompanied by Field Marshal Erhard Milch, visited him the morning after the attack. As the two men arrived, the Reichsmarschal was on the telephone to Cologne's Gauleiter, who had already reported the scale of the destruction to Hitler himself. "The report from your Police Commissioner is a stinking lie," Goering shouted. "I tell you as the

Reichsmarschal that the figures cited are simply too high. How dare you report such fantasies to the Fuehrer?" Unfortunately for him, Hitler believed the Gauleiter.

Hitler demanded that the Luftwaffe take reprisals. In April, the so-called Baedeker Raids were launched, targeting small, more or less undefended British towns—York and Norwich were prime examples—of significant historical and architectural importance. The Luftwaffe could only muster a handful of aircraft to carry the raids out—a pitiful 30 fighter-bombers for daylight attacks and a maximum of 130 bombers for use during the hours of darkness. They achieved nothing of military significance. Attempts to bomb London again in spring 1944 were as unsuccessful. Much to the Fuehrer's disbelief, many of the bombers could not even find the city.

Total destruction

Cologne was just the beginning. In 1943, the US 8th Air Force joined the RAF in the attack. Certainly Goebbels appreciated that there was a potential disaster in the making. "We find ourselves in a situation of helpless inferiority," he confided to

his diary, "and have to receive the blows of the English and Americans with dogged fury."

Night after night, Bomber Command pounded the Ruhr, the Reich's industrial heartland. In July, Harris and the Americans struck at Hamburg; the RAF triggered a firestorm that reduced much of the city to ashes. Some 900,000 were made homeless and an estimated 40,000 lost their lives. Finally, Harris turned the full might of Bomber Command against Berlin. However, despite the devastation and destruction inflicted on the city, it proved too tough a nut for him to crack.

It was the 8th and 15th US Air Forces, with their Flying Fortresses and Liberators protected by a new generation of long-range escort fighters that could reach the heart of the Reich, which brought the Luftwaffe to its knees. During "Big Week," a series of mass attacks on the German aircraft industry in spring 1944, over 4,000 German fighters were downed. Then, the Americans turned on Hitler's precious oil plants. The results were even more dramatic. The Luftwaffe's supply of aviation spirit fell from 180,000 tons in April 1944, to 50,000 in June, and to a derisory 10,000 tons in August. From then on, the Luftwaffe lacked the fuel to fly anything like the number of fighters it actually had available. Even the new jets, which might have turned the tide of the air war against the Allies had enough of them been produced earlier, were affected.

By the end of the year, as the Reich neared the point of collapse, the bombers were flying virtually unchecked. Day and night, huge palls of smoke and fire rose from the Reich's devastated cities. "The situation grows daily more intolerable and we have no means of defending ourselves against this catastrophe," Goebbels wrote. It was, indeed, the end.

Pull away the chocks — night operations!

The Ju 88 has taken its bombs on board, the humming of the propeller changes to a loud droning. Lit up by the floodlight on the taking-off ground the hubs of the engines which are running at full speed look like circles of glistening fabric. And now the giant metal bird glides down the landing-ground; it rises and disappears into the night. One after the other the bombers take off on their flight against Britain which was relying on a lull in the German attacks on the island after the beginning of hostilities on the eastern front   Photographs: PK. Stempka

The dawn after the night of terror. *Smoke is still rising from the burnt-out opera house (on the right) and a large hotel; it hangs over the square where men belonging to a salvage corps are seeking a few minutes' rest on mattresses which have been saved*

The dawn after the night of terror. *"I put out three incendiaries," says Gardener Thiessen who looks after the swans in the city park. A few weeks ago his home in the old part of the town was destroyed by an explosive bomb. His face tells the story of the night of devastation*

A NIGHT OF TERROR...

War Correspondent Hanns Hubmann experienced one of the heavy night raids on a town in the west of Germany. Ten days later, he revisited the same town and its inhabitants. SIGNAL here publishes his report

This town in western Germany has already been the object of a hundred night air raids. Of more than a hundred, but this one was one of the worst. War Correspondent Hanns Hubmann was there and saw the innumerable conflagrations. The opera house and many of the large hotels were destroyed. Reich Minister Speer, with whom Signal's War Correspondent was travelling, helped to salvage mattresses and other things. Hundreds and thousands of people lost their homes. Everybody helped in saving what could be saved. On the morning after the raid, the smoke was still hanging like a pall in the streets, but the people were already hastening to their work again. Yet their

faces reflected the terrors of the night. Ten days after this night raid, Hubmann returned to the town. The marks of destruction on the housefronts were naturally still unchanged. But the faces of the people and their whole life clearly showed that they are overcoming the hardships of the nights of terror. How they are doing so is shown by Signal's photographs. Men who take home a bunch of flowers to their wives ten days after such an air raid and women who cannot hide their so disarming anxieties about hats and handbags, people who stream to their work in the early morning after the night of devastation as though nothing had occurred—such people are stronger than their fate.

The dawn after the night of terror. *On their way to work already, they pass ruins and wounded people. They have had no time to shave, because they all want to be at their machines at 6 a.m. as usual. The trams are not running and at most they have a bicycle at their disposal for getting to the factories*

←
Under the glass roof of his cockpit. *The wireless operator at the M. G.*
PK. Photograph: War Correspondent Speck

The dawn after the night of terror. *Their appearance still bears marks of the night of devastation. They have taken off their collars to be able to fight the flames and do salvage work. The alert had brought them together by chance in an air-raid shelter—Schäfer, the municipal inspector, Strathmann, the grocer and Arenswald, the master basket-maker. They had done good work. Ten days later? (See below)*

They have recovered their good spirits . . .

. . . for they still have their Rhineland humour. These three men are a municipal inspector, a grocer and a master basket-maker. Ten days after the heavy air raid things are taking their normal course again—the one is selling sausage, the second is carrying on his office work between makeshift walls and the third is again making neat baskets.

"This is my office now. Don't you agree, cupboards take the place of a wall nicely?"

"Would you like some real Brunswick tongue sausage again? It has just come in fresh!"

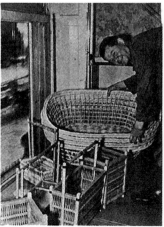

"I've just finished making these baskets. And there is a new pane in my shop window, too"

The waitress Kate

The morning after the night of terror, *Signal* came across her sitting with a colleague on a few stools she had saved together with a number of other things including the cash register from her café (on the left of the picture)

↓ **Ten days later,** *the reporter happened to see her working as a National Socialist People's Welfare helper distributing food (on the right of the picture)*

Architect and photographer...

"Hallo, where are you taking that pail?" "Up the ladder to the staircase and then to my atelier!" Mrs Hehmke-Winterer, a photographer, lives on the 5th floor. The atelier was not wrecked. Her husband, the architect Konrad Wagner, has built a makeshift hearth out of a few bricks. They fetch water from a pump in the yard. She has a smile on her face for life is still going on as usual.

The dawn after the night of terror. *Wagner and his wife, in front of their house*

Ten days later *the architect Wagner is again at work with his women assistants in a makeshift office in the heavily damaged house*

She wanted to buy a pair of stockings...

"What a lovely dress!" Two friends strolling past the glittering show-cases in Kurfürstendamm in Berlin stop to admire the pretty things displayed (below). "Do look at these adorable undies!" — "Darling," sighs her friend, "I only want to buy stockings. Besides think of the clothes card! But maybe it would do no harm just to ask in the shop..."

Horseshoes bring good fortune

according to a super-
stition know all
over the world. But to
the army blacksmith
they bring work, the
careful execution of
which exercises a
particular influence
of its own on the
"fortune of war"

PK. Henisch

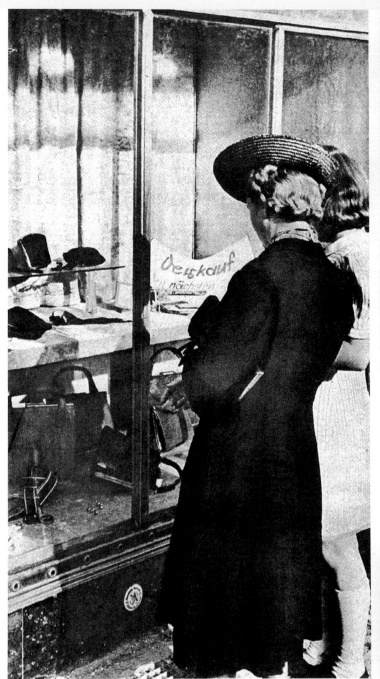

"I'll have the second from the right" *says Hilde as she admires the new handbags which have just been placed in the repaired shop window. A notice says that business will begin again in a few days time*

Ten days later . . .

"Yes, we begin business again tomorrow" *the girls in a stocking shop say with a smile. But it will be in a shop being shared with three other firms. Now they are busy fetching stocks from a warehouse which was not h...*

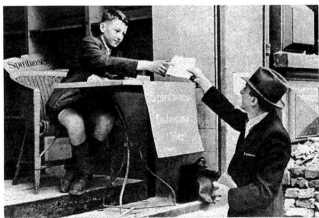

"We're getting brandy," *the boy says as he registers customers for spirits to help his mother. There are special rations for the population of the bombed cities*

w good the army bread tastes!" Par-
arly is this the case when Rhineland
help to distribute the bread from the
bakeries at food centres for people
e homes have suffered damage from bombs

Roses and marguerites. Flower-sellers have
set up their gay stalls again in front of the
burnt out façade of a departamental store. Hus-
bands come and buy bunches of flowers for their
wives. Ten days after the night of terror . . .

...And the main thing:
The work goes on

TWILIGHT OF THE GODS

As bad news poured in from all the fighting fronts, Hitler still refused to admit that the war was lost; Josef Goebbels assured him that for "reasons of historical necessity and justice," something had to happen to transform the military situation. *Signal*, too, ignored the unfavorable war news as much as it could. From time to time, it did condemn the devastation caused by Allied "terror bombing;" naturally enough, it celebrated the coming of the Fuehrer's "wonder weapons"—the VI flying bomb and the V2 rocket—which, it assured its readers, would turn the tide of war back in the Reich's favor. What it could not disguise was how the deteriorating situation was affecting the magazine itself. Edition after edition shut down as more and more of Occupied Europe was liberated; publication dates became more and more sporadic. The last issue of all appeared in March 1945, just a few weeks before the Fuehrer committed suicide in his Berlin bunker and the Third Reich's final capitulation.

The fighter and his victim. This Americ...
Short-Stirling bomber with its crew of twe...
could not cope with the German figh...
PK. Photograph: War Correspondent Hubm...

From Normandy to Berlin

In June 1944, when the Western Allies finally landed in Occupied France, Hitler lost the battle of "the longest day." Eisenhower's forces powered their way across France, into Belgium, and forward to the Reich's western frontier. Then, amazingly, the situation stabilized. Hitler seized the opportunity to launch a last-ditch offensive in the Ardennes; despite initial success, it soon turned into yet another military failure. As the Allies crossed the Rhine, and the Russians smashed their way into Berlin, it was only a matter of days before Grand Admiral Doenitz, whom Hitler had made his successor following his suicide, was forced into unconditional surrender.

Imminent defeat in the west and east was not the only potential disaster facing Hitler in the summer of 1944. As it transpired, he also had to face a determined threat to kill him and overthrow the Nazi regime from within. On July 20, a determined attempt was made to blow him up at his Rastenburg field headquarters. It was the closest the Fuehrer was to come to death during the entire war until his eventual suicide in his Berlin command bunker in April the following year.

The July bomb plot

Lieutenant-Colonel Claus von Stauffenberg was the man chosen by the conspirators to assassinate the Fuehrer. It was by no means the first time that a plot had been organized to kill him. On March 13, 1943, an attempt had been made to blow up his plane as it flew him back from the Eastern Front—it failed because the bomb's detonator failed to work at high altitude—and again in March 21, when a young officer took a bag stuffed with explosives to an exhibition of captured Soviet military equipment in Berlin, hoping to kill Hitler as he inspected it. The Fuehrer hurried through the exhibition at such a pace that the opportunity did not present itself.

It seemed as if the Fuehrer enjoyed a charmed life, but, this time, Stauffenberg was determined to succeed. Summoned to confer with Hitler at Rastenburg in his capacity as chief of staff to General Friedrich Fromm, commander of the Reserve Army, he took two bombs with him, though in the event he had time to prime only one of them. He slipped it into his briefcase, which he propped up against one of the legs of a heavy wooden map table over which the Fuehrer was leaning. Then, he excused himself, saying he had to make an urgent telephone call.

As Stauffenberg watched from a safe distance, the bomb exploded. Convinced that Hitler could not have survived, he bluffed his way through the security cordons, reached the nearby airstrip and flew back to Berlin, where his fellow-conspirators in the War Ministry were primed to launch a coup d'etat. They were supposed to put Operation Valkyrie, the codename for a military takeover of the government into operation, as soon as they received confirmation from Rastenburg that the Fuehrer was dead. Instead of taking immediate action, however, they dithered. Eventually they decided to wait for Stauffenberg to return to Berlin before giving the go-ahead.

Not waiting to ensure the Fuehrer was dead proved to be a fatal blunder. Hitler had survived. Staggering out of the conference room, he was embraced by Field Marshal Wilhelm Keitel, head of the Wehrmacht High Command, with the words "My Fuehrer, you are alive, you are alive!" Hitler's clothing was torn to shreds. He had burns and abrasions on his arms and legs, and burst ear-drums, but no serious injuries. Once again, he had escaped assassination.

Back in Berlin, a furious Stauffenberg urged his fellow-conspirators into action, but counter-orders were already pouring out of Rastenburg saying that the Fuehrer was alive and ordering the conspiracy's suppression. In Berlin, loyal troops stormed the War Ministry and released Fromm, whom the conspirators had arrested. He promptly had them shot. Stauffenberg called to the firing-squad: "Long live our sacred Germany!" With the failure of the Berlin coup, the simultaneous risings in Paris, Prague, and Vienna also collapsed.

Decline and fall

Just before 1.00am, Hitler himself broadcast to the nation to assure Germans everywhere that he was alive and unharmed. "A

very small clique of ambitious, irresponsible, unscrupulous, and at the same time senseless and criminally stupid officers, have hatched a plot to eliminate me, and with me, to exterminate the Wehrmacht High Command," he began. "It has again been granted to me that I should escape a fate which would have been terrible not for me but for the German people. They see in this again the pointing finger of Providence that I must and will carry on with my work."

Only ten minutes warning was given of the broadcast. Those who heard it noticed how Hitler's speech was slow and halting at first; it was only toward the end of his address, when he pledged to be avenged on the plotters, that he speeded up into his customary ranting. He had not spoken to his people for months. Letters poured into the Propaganda Ministry asking why the Fuehrer remained silent. His popularity plummeted as the war news went from bad to worse. His last speech, broadcast on January 30, 1945, certainly did nothing to raise German morale. "His

voice," wrote Mehta Maschmann, a young activist in the League of German Girls, an offshoot of the Hitler Youth, "sounded shrill with despair."

By this time, Hitler was nearing the point of physical collapse. Over the years, he had come to rely more and more on the somewhat dubious remedies prescribed by Dr. Theodore Morell, his personal physician since 1936, to keep him going. By the later stages of the war, the Fuehrer was swallowing twenty-eight different varieties of pill a day, and being injected so frequently that Goering sarcastically dubbed Morell "the Reich Master of Injections."

Nothing Morell did could alleviate Hitler's increasing physical deterioration. Electrocardiograms indicated that the Fuehrer was suffering from progressive heart disease, probably caused by sclerosis of the coronary arteries. From 1943 onward, he also suffered from chronic indigestion and periodic stomach cramps. A tremor developed in his left hand. It grew markedly worse, accompanied by a growing stoop,

A sentry stands guard of a massive gun emplacement in the Pas de Calais section of the much-vaunted Atlantic Wall. Parroting Hitler himself, Signal *boasted that Fortress Europe's defenses were impregnable. The truth was that they were far from complete.*

and jerking movements in the left leg. At the beginning of 1945, Morell diagnosed Parkinson's disease.

Outside observers noted how rapidly the Fuehrer was ageing. His hair was turning gray; he looked far older than he was, and seemed to be increasingly debilitated. As he descended into the bunker complex beneath the Reich Chancellery to fight his last battle as the Soviet Army prepared to storm Berlin, the deterioration became more and more marked as Hitler stormed at his generals and ordered phantom divisions to the relief of the city. On April 22, he finally broke down in despair, admitting openly for the first time that the war was lost. On April 29, as Soviet troops started to penetrate the heart of Berlin, he shot himself.

The Thousand Year Reich was at an end. It surrendered unconditionally just days later.

becomes a reality: **Evening at home.** *The children romp on the soft carpet. The father is occupied with the paper, the mother with her needlework. The daughters are poring over their books. The table is placed in the corner in accordance with an ancient German custom. It was not until the 19th century that the love of "cold splendour" brought it into the middle of the room, completely spoiling the proportions*

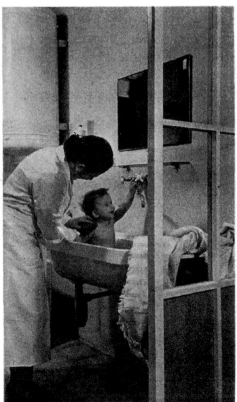

Johnny's little paradise. *In the deep bathlike basin which the family normally uses as a wash-basin the little fellow kicks about to his heart's content. Beside the baby's bath stands the table on which he is dressed. The electric geyser provides hot water in a few minutes for the bath*

The kitchen is small—*on purpose. Long distance running belongs to the sports grounds. The equipment is convenient, modern and complete; every detail was carefully planned and tested. A small refrigerator is used for storing foodstuffs. The meals are handed in through a hatch in the wall*

The girls' room. *The beds are made of plain larchwood, less attractive in appearance but excellent to sleep in. And girls sleep well at this age especially when they can look forward to all the little joys of a family breakfast-table such as is found in every real home*

Question: Has Germany a programme for which she is fighting? Answer: What the German soldier is defending is not a programme. It is the very substance of his existence, the richness and variety of his civil life in peacetime. What he desires to acquire by victory, however, is the fulfilment of the claim that an individual shall be respected for his own self. This, too, is not a programme but an idea, to explain which SIGNAL publishes the following pages

WHAT WE ARE FIGHTING FOR

Wilhelm Leibl:
The three
women in the
church (1881)

The theme of this number is what Germany is fighting for. The picture by the Munich painter Wilhelm Leibl, portraying the three women in the church as they can be seen in that part of the country, has been placed at the beginning. The aim of the following pages is to show what we are and what we possess, what is indispensable and sacred to us

THINGS THAT MAKE LIFE WORTH LIVING FOR US

What we are fighting for:

For man's right to culture

The problem of the masses is the special problem of our age.

In the plutocratic countries, the number of those people having any part in the benefits of culture has become increasingly small. On the other hand, the wretched products of the proletarian cult in the Soviet Union have proved that the nation's need for culture cannot be satisfied by levelling processes and standardization.

It is consequently one of the most important of Europe's war aims that every worker should have at his disposal sufficient leisure time to be able to shape his life so that it is not completely filled out by the dreariness of offices and factories. This need for culture benefiting every individual and every family appears to us no less important than the struggle for a just wage which is essential for providing security and removing that uncertainty which more than anything else has rendered people homeless in great towns. By this means alone is it possible to give talented and ambitious people opportunities for advancement. We are consequently opposed to both standardization and class supremacy.

The right of talented people to receive training is the logical continuation of the right to work which must be the basis of any new social order in Europe. Ability must be the deciding factor and not class, money or profit. The capable individual must be able to occupy by his efforts the place for which he is fitted. That appears to us to be the expression of real culture. It was a fundamental mistake of previous socialist movements to instigate the people to make claims without simultaneously stating that every claim could justifiably be attained only as the result of improved performance. There, however, where the capable individual is cast back into the hopelessness of proletarian existence, social justice can never hold sway. We are passionately opposed to such a system.

Two examples among many: A Beethoven concerto played by a State orchestra conducted by Wilhelm Furtwängler during the lunch hour in a big German industrial plant. One of the German pleasure steamers which give the less well-to do the opportunity to appreciate the beauties of the world which are otherwise available only to the favoured few

What we are fighting for:

For the final solution of the question regarding the worker's standing

The chief point at issue in this war is the question regarding the individual of the future.

Will this individual be the servant of machinery or of money? Or will he, on the other hand, be the master of machinery and capital? That is the great question now raised in this world struggle.

Not only for the rule of the machine, the characteristic feature of the Soviet Union, but also for the mastery of capital in the British and American plutocracies, the working man is a proletarian.

The rule of capital and of the money market is founded on the uncertainty in the existences of millions of people. On the other hand, the aim of Marxism and of Sovietism is to make the proletariate a thing of permanence. Both Sovietism and the plutocracies have tried to construct an ideology of human ideals based upon a mistake in the social system. In every country capitalism has deprived the worker of his rights, rendered him homeless and made him antagonistic to his people. Sovietism has done the same but by the reverse process. In the vast areas of the Soviet Union, man has been reduced to the state of a slave of machinery and a Stachanov proletarian without rights and without a just wage.

We, on the contrary, aim at social security for the working man: Only he can bear the honourable name of worker who possesses both for himself and his family the security of a definite wage, comfort during the last years of his life, help in cases of illness, a pension should he be injured, benefits for motherhood, and also knows that in the event of his decease, provision will be made for his wife and children.

Insecurity is characteristic of the proletarian system whether it be in the shape of the wage struggles and unemployment in the capitalist countries or in that of debasement to the level of cattle which is first sent to work at one place and then to another as in the Soviet Union.

On the other hand, we are fighting for the individual's security in the community of the people. That is the most important aim of our European struggle.

These four pictures symbolize the path leading the worker to a secure existence which has already been trodden in Germany where, by the outbreak of this war, a large proportion of everything which turned the worker into a proletarian had already been suppressed. The German worker has a legal claim to work, an adequate wage, sick treatment, medical care, holidays and an old age pension. As far as possible, the factories have provided sanitary installations, clean and sunny recreation rooms and no less clean and sunny workshops. Besides all this, kindergartens have been established by the State or by private concerns. Continuation schools can be found everywhere. The gifted can there gain by their work both the right and the opportunity to climb the social ladder. The most important thing, however, is: (see the following page)

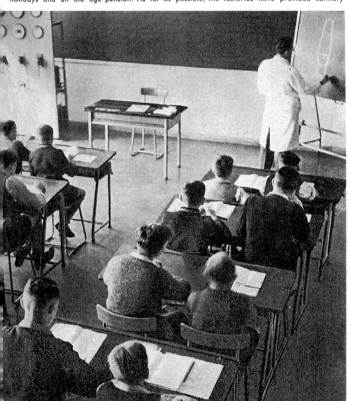

Fiodr Ivanov is a Russian. Since the beginning of the eastern campaign numerous members of this people have volunteered to take part as soldiers, farmers or mechanics in the liberation of their native land from Sovietism. The Russians, who had been cut off from the rest of the Continent by the wall of Bolshevism, have thus joined in the fight for the liberation of Europe. Their conception of Germany derived from more than twenty-five years of Bolshevist propaganda is undergoing a complete revision

Tatashvill is a Georgian. His people, which numbers about two millions, inhabits the southwest of the Caucasus. For the most part, they have retained their traditional Christianity. Ever since 1801, when they were annexed by the Russian Empire, they have fought again and again for freedom or for genuine autonomy. Before the First World War many of the Georgians hoped that the Russian Socialists would bring about a change and give them their liberty. They were bitterly disappointed by Bolshevism and Stalin, who is himself a Georgian, and are now fighting with dogged enthusiasm against the Soviets

Vladimir Maximenko is a Ukrainian and thus belongs to the second largest people in the Soviet Union. The total number of Ukrainians is something more than 40 millions. The cold, unnatural theory of Sovietism is entirely foreign to the deeply optimistic nature of this vivacious people living in the fertile black earth country. There is a lively tendency in the Ukraine towards both economic and intellectual incorporation in Europe. It has now come to the surface again as strong and vigorous as ever. Ukrainian soldiers have always fought courageously against Bolshevism

For the rights of their peoples

Sigerbai Kusherbai is from Turkestan. The Turkomans, including Usbeks, Kirghiz, Kalmucks, Kasachs, Tadshaiks, Karakalpaks and hordes of other names, settled in the vast territory stretching from the Caspian Sea to Pamir and to the borders of China. The Turkomans number between 25 and 30 million people. A recent census taken by the Soviets numbers them at less than half this figure, but these statistics were dictated by political intentions. Today many of the Turkomans, who never willingly submitted to the Soviet system for national reasons, are fighting with the Germans

Idris Shakirov is a Volga Tartar. His people, which lives on the Upper Volga, numbers approximately four millions. In spite of close contact with the Russians when it was exposed for many years to intense attempts at Russianization, this people has defended its national individuality and its own religion with conscious obstinacy and preserved its national integrity intact. Like their cousins in the Crimea, the Volga Tartars have taken advantage of the opportunity offered by the great international conflict of our day and are fighting for the rights of their people

Hasmik Nasarian is an Armenian. This tiny people of approximately 2 millions has retained Christianity ; it was the first people in the east to adopt this religion to which it is consequently particularly attached. There have always been religious martyrs among the Armenians so it is easy to understand that the Armenians are natural enemies of Bolshevism and that especially large numbers of deserters come from the Armenian divisions as convinced antagonists of the Red Army. As soldiers, they are grim and steadfast, as grim as their history and as steadfast as their loyalty to their own tradition

Timer Gallamov is a Crimean Tartar. The Crimean Tartars settled in the Crimea at the time of the Golden Horde. They are Mohammedans and, like all Islamic peoples, have always fought to preserve their national customs against all foreign influences. Bolshevism went so far as to grant them on paper the autonomy they demanded, but this was never realized. During the struggle for their rights, many Tartars were banished to Siberia. In consequence, the percentage of Crimean Tartars, who have joined the volunteer units from the eastern territories is especially high

Vassili Kigorovitch is a Ruthenian. The Ruthenians, numbering about eight millions, played a special rôle even in the Grand Duchy of Lithuania. Later the intellectuals were absorbed by the Poles and Russians, so that today the nation has more the character of a peasant people. As far back as the First World War, however, the Ruthenians remembered their individuality and, in spite of all the attempts of the Soviets, this national consciousness remained awake. Today, with the doors of freedom open to them, they are proving particularly receptive to European tendencies

Alexei Sovichenko is a Cossack. He thus belongs to the warlike community of the east. Although the Cossack lands suffered exceptionally during the Civil War in 1917, and though the Bolshevists destroyed the last remnants of Cossack independence, what are known as the "Cossack Armies" have preserved intact the laws of Cossack tradition. Once they lived on the banks of the Don, the Terek, the Kuban and the Volga as farmers, but now they are fighting as volunteers with the Germans in the hope that one day they will be able to live there under their own laws once more

The volunteer units from the eastern territories personify the natural rights of over 160 peoples who lost their individuality when forcibly banded together as the Bolshevist U.S.S.R. SIGNAL here introduces 12 examples

PK. Photographs: War Correspondents Pabel, Grimm, Frenske, Modl, Arndt, Kirsche, Mittelstaedt, Knaack

S. Havibakshi is an Aserbeidjan. He is wearing the award for wounds. This mountaineer people from the Northern Caucasus is famous for its horsemen and marksmen. For years it has waged bitter warfare against Bolshevism of which it was the declared enemy from its earliest days. It withdrew before the overwhelming terror into remote mountain valleys without giving up the struggle. When the Germans came, the Aserbeidjans greeted them as liberators and joined them by the hundred. When the Caucasus was evacuated, many families followed in the Germans' train

Machmet Hadaiuhov is a North Caucasian. His tiny people of slightly more than 150,000 inhabitants are Mohammedans. When the North Caucasian territory was occupied by German troops in 1942, it transpired that the Soviet rule had been particularly violent there. Numerous North Caucasians accompanied the German Army when it evacuated the country again. They are freedom-loving mountaineers who have been to a certain extent pressed into the North Caucasian industries by the Soviets, though they take every opportunity to evade this oppression. The North Caucasians are excellent marksmen

Ivan Kulkaanen is a Carelian. The Finnish linguistic group in the Soviet Union numbers about 4 million people. The Finns and Carelians on Soviet soil do not differ racially from their brothers in Finland. The division line between the Russian and Finnish racial areas runs approximately along the Murmansk Railway. The frontiers of the Carelian Soviet Republic had been intentionally so drawn that the Carelians and Finns formed a minority. Today the Carelians are fighting with heart and soul side by side with their people against Bolshevism

See the colour pages following.:

THE WAR AIM OF THE CONTINENT

A theme certain to interest the whole world but which cannot be broached without a few introductory remarks to explain the situation

"Europe must be wiped out... *Tanks 30 feet high raze Berlin mercilessly to the ground, crushing walls, men, women and children beneath them... In Copenhagen there are no survivors. Stockholm is as silent as the grave. While the clouds of gas are descending over Paris, the population flees to take refuge in the Underground... But all in vain! Bolshevism deals its blow. Paris and France are extinguished. One year suffices to annihilate the Continent with its 350 million inhabitants... The peoples of Europe are deported to Siberia..*

From the "Trust for the destruction of Europe," a book by the Soviet journalist Ilia Ehrenburg published in England and the U.S.A.

Looking back, the first shots in this war were provoked by a purely local quarrel. The bone of contention was a certain Corridor and a certain Free City of Danzig. It was a matter of the revision of a frontier in which every nation with a sense of honour was deeply interested. Documents prove how easily this revision could have been carried out in a peaceful manner without wounding any feelings.

Why, in spite of all, were the first shots in this war fired in the north of Europe, on the German-Polish frontier? Why did this strip of territory and this city of less than 200,000 inhabitants set alight the flame which a few careful hands could easily have extinguished and which has now become a conflagration spreading over the five continents and the seven seas. Is not the lack of proportion between the cause and the effect of such a monstrous historical phenomenon enough to shake one's belief in mankind? Or have we put the question badly? Should we not rather ask whether the Corridor and Danzig are really the cause or merely the occasion of this war?

A world-wide struggle

It is a fact that in 1939 Britain gave as the reason for war her desire to protect the smaller states and in the same year France declared her anxiety for her own safety. A little later, beyond the ocean, the United States felt threatened by a Germany which was involved in one of the bitterest struggles in its history taking place before its very frontiers.

But these war motives or war aims scarcely justify the magnitude of the struggle. They have been refuted or explained by confiscated archives. To a certain extent these explanations have something satisfactory about them. When people see that Britain meant neither Poland nor Denmark, neither Norway nor Holland, neither Belgium nor France and neither Greece nor Yugoslavia when she declared war but the maintenance of the European balance of power in her own favour and the freedom of the seas as she understands it, the realists of the 20th century are facing facts to which it is easy for them to define their attitude. They understand too that a French Government which sees the country's centre of gravity abroad, and in Britain at that, cannot avoid going to war. Meanwhile Lend and Lease Acts and other diplomatic-military actions have revealed the real war aims of the U.S.A. The American policy to obtain control of bases is slowly materializing and is obviously a move on the way to world dominion in the future, while the monopoly for the building of bombers, about which "Signal" published a report recently, points to the fact that it is to be a policy of air supremacy. Clearest of all are the real war aims of the Soviets who for 26 years have made no attempt to disguise their plans for world revolution which they have

partly realized in exemplary fashion on their western frontier whenever the opportunity offered itself.

Germany's war aim, too, has been clearly revealed. The Germans maintain that they are fighting for the fruits of their internal revolution which has solved the problem of the century for them, the social problem. This revolution has brought them into deadly combat with the modern forms of human enslavement, Capitalism and Bolshevism, and placed them in the forefront of an intellectual struggle involving the whole world.

That brings the war aims on to another plane: the United States have plans for world domination against which the British Empire is on the defensive. The Soviets are trying to create a Bolshevist empire. Germany, the bulwark of Europe and the world against the threat of Bolshevism, is holding the front in the east and defending herself like Japan in the west who is fighting for her historical claim to leadership in the Pacific against the tyranny of foreign interests.

The demands of the hour

Seen from this point of view the question of the Corridor and Danzig vanish into thin air, for such causes are in proportion to the effects of this world-wide struggle. At the same time, however, the relentlessness of what the hour demands from the living becomes clear as crystal. The whole universe is involved in a dispute from which there is no escape and which must be faced. It has to be coolly considered and weighed up. Even the most idyllic spots on this earth will be involved and everyone must be prepared for questions of life and death which have to be answered precisely and quickly. It is just like an examination: the candidate is given a quarter of an hour and what he thinks of afterwards is of no avail.

If fate were to ask the European Continent about its attitude and aims in this universal struggle (and we believe that this question has already been asked), what would Europe answer?

One thing is certain: It would fail miserably in this examination were it to bring before the Supreme Court of world history all the details of its internal affairs. Minor problems are solved automatically according to the lines laid down by the main verdict. But in order to secure a favourable main verdict, Europe must have a strong case, and she has it.

The case is made up of sober facts; it is an argument that has been fought and suffered for with bravery and industry, with wisdom and tears and with the blood of every nation of this hemisphere throughout its history. It is the outcome of the natural and dynamic development of history—it is the path leading to the synthesis of Europe's power.

On the four pages following, "Signal" attempts to give details on this theme.

Whither is Europe going?

A question to the history of the Continent—and the answer in five pictures

In the middle of the 9th century when Charlemagne's Reich, the first Central European Empire, decayed, Europe broke up into the scene of innumerable miniature struggles, for in the minor empires that came into being the previous vassals became supreme lords at the cost of the various central powers. The rivalry between the different houses was the beginning of the struggle to form the society, economics and State of Europe

In the early years of the struggle against the East the outlines of a national German state were visible although it did not become a reality until a thousand years later. Meanwhile France, with the Ile de France as its centre, overcame its vassals and stabilized the state during the Hundred Years' War with England. At the same time Spain was acquiring strength by defeating the Moors. But on the whole, the Middle Ages, resounding to the march of mercenary soldiers, were drawing to a close

The great turning-point

The turning-point between the Middle Ages and modern times was also the hour of birth of the Continental idea. Whilst European explorer impetus and courage discover the wide areas of the earth, it simultaneously outlines the frontiers of the Continent and teaches us for the first time to look upon it as a cultural, economic and political unit. Europe has become a home. Whilst in the Italy of the Renaissance period the intellectual torch of antiquity is again being kindled in order to throw a new light on universal space and mankind, the Portuguese, Spanish, Dutch and French are conquering the world for western culture. But this enormous and unique achievement in the history of humanity appears to grudge its performer his own perfection: The heart of Europe is bleeding from the blows dealt by the first social struggles of

reorganization during the Peasants' Wars. The commencing world trade develops new friction and civil life becomes a war-influencing factor. The ceaseless fighting for new territory gains, moreover, a fresh impulse resulting from tragical religious differences. The great turning-point will not allow a great unity. Even the next step which Europe must inevitably take, that is the step towards the reorganization of peoples and states, leads only to a dynastical allotment of the Continent. For two centuries it will continue to groan from the results of heritage and Cabinet wars. On the other hand, the island on its outskirts, England, will realize its unique maritime position and, by skilfully betraying one Continental power to the other, will inherit all of them. Therefore, Europe stands — still divided into more than 200 sovereign states — on the threshhold of modern history

The last stage

At the beginning of the latest period of history, too, Europe has placed a milestone. The obsolete forms were wiped away by the French Revolution and its great son tried to create a Continental State out of the ruins. Napoleon recognized the necessity but fate forbad him to accomplish his plan. He cleared the way along which European history was to advance from the idea of the dynastic principle to that of the national state. Napoleon recruited his legions from the first levée en masse of the peoples of Europe which, however, began to be inflamed with national enthusiasm. A century of struggles for national unity followed during which the number of sovereign states sank from 200 to 20. While this simplification was in process the spirit it liberated created the magnificent tools of civilization. And while Europe was occupied with her own affairs the rest of the goods of the earth were being newly distributed for the technical age brought with it a new grouping of all political powers. The first World War for which considerations of foreign policy were chiefly responsible was the result. These considerations decided the issue and contrary to its own interests split the Continent into an uneasy conglomeration of 36 states. Meanwhile grossraum economy was beginning. Europe with its 8 additional states barricaded itself behind the unsurmountable walls of mutual distrust and rearmament and remained inferior to the rest of the world in economics and politics. But from the East came the menace of Bolshevism that appeared like a new storm threatening the whole world.

The final decision

The heavy damages suffered by almost all the States of Europe, the victors not excepted, during the first World War were a profitable lesson from fate to the Continent showing that in future capital and oil, wool and rubber, coal and iron which had assumed an incomparably greater importance in wartime played a decisive rôle in history like traditional questions of frontiers and sovereignity. The sequence of interminable economic crises between 1918 and 1938 are a proof of this fact. Has Europe understood or is the old rivalry between the 36 States continuing while the development of world history is confronting continent with continent? It is continuing. Only the most profoundly affected European States, that is Germany and Italy, recognize the first demand of the hour, the dangers of West and East. They are modernizing their conception of technics and capital, of socialism and society and within their frontiers are solving the problems of the time in exemplary fashion. It is one of the most tragic things in European history that at this moment the smouldering passions of the world should flare up for a second time and try to plunge Europe into chaos. Today, now that the Axis has established its outposts along all the coasts and frontiers of Europe and now that she has been forced to oppose Bolshevist imperialism in arms revealing in the attack the extent of the danger, the powers of Europe who look forward to the future with confidence have recognized the second demand of the hour, the dynamic demand of European history and have formed a common front regardless of frontiers. The road to the synthesis of Europe has been opened up—perhaps for the last time.

A dream becomes reality:

A journey to Italy! Who was formally able to travel to Italy? There were only a few who were privileged to satisfy this longing. It is now possible to travel to foreign countries with the "Strength through Joy" organisation, to spend one's vacation on the Riviera or on even more distant shores

Recreation every evening for thousands:

The world of variety! Two decorative and boldly stylicized programmes of the Berlin variety theatre "The Plaza". Instead of cheap printed programmes in two colours, the best is just good enough for the audience. (Above and right). Not a few keep and collect these programmes in memory of happy hours

Yachting — an exclusive sport?

This is no longer the case in Germany. Anybody is able to take up yachting in the same way as he can indulge in riding, tennis, hockey etc.